Conari Press books are distributed by Publishers Group West

ISBN: 1-57324-061-3

Cover Design: Rex Ray
Cover Background Photo: Rex Ray

Library of Congress Cataloging-in-Publication Data
Women of the Beat generation : the writers, artists and muses at the heart of a revolution / edited by Brenda Knight; foreword by Anne Waldman; afterword by Ann Charters.
        p.   cm.
    Includes bibilographic references and index.
    ISBN 1-57324-061-3
        1. American literature—Women authors. 2. Beat generation—Literary collections.
        3. Women authors, American—20th century—Biography. 4. Women artists—United States—Biography.
    5. Women and literature—United States. 6. American literature—20th century.   I. Knight, Brenda, 1958– .
PS508.W7W585   1996
810.8'09287'09045—dc20   96-9237

Printed in the United States of America on recycled paper
10 9 8 7 6 5 4 3 2 1

WOMEN of the BEAT GENERATION

The Writers, Artists and Muses at the Heart of a Revolution

BRENDA KNIGHT

Foreword by ANNE WALDMAN

Afterword by ANN CHARTERS

CONARI PRESS
Berkeley, CA

WOMEN of the BEAT GENERATION

To Robert Kent Leffler
who encouraged me to pursue my vision
and
to Leslie Rossman and Nancy Fish
who kept me going when I didn't think I could.

Contents

Foreword by Anne Waldman, ix
Sisters, Saints and Sibyls: Women and the Beat, 1

The Precursors, 7
Helen Adam: Bardic Matriarch, 9
Jane Bowles: A Life at the End of the World, 18
    Ilse Klapper, 25
Madeline Gleason: True Born Poet, 29
Josephine Miles: Mentor to a Revolution, 39

The Muses, 47
Joan Vollmer Adams Burroughs: Calypso Stranded, 49
    Vickie Russell, 50
    Helen Hinkle, 52
Carolyn Cassady: Karmic Grace, 57
    LuAnne Henderson, 60
    Anne Murphy, 64
Edie Parker Kerouac: First Mate, 76
    Stella Sampas, 78
Joan Haverty Kerouac: Nobody's Wife, 87
    Gabrielle "Mèmére" Kerouac, 88
Eileen Kaufman: Keeper of the Flame, 103

The Writers, 115
Mary Fabilli: Farmer's Daughter, 117
Diane di Prima: Poet Priestess, 123
    Barbara Guest, 125

Elise Cowen: Beat Alice, 141
Joyce Johnson: A True Good Heart, 167
Hettie Jones: Mother Jones, 183
    Billie Holiday, 186
Joanne Kyger: Dharma Sister, 197
Denise Levertov: Fortune's Favorite, 205
Joanna McClure: West Coast Villager, 214
Janine Pommy Vega: Lyric Adventurer, 223
    Elsie John, 225
ruth weiss: The Survivor, 241
    Aya Tarlow, 244
Mary Norbert Körte: Redwood Mama Activist, 257
Brenda Frazer: Transformed Genius, 269
Lenore Kandel: Word Alchemist, 279
Anne Waldman: Fast Speaking Woman, 287
Jan Kerouac: The Next Generation, 309
    Natalie Jackson, 311

The Artists, 319
Jay DeFeo: The Rose, 321
Joan Brown: Painter and Prodigy, 327
    Gui de Angulo, 328

Worthy Beat Women: Recollection by Ted Joans, 331
Afterword by Ann Charters, 335

Appendix: Lists of Collected Works, 343
Acknowledgments, 353
Permissions Acknowledgments, 355
Index, 359

Foreword
by Anne Waldman

As a teenager and aspiring writer in the 1960s I looked to creative female comrades and role models among both elders and peers. Of course there were the earlier examples of Gertrude Stein and HD—brilliant writers who chose to be exiles from the social pressures of their own cultures and were able to manage their creative lives abroad. Or Marianne Moore—quirky intellectual with a disciplined mind whose most intense relationship was with her mother. Yet so many of the women I knew—like many of the women represented and conjured in these pages—were more troubled characters—driven, desperate, fighting against the constraints of culture, family, education and often dwelling in the twilight of a "great" man's personality or career. A brilliant, sensitive lot—not unlike my own mother who had dropped out of Vassar College her freshman year, marrying at age nineteen the son of celebrated Greek poet Anghelos Sikelianos and living abroad a decade before World War II. She found herself a part of a lively bohemian circle and helped mount the classical Greek revival of plays in Delphi under the tutelage of her energetic mother-in-law Eva Palmer Sikelianos. Eva herself—although part of the Nathalie Barney circle of feminist and lesbian persuasion—lived in her husband's shadow, always deferring to Sikelianos as the greater artist. He was a god! He was known to raise the dead! Never mind his sexual exploits and rampant egoism! My mother had been raised by a widowed invalid, a passionate Christian Scientist who regretted she had not the requisite strength to be a missionary in Africa. Not exactly thwarted lives these womens' by any means, but difficult, restless, and most definitively outside the norm. Lives that exacted an emotional and psychological toll. And remained unfulfilled to a certain extent. Later my mother struggled with her own lack of confidence as a writer and a translator, feeling she had been distracted by marriage, children and a societal need to conform. She was a fierce autodidact yet panicked on her deathbed she had not studied or accomplished enough ("I should have been a scientist. An anthropologist? Something!"). I grew up in Greenwich Village and my closest friends were an "arty" bunch, mostly from the lower-middle class and predominantly white. We benefited from the examples and trials of young women who had struggled to be creative and assertive before us, and we were certainly aware of the exciting artistic and liberal heritage of our New York City environs and yet many of us fell into the same retrograde traps. Being dominated by relationships with men—letting our own talents lag, following their lead—which could result in drug dependencies, painful abortions, alienation from family and friends. I remember my mother cautioning me not to be too "easy" with men on the one hand, and on the other hand the advice to appease their egos! She had suffered as an intellectual; men didn't want you to be smarter than they were. And so on. I knew interesting creative women who became junkies for their boyfriends, who stole for their boyfriends, who concealed their poetry and artistic aspirations, who slept around to be popular, who had serious eating disorders, who concealed their unwanted pregnancies raising money for abortions on their own or who put the child up for adoption. Who never felt they owned or could appreciate their own bodies. I knew women living secret or double lives because love and sexual desire for another woman was anathema. I knew women in daily therapy because their fathers had abused them, or women who got sent away to mental hospitals or special schools because they'd taken a black lover. Some ran away from home. Some committed suicide. There were casualties among the men as well, but not, in my experience, as legion. Has all that much really changed, one might be tempted to ask? Yes and no. The subject is a convolutional one, albeit a problematic one. Socio-political, economic, environmental, karmic. Afflictions seem greater now on the whole culture, on the entire planet. It is in certain interests, however, to keep women down and silenced. Certainly the feminist movement has advanced the "cause" of women. And the contemporary literary scene is extremely strong and vital. An unprecedented amount of brilliant, imaginative and highly experimental writing by women is being recognized, available, applauded. It now behooves us to look at the antecedents for this greater liberty of expression.

This anthology—a collection of hagiographies and writers by and about an astonishing array of women—is a kind of resurrection. Interesting that it comes at the millennium as if there is, in fact, a necessary reckoning. This book is testament, primarily, to the *lives* of these women, lest they be ignored or forgotten. For what comes through is the searing often poignant hint or glimpse of an original—often lonely—tangible *intellectus*—a bright, shining, eager mind. And these very particular "voices" as it were form in unison a stimulating and energetic forcefield of consciousness that manifested at a rich and difficult time in cultural history, spanning half a century. The men, yes, have gotten most of the credit as the movers and shakers of the "Beat" literary movement. But here we may be privy to what else—what "other"—was going on at the same time, in parallel time, and how the various lives—of both men and women—interwove and dovetailed with one other. I've always appreciated ethnologist Clifford Geertz's notion of "consociates," a useful paradigm that touches on the inter-connectedness of shared and experienced realities. It takes into consideration the influences of time, place, mutually informed circumstance on individuals existing in proximity—yet not necessarily intimates—to create a larger cultural context for action and art. There is an extremely vibrant twinge to the occasions noted, suffered, recorded and refined into literature in these pages by a range of folk very much on their own time cycles yet intersecting at crucial moments. I've always considered the memoir to be the strongest literary genre by the women of the so-called Beat generation, although there is also memorable poetry by major poets included here. But the quintessential "rasa" or taste of that historical period is often captured by the diaristic accounts which substantially strengthen and give a historical viability and narrative to this collection. For, in a sense, the women were often present as the most observant and sober witnesses—see the selections by Joyce Johnson, Hettie Jones, Carolyn Cassady, Eileen Kaufman, Brenda Frazer, Janine Pommy Vega to name a few. The already known and acknowledged poets soar—Helen Adam, Denise Levertov, Josephine Miles, Mary Fabilli, Diane di Prima, Joanne Kyger—among others. There are lesser known illuminati, such as the poet Mary Norbert Körte, former Catholic nun who became an environmental activist in the 1970s. Disturbing glimpses of Joan Vollmer Adams Burroughs, others. Real surprises in the work by Elise Cowen, tragic misfit with her "diffident sulky air." A quirky, elegant language inhabits a shaky yet sharp sensibility:

Emily white witch of Amherst
The sly white witch of Amherst
Killed her teachers
    with her love
I'd rather mine entomb
    my mind
Or best that soft grey dove.

Elise Cowen jumped out a window to her death in 1962 at the age of twenty-nine.

The portraits that crystallize are quite haunting. Helen Adam—brilliant Scots balladeer who could chant in the voice of an Amsterdam prostitute:

A spangled garter my only clothing
A candle flame in my hand

—dies alone in a nursing home. Jane Bowles, also alone, sick and broken at the end of her life in a hospital run by nuns in Spain. I am struck by the remark of Mary Greer, Madeline Gleason's lover and companion of twenty-five years, who said on Gleason's death "Madeline died of despair, what all poets die of." True now as well for writer Jan Kerouac, dead this past month of kidney failure fighting until the end for her identity and what she considered her rightful legacy as the daughter of Jack Kerouac, reigning giant of the Beat literary movement.

It is time for cultural historians, critical theorists, feminist literary critics, other poets and writers to take heed of this rich compendium of lore, literary history, and serious creative endeavor. And to acknowledge, as well, the suffering, difficulty, and dignity of these lives.

I see this book as opening the field of an extraordinary unsung legacy.

Anne Waldman
The Jack Kerouac School of Disembodied Poetics
July 1996

Sisters, Saints and Sibyls
Women and the Beat

Brenda Knight

"If you want to understand Beat women, call us transitional—a bridge to the next generation, who in the 1960s, when a young woman's right to leave home was no longer an issue, would question every assumption that limited women's lives and begin the long, never-to-be-completed work of transforming relationships with men."

—Joyce Johnson

This book came about after a modern poetry class I took from the venerable Michael Krasny, an informed and inspiring teacher if ever there was one. I looked forward to that class every Wednesday night because it was so lively. When we came to the Beats, lively sometimes meant heated. I saw how, even after all these years, Beat writing could set off sparks and had such power to move people. When, sadly, the term ended, I hungered for more Beat writing, the energy and raw passion, and soon discovered a motherlode of writing I had never seen in bookstores and curriculums before—Beat women! And thus, this book was born with a desire to share the wealth of brilliance and beauty of these women.

The fifties had a choke hold on consciousness, the industrial age at its most insidiously rote and conformist. The Beats were the only game in town or, as journalist Bruce Cook says, "the only revolution going on at the time." The women of the Beat Generation, with rare exception, escaped the eye of the camera; they stayed underground, writing. They were instrumental in the literary legacy of the Beat Generation, however, and continue to be some of its most prolific writers.

This book is a collection of women who participated in a revolution that forever changed the landscape of American literature. Before the late forties and early fifties, poetry was buttoned up tight. The Beats helped make literature a democracy, a game with no rules. All you needed, they believed, was passion and a love of the written word. As the movement spread, the Prufrockian ennui and weltschmerz of Eliot gave way to Beat vision and word jazz, and the literary world was never the same.

Beat was first coined when Times Square hustler and writer Herbert Huncke picked up the phrase from carnies, small-time crooks, and jazz musicians in Chicago, who used it to describe the "beaten" condition of worn-out travelers for whom home was the road. Huncke used it to explain his "exalted exhaustion" of a life lived beyond the edge. Jack Kerouac took it one step further, saying, "I guess you might say we're a Beat Generation" when talking to his friend, writer John Clellon Holmes, who included the quote in an article for the *New York Times Magazine.* Kerouac and Allen Ginsberg further refined the concept as "beatific" and containing a spiritual aspect, invoking Catholicism, William Blake, and Buddhism, respectively. Toward the end of his life, Kerouac explained that he was really just a Catholic mystic all along.

Beat was a countercultural phenomenon, a splash of cold water in the face of a complacent society, that radiated out from certain places in America, primarily New York City and San Francisco, and consisted of many people, not all of whom received the attention of the mass media. Diane di Prima, considered by many to be the archetypal Beat woman, started her own press rather than wait for a publisher to come knocking. When a major house finally did pursue her, it was for erotica—*Memoirs of a Beatnik*—not her poetry. Elise Cowen, who typed *Kaddish* for Allen Ginsberg, was in her own right a strong and prolific poet whose work has never been published until now.

The women included in this anthology run the gamut from the famous—Carolyn Cassady and Jan Kerouac—to the as yet undiscovered—Mary Fabilli and Helen Adam. The art, prose, and poetry selected represent the range and development of their work, from pre-Beat to, in many cases, new work that has never before been published. For those readers who want a fuller experience of these talented females, I have also included a list of collected works of each woman in the appendix of this book.

To place their accomplishments in context, it is important to understand why, in the seemingly idealized fifties' America of comfort and capital, anyone, man or woman, would choose to live marginally, to struggle and oppose. Postwar America was the richest, most powerful nation in the world, bustling with industry, pride, and the Puritan obsession with work and perfection. Or so it seemed. As it turns out, not everyone in America shared this swaggering posture. The Beats were simply the first to very vocally and artistically decry American materialism and conformity. Toward the end of the decade, after years of struggling in obscurity, perseverance and timing conjoined to catapult the Beats into the public eye, where they caught the attention of millions who were similarly disenchanted with the American myth. In a very real sense, the Beats helped the Silent Generation find a voice and paved the way for the explosion of the sixties.

Women of the fifties in particular were supposed to conform like Jell-O to a mold. There was only one option: to be a housewife and mother. For the women profiled here, being Beat was far more attractive than staying chained to a brand-new kitchen appliance. For the most part, the liberal arts educations these young women were given created a natural predilection for art and poetry, for living a life of creativity instead of confining it to the occasional hour at the symphony. Nothing could be more romantic than joining this chorus of individuality and freedom, leaving behind boredom, safety, and conformity.

The women in this anthology were talented rebels with enough courage and creative spirit to turn their backs on "the good life" the fifties promised and forge their way to San Francisco and Greenwich Village. Long before the second wave of feminism, they dared to attempt to create lives of their own. From Sister Mary Norbert Körte, who left the convent to be a Beat poet under the tutelage of Denise Levertov, to Helen Adam and Madeline Gleason, co-founders of the San Francisco Poetry Festival, these women made their own way.

In many ways, women of the Beat were cut from the same cloth as the men: fearless, angry, high risk, too smart, restless, highly irregular. They took chances, made mistakes, made poetry, made love, made history. Women of the Beat weren't afraid to get dirty. They were compassionate, careless, charismatic, marching to a different drummer, out of step. Muses who birthed a poetry so raw and new and full of power that it changed the world. Writers whose words weave spells, whose stories bind, whose vision blinds. Artists for whom curing the disease of art kills.

Such nonconformity was not easy. To be unmarried, a poet, an artist, to bear biracial children, to go on the road was doubly shocking for a woman, and social condemnation was high. Joyce Johnson and Elise Cowen fled respectable homes and parental expectations. Others married and raised families, but in an utterly unorthodox manner. Joan Vollmer Adams' common-law marriage to William Burroughs, for example, was shocking to their wealthy, upper-class families. Diane di Prima raised five children, taking them with her to ashrams, to Timothy Leary's psychedelic community in Millbrook, and on the road in a VW van for a cross-country reading tour. Hettie Jones' biracial marriage and children were a scandal even in New York's Greenwich Village, causing irrevocable rifts with her parents.

Their iconoclastic lifestyle matched their literary work. But though they were revolutionary, Beat poetry, art, and prose didn't spontaneously generate—although many literary precursors would not dare lay claim to it. The Beats themselves are quick to name their inspiration, and several names come up consistently: HD (Hilda Doolittle), Ezra Pound, William Carlos Williams, Walt Whitman, Gertrude Stein, and Emily Dickinson. In particular, the Imagist poets—HD and Ezra Pound—changed the course of poetry from strict formalism, loosened the corsets, so to speak, and freed the form. Immediately prior to the raw, unvarnished confessional writing of the Beats was a different breed of poet, a liberated artist, albeit embraced by academia, but prophetic in the cryptic, blunted free verse and experimentalism with style from haiku to rant. William Carlos Williams and the Imagists were, like the Beats, unrepentantly individual and beyond the ken of their peers. Like the Beats to come, they were very concerned with encouraging other poets, especially younger writers, and often found themselves in trouble for unpopular politics, poetics, and lifestyles.

The Black Mountain College in North Carolina was founded in the wake of this "liberated arts" movement by a group of brilliant individuals and boasted a world-class faculty—Charles Olson, Merce Cunningham, artist Robert Rauschenberg, and musician John Cage. Poet Charles Olson went to Black Mountain after the eminently successful publication of his Melville study, *Call Me Ishmael.* There, Olson, Robert Creeley, and Robert Duncan took an antiacademic stance on poetry and literature, propounding the belief that the energy the poet transfers to the writing is more important than form, content, or the judgment of critics. This stance attracted legions of young artists to the Black Mountain oeuvre, including a cadre that would soon be known as the Beats.

A few years after the antiacademy movement emerged, the New York art-and-poetry scene erupted—as depicted here in the memoirs of Hettie Jones, Diane di Prima, and Joyce Johnson—with constant readings, showings, performances, salons, plays, parties, and happenings, providing one of the two poles for the Black Mountain diaspora upon the demise of Black Mountain College. Robert Duncan went to San Francisco, where he encountered and encouraged such mavericks as Helen Adam and Madeline Gleason with whom he kick-started the poetry movement known as the San Francisco Renaissance. Meanwhile Creeley and the others went to New York, often to be found at the Cedar Tavern, a favorite Beat gathering place. Although the writing and philosophy of these Beat progenitors is very different from that of the Beats, what they all have in common is a reaction to and a rebellion against rigidity.

Jack Kerouac would be the first to tell you that the mainstream and the media were the death of the Beat Generation. Sensationalism and mass success, by its very nature, negates that which is Beat. Beat is underground, raw, unedited, pure, shocking. Beat can't be refined, sanitized, second-guessed, premeditated; it must be immediate. Beat is an expulsion, a vomiting of vision. To pretty it up for the cameras and papers is to snuff the very essence of Beat. Ironically, because the women in the movement have, to a certain degree, been ignored and marginalized, they represent the precious little of that which remains truly Beat.

Why is it that the fascination with the Beats, far from dying down, continues to grow? Each of these women offers her own answer to this question, but all agree that, in a time of skyrocketing rents, mass layoffs, and the cultural desert of the sixty-hour work week, the Beat credo has much to offer in the way of courage and the creative identity of the individual.

The women of the Beat are the epitome of cool. They were the black-stockinged hipsters, renegade artists, intellectual muses, and gypsy poets who helped change our culture forever. They were feminist before the word was coined, and their work stands beside that of the men. To the Beat men, these women are sisters, saints, and sibyls. Jack Kerouac, who had many women in his life, once said, "The truth of the matter is we don't understand our women; we blame them and it's all our fault."

Women of the Beat Generation is an opportunity to finally understand these women as important figures in our literature, our history, and our culture and as some of the best minds of the Beat Generation.

Read on.

THE PRECURSORS

Helen Adam and her sister, Pat, in New York City.

Reverse: Expat literati in Tangier: Jane Bowles, William S. Burroughs, and Paul Bowles against the back wall.

Helen Adam
Bardic Matriarch
(1909–1992)

"Be quiet. A talking woman likes a silent man."

—from *San Francisco's Burning*

Although she is almost a generation older than most of the others in *Women of the Beat Generation,* Helen Adam was an important influence on the up-and-coming poets who would later be known as the Beats. Godmother and matriarch of the San Francisco Renaissance, she mystified the younger poets by staying true to the ballad form; but all who knew her were struck by her unique vision of the world and impressed by the power of her public readings. During the fifties, her performances in San Francisco were great happenings during which she chanted her poetry in a light Scottish brogue that crept up behind the listener, weaving an uneasy spell. Folksingers, poets, and artists were influenced by the haunting burr of her voice which, some claimed, was so magical it could cause a mist to rise in the air.

Helen was born in Glasgow, Scotland. There she was hailed as a prodigy for her uncanny ability to read at the age of two. She was writing ballads as soon as she could, and many superstitious Scots considered her everything from a reincarnated bard to a witch's changeling. By the age of twenty, Helen had published three books of poetry with a major English press, Hodder and Stoughton.

Her first book, *The Elfin Pedlar,* was published when she was fourteen years old and includes 120 ballads composed from the time she was two, when, according to the book's foreword, the child "talked to her dolls in rhyme. She would tell them stories of fairies and flowers all clothed in beautiful language and in faultless rhythm." The book was met with enthusiasm, and Helen was hailed as having "an extraordinary sense and handling of rhythm and rhyme" with a "perfect ear and a delicate imagination" and "a mind elect" which was "entirely free from self-consciousness or any thought of posing." Upon its publication, Helen Adam became the pride of Scotland; *The Elfin Pedlar* even elicited a note of praise from the queen of Scotland herself.

Helen spent most of her childhood in Dundee and Edinburgh and graduated from the University of Edinburgh with a degree in English literature. Upon graduation, in addition to writing poetry she also began a singing career, performing in both Scotland and London, often under the stage name Pixy Pool. Ultimately, she adopted the Celtic tradition of singing ballads, honing her writing and singing skills into a unique form of chanted poetry that took the nature of a mystical incantation, touching the listener with an eerie and compelling word music.

Very deliberately, Helen set out to create a new life for herself, away from the notoriety her prodigality created. In 1939, accompanied by her mother, Isabella, and her sister, Pat, a novelist, musician, and poet, Helen came to the United States, arriving in San Francisco in 1948. The three of them lived in a pleasant apartment on 17th Street. One might say there were four of them, for their household included a beautiful Siamese cat named Kiltie. Kiltie was considered an equal member of the household, sometimes referred to as Helen's "familiar." Kiltie was so named by Isabella "because when he walked, his wee backside reminded one of a kilt rocking back and forth." Like her friend and fellow poet Madeline Gleason, Helen made her living as a message runner in stock exchanges in the financial district, rising before dawn to head for downtown San Francisco.

For Helen Adam, San Francisco in the 1950s could not have been a more perfect place to reinvent herself. There poetic license and the mastery of form were combined with a disregard for social expectations and a rebellion against the mundane. She was counted among the oldest of the San Francisco poets, but the mystery and knowledge she brought excited the wild young poet scholars of its Renaissance with a special kind of mad spirit. Her lyric craft was celebrated for both originality and tradition. Other poets used her work not so much to copy, but to study as an example of purity in art.

Helen quickly formed a relationship of creative inspiration and mutual support with Robert Duncan and his lover, the artist Jess. She brought a completely new element to Duncan's poetry workshops with her modern medievalist tales of witches, possessed knights, and lovely, alluring but deadly women. The Adam sisters were regular guests at the Jess/Duncan household, and Robert stated that it was Helen's recitation of William Blake's "Songs of Innocence and Experience" at a poetry reading that entirely shifted the direction of his sense of poetics. Similarly, Helen claimed his play *Atlantis* as the key inspiration for her play *San Francisco's Burning*.

Helen was very protective of Robert. When he complained about critical attacks on his poetry, she would do a tarot reading and threaten to put curses on the critics, saying of one, "If I ever meet this character, I am going to put a spell on him to rot his bones. Daring to condescend to Duncan, the cheap, trashy, brainless rat."

She was fond of the very controversial poet Jack Spicer and was a participant in his Magic Workshop, although she was dubious as to the depth of Spicer's understanding of magic—a subject of great familiarity to her. Helen wrote a play entitled *Initiation to the Magic Workshop* in which most of the circle, including Spicer himself, had a part. In it, Spicer is removed from his status as magus for being a demon from hell, and is then exorcised: "Before the circle can spit complete / My burning babe you must cook and eat. / Will it taste nicer / than roasted Spicer?" Then Robert Duncan is acknowledged as the true and rightful magician. No one in the art-and-poetry scene of San Francisco at the time failed to see Helen Adam's judgment on the poets of the day.

Helen's creativity couldn't be contained by her poetry. She also made artworks, preferring collages. Cutting edge for the fifties, they show women undergoing varying stages of metamorphosis accompanied by fragmentary poems. Often, the women were changing into insectlike creatures, mythical beasts, or worm queens, with a male counterpart in the margins in complete dismay.

She also collaborated on several experimental films including *Daydream of Darkness* with William McNeill—a grand menagerie of dream images, such as statues of mythological animals from Golden Gate Park, a candlelit deer's head, and the trademark "moon-maiden" head. Helen plays the seer/witch who is beckoning the viewer to follow. She read her manuscript live while the silent film was projected onstage. The debut for this performance was at the Peacock Gallery, November 22, 1963, the day John F. Kennedy was assassinated, despite complaints it should have been canceled.

In 1957, Helen started her own magical poetry and performance troop called the Maidens that included Jess, Madeline Gleason, Robert Duncan, Eve Triem, and James Broughton. Writer Robin Blaser would sometimes attend as an honored guest at the elaborate dinner events with poetry and theater. That same year, several important events catapulted the Beats to fame, notably the publication of Jack Kerouac's *On the Road* and the "Howl" obscenity trial. The Maidens were intrigued by these new literary radicals, welcoming them at readings and offering encouragement.

Helen Adam's influence upon the Beat poets wasn't always immediate, aside from a mutual love of words and a ready stage. Allen Ginsberg, who introduced Helen when she read at the Naropa Institute in 1975, said it took many years for him to realize the impact of her poetry and her mesmerizing readings.

In 1964, Helen Adam received national attention when her play *San Francisco's Burning* was staged off Broadway in New York. Sadly, a series of difficulties coincided with this success. Helen was fired from her filing job of ten years and suffered from stress and depression, leading to hospitalization and a series of shock treatments. Helen and her sister, Pat, never parted, eventually moved to New York City and lived in solitude together until their deaths.

"When I write I am not thinking of an audience," Helen would say with a disarming smile. "I just sort of get caught up in the ballad. Of course, I am delighted if an audience likes my poetry. To me poetry is a terrific force. If you don't write it for its own sake, you are not a writer."

That poetry was indeed a terrific force in the hands of Adam is illustrated in the poem "The Queen O' Crow Castle" with its strange, dark imagery and insistent rhythms:

> Black banners beat in the onrushing dark
> Frae the tower o' Crow Castle there flies
>   a red spark
> Rash is the man, when the black banners blow,
> Wha weds wi' the Queen o' the Castle o' Crow.

At times the lines pulse with a savage violence:

> Ain, twa, three, four, five, six, seven, Craw!
> Swaked doon, bogle bit, caught up skirlin',
>   banes brackled, skulls crunched,
>   clapper clawed, dunted, dust and ashes,
>   dead gone, dead gone,
> Kra, craw, clap, slap,
> Eight will be you.

From time to time, Helen tried her hand at free verse and more experimental forms, but she found in the ballad her natural element. Most of her poetry is narrative, blending satire, diabolic images, and the music of words in her unique style.

According to Helen Adam scholar and biographer Kristin Prevallet, "Helen Adam was not an aside of the San Francisco Renaissance—she was a vital and central figure who had a unique influence on poetry and the way it was performed during that time."

The best description of Helen Adam came from a review of her work in a news-letter called *The Galley Sail:* "Miss Helen Adam's appreciative audience grows for she is without a doubt no ordinary woman. Who has a defense after all against witch-craft?"

APARTMENT ON TWIN PEAKS

I remember, when the moon shines clear
How I'd whisper in my husband's ear
Like a dentist saying "Open wider"
"Don't you want to be a good provider?"

"Don't you want to be the gracious host
In a lovely home of which you're proud to boast?
When my girl friends come to call
We've got to have carpeting from wall to wall."

After the carpeting he fought and bled
Trapped in the jaws of the Davenport bed!
He screamed as he vanished up the vacuum spout.
In triple-sealed bags it spat him out.

We chased his skull across the Twin Peaks stones.
Maud's pet chihuahuas ate the rest of his bones.

$*\quad*\quad*$

Another gnawed ghost, another gone man,
Another mild husband in the garbage can
Served up colder than his marriage vows
On his bones let chihuahuas browse.

■ ■ ■

MARGARETTA'S RIME

In Amsterdam, that old city,
Church bells tremble and cry;
All day long their airy chiming
Clavers across the sky.

I am young in the old city,
My heart dead in my breast.
I hear the bells in the sky crying,
"Every being is blest."

In Amsterdam, that old city,
Alone at a window I stand,
A spangled garter my only clothing,
A candle flame in my hand

The people who pass that lighted window,
Looking my up and down,
Know I am one more tourist trifle

For sale in this famous town.

Noon til dusk at the window waiting,
Nights of fury and shame.
I am young in an old city
Playing an older game

I hear the bells in the sky crying
To the dead heart in my breast,
The gentle bells in the sky crying
"Every being is blest."

■ ■ ■

LAST WORDS OF HER LOVER
The bald parrot said,
"Better dead! Better dead!"
The bats nestled thick on the wall.
The sheets of my bed
Felt like lead, felt like lead,
And dust smothered all, smothered all.

A glum thunder cloud
Like a shroud, like a shroud,
Flowed over the vanishing sky,
While the bones 'neath my skin
Raised a querulous din,
"Let us out! Let us out! Time to die!"
"Oh! where will you run
In the beams of the sun,
Snarling bones, when my body is dust?"
They replied "We will haste
To your lady so chaste.
And seize her with skeleton lust."

"Yes, skeleton run
To that arrogant one
Who is colder, far colder than stone.
She who refused
The delights of my love,
Let her try the embraces of bone."

"Her favor We'll win"
Laughed the bones 'neath my skin,
"With a chill wooing more to her taste
Than the fires of the flesh.
Never waiting for "Yes"
We will tumble your lady so chaste."

"She deserves such a fate."
Croaked the bones in their hate.
But my heart sighed "Forgive her, forgive.
Her beauty" it sighed
"Every pang justified.
To look on her face was to live."

Then shaken with flame
As I whispered her name,
I opened my eyes to the light.
But the bald parrot said,
"Better dead! Better dead!"
So I closed them on infinite night.

■ ■ ■

THE LAST SECRET

Grains of Sand Sing

What is the holy secret this planet hides
That the race of man has forgotten, or dare not guess?

Queen of Cups Answers

It is something to do with silence and loneliness,
Something to do with sunlight and idleness.
Something dying that lives only to bless!
But I have forgotten, forgotten, or dare not guess.

Grains of Sand Sing

Something to do with sunlight and loneliness,
Something to do with silence and idleness.
A holy and hidden secret powerful to bless!
We have all forgotten, forgotten or dare not guess.

Queen of Cups

Nothing to do with striving against ones fate
Nothing to do with raging in love or hate.
This is a secret calm as the evening sky
Empty of clouds when the first star trembles high.

Grains Of Sand

What is the holy secret this planet hides?
A child may find it at last by the deep sea tides,
Or in some meadow at dusk exploring alone
The House of the Broken Heart, or the haunted stone.

Queen of Cups

It has something to do with silence and idleness
More than a little to do with loneliness.
A holy and hidden secret powerful to bless,
Answering all Earth's prayers with one word "Yes!"

Jane Bowles
A Life at The End of The World
(1917–1973)

"I liked the kind of writer you could recognize in one sentence. Jane Bowles' writing you can recognize in one sentence."
—William Burroughs

Jane Bowles is by no means a Beat writer. But she was certainly a bridge between the Lost Generation and the Silent Generation and was part of the social and literary circle that included many of the Beats. A writer's writer, she never attracted a mass audience, but appealed to critics, her peers, and an underground readership, including the Beats. Both Hettie Jones and William Burroughs cite her unique voice and world view as an inspiration; her black humor especially appealed to the Beat expatriates she and her husband Paul hosted in their home in Tangier, Morocco.

In terms of literature, Jane represents the transitional years of the forties and fifties, a modernist with roots firmly in the classic traditions of American literature. Her writing is sharp and smart—close to the bone. Her early work is filled with light, bright comic sarcasm, but there is a steadily darkening tone in later works such as *Camp Cataract*. She is at her best in describing the odd tensions between people, frustrated relationships, and human loneliness.

Born in New York City in 1917, Jane Bowles is remembered by all who knew her as a lively spirit with a gamine charm and quick wit. Her good friend Truman Capote describes "her dahlia-head of cropped curly hair, her tilted nose and mischief-shiny, just a trifle mad eyes . . . the eternal urchin, yet with some substance cooler than blood invading her veins." Tennessee Williams wrote that she was "a charming girl, so full of humor and affection and curious, touching little attacks of panic—which I thought at first were bits of theater but which I soon found were quite genuine." In her writing, Williams found an "acute mixture of humor and pathos" which reflected "a unique sensibility...that I found even more appealing than Carson McCullers." He once lauded her as "the most important writer of prose fiction in modern American letters."

Jane was a gifted linguist and spoke several languages fluently. Her first novel, *Two Serious Ladies,* was published while she was in her twenties during World War II. It was very well received by critics as a strikingly original work by an important new voice.

When Jane and Paul met, Paul was a composer and protégé of Aaron Copeland, with a spare musical style often compared to pianist Erik Satie. The high point of the couple's creative partnership probably came when her play *In the Summer House* was staged on Broadway with an original score by Paul, who also scored the original productions of many of Tennessee Williams' plays. He was inspired to take up writing when he saw his wife's success and proved to be both skilled and prolific. When his success as a writer eclipsed Jane's, it seemed to destroy something inside her. The ease with which he wrote was a source of endless frustration for her, because she always worked very hard at her stories. Writing became so agonizing that she once claimed to be dying of writer's block.

Ultimately, the two seemed to exchange places, and he became the writer in the family while she experimented with life itself. The transition from artist to muse tormented Jane for the rest of her life. Without writing, she turned other things into art: cooking, talking (she was an incredibly gifted mimic and storyteller), traveling, letter writing, as well as conducting a number of amorous liaisons with women. She pulled off what was surely a difficult feat in Tangier at that time when she had an affair with Cherifa, a Moroccan country girl and grain-seller she met in a crowded souk and ardently wooed with gifts and money. Cherifa was unlike most Tanjawi maidens; beneath her red-and-white-striped Berber blanket, she wore jeans and golfing shoes, sported a downy mustache, and had several gold teeth. Paul claimed that she was "crazy" and carried a switchblade, which she would draw and show him what she could do to men with it. Later it was said by some that Cherifa dabbled in witch-craft. "I've never understood why," Jane confessed at one point, "but I am terrified of going against [Cherifa's] orders."

As a couple, Jane and Paul always seemed to be surrounded by writers and other creative types. They began their life together, rather auspiciously, in the now-legendary Brooklyn Heights boarding house run by George Davis. Fellow tenants included W. H. Auden, Benjamin Britten, Gypsy Rose Lee, Carson McCullers, and Richard and Ellen Wright. This glamour followed them everywhere; Paul was a special favorite of Alice B. Toklas and Gertrude Stein, and Jane was dear friends with Truman Capote and Tennessee Williams.

Ultimately the Bowles settled in Tangier, and the Beats began to intersect their lives. William Burroughs, Jack Kerouac, and Allen Ginsberg were drawn to the mystery and danger of the North African port and the spirit of outlaw literati that Jane and Paul created. Tangier was a place where no rules applied. In visiting Tangier, the Beats were following in the footsteps of William Burroughs, who had moved there in 1954. Granted a special international status in 1912 when Morocco was divided into protectorates governed by France and Spain, Tangier had long been a haven for desperadoes and renegades of every description. The postwar boom saw a new wave of misfits descend on the city. To the expatriates who landed there in the late forties—romantic adventurers and iconoclasts like the Bowles bent on escaping the restrictions of Western culture and consistently fascinated by the bizarre—its International Zone was an exotic utopia where homosexuality was acceptable, drugs readily available, and outlaw artists, in particular those fleeing the McCarthy terror in the United States, could give full expression to their ideas and explore forbidden impulses.

In a letter to his mother, describing the arrival of the Beats, Paul wrote: "The Beatniks have invaded Tangier at last. Every day one sees more beards and filthy blue jeans, and the girls look like escapees from lunatic asylums, with white lipstick and black smeared around their eyes, and matted hair hanging around their shoulders."

Jane was both titillated and terrified by the Beats. Paul loves to tell the story of when Allen Ginsberg called one day and happened to get Jane on the phone.

"This is Allen Ginsberg, the bop poet."

"The what?" asked Jane. This went on for some time, but eventually Jane understood and simply said, "I see."

"Do you believe in God?" asked Allen.

"Well, if I do I'm certainly not discussing it on the telephone," sniffed Jane and hung up.

Jane, in turn, loved to tell about the day that Allen, Jack, and Peter Orlovsky came to visit Bill in Tangier. Jack went up to the rooftop of Bill's house, evidently disgusted with Bill, who stayed in his room eating hashish with a young Moroccan boy. Bored, Allen and Peter yelled up to Jack, imploring him to come down. Jane was especially amused by Allen's plaintive cry of "Jacky, please come down!" which reminded her of boys in a schoolyard.

When William Burroughs moved to Tangier, he got to know Jane and Paul Bowles quite well. He saw something special about Jane and commented that she exuded a radiant energy that touched everything around her: "She was very, very funny, and she had a sort of chic quality that everyone commented on . . . she has this very admiring set of [followers] whose eyes would get all misty when they said, 'Oh, Janie!'" Although he had hoped to get to know Paul Bowles better during his stay, it was Jane and her bittersweet stories he came to like enormously. Bill even got on with Jane's menacing inamorata. "Cherifa," he remembered, "thought I was a holy man."

Many people mistakenly believe that they know all about Jane Bowles from Paul's popular novel, *The Sheltering Sky*, about a couple living in Tangier and traveling together through the desert. Although Kit and Port bear similarities to Jane and Paul, the book is, at its core, a work of fiction and doesn't begin to tell the true story of Jane's frustration as a writer and her feelings about being replaced, to a great extent, by the men in Paul's life.

As Jane got farther and farther away from her origins, the years of self-imposed exile in Tangier affected her strongly. In an autobiographical essay, written in 1967 and published in *World Authors,* Jane wrote: "I started to 'write' when I was fifteen years old. . . . I always thought it the most loathsome of all activities, and still do. At the same time, I felt even then that I had to do it. . . . From the first day, Morocco seemed more dreamlike than real. I felt cut off from what I knew. In the twenty years that I have lived there I have written only two short stories, and nothing else. It's good for Paul, but not for me."

Toward the end of her life, Jane became depressed and anxious and, in her words, "a little crazy," not unlike one of her characters in *Camp Cataract*. She died alone in a hospital in Spain in 1972.

Interestingly, Jane has gone on to much more acclaim since her death. There are a half-dozen biographies of her, and her work is now being reprinted, once again receiving the highest praise. John Ashbery, critic for the *New York Times Book Review,* has hailed her as "one of the greatest writers of fiction in any language."

Although Paul has continued to write, he has produced no novels after Jane died. Years after her death, he told a visiting journalist: "I think I lived vicariously . . . and didn't know it. When I had no one to live through or for, I was disconnected from life."

The short story included here is one that Jane wrote shortly before her death.

"Emmy Moore's Journal"

On certain days I forget why I'm here. Today once again I wrote my husband all my reasons for coming. He encouraged me to come each time I was in doubt. He said that the worst danger for me was a state of vagueness, so I wrote telling him why I had come to the Hotel Henry—my eighth letter on this subject—but with each new letter I strengthen my position. I am reproducing the letter here. Let there be no mistake. My journal is intended for publication. I want to publish for glory, but also in order to aid other women. This is the letter to my husband, Paul Moore, to whom I have been married sixteen years. (I am childless.) He is of North Irish descent, and a very serious lawyer. Also a solitary and lover of the country. He knows all mushrooms, bushes and trees, and he is interested in geology. But these interests do not exclude me. He is sympathetic towards me, and kindly. He wants very much for me to be happy, and worries because I am not. He knows everything about me, including how much I deplore being the feminine kind of woman that I am. In fact, I am unusually feminine for an American of Anglo stock. (Born in Boston.) I am almost a "Turkish" type. Not physically, at least not entirely, because though fat I have ruddy Scotch cheeks and my eyes are round and not slanted or almond-shaped. But sometimes I feel certain that I exude an atmosphere very similar to theirs (the Turkish women's) and then I despise myself. I find the women in my country so extraordinarily manly and independent, capable of leading regiments, or of fending for themselves on desert islands if necessary. (These are poor examples, but I am getting my point across.) For me it is an experience simply to have come here alone to the Hotel Henry and to eat my dinner and lunch by myself. If possible before I die, I should like to become a little more independent, and a little less Turkish than I am now. Before I go any further, I had better say immediately that I mean no offense to Turkish women. They are probably busy combating the very same Turkish quality in themselves that I am controlling in me. I understand, too (though this is irrelevant), that many Turkish women are beautiful, and I think that they have discarded their veils. Any other American woman would be sure of this. She would know one way or the other whether the veils had been discarded, whereas I am afraid to come out with a definite statement. I have a feeling that they really have got rid of their veils, but I won't swear to it. Also, if they have done so, I have no idea when they did. Was it many years ago or recently?

Here is my letter to Paul Moore, my husband, in which there is more about Turkish women. Since I am writing this journal with a view to publication, I do not want to ramble on as though I had all the space in the world. No publisher will attempt printing an *enormous* journal written by an unknown woman. It would be too much of a financial risk. Even I, with my ignorance of all matters pertaining to business, know this much. But they may print a small one.

My letter (written yesterday, the morrow of my drunken evening in the Blue Bonnet Room when I accosted the society salesman):

> Dearest Paul:
> I cannot simply live out my experiment here at the Hotel Henry
> without trying to justify or at least explain in letters my reasons for being
> here, and with fair regularity. You encouraged me to write whenever I felt I
> needed to clarify my thoughts. But you did tell me that I must not feel the
> need to *justify* my actions. However, I *do* feel the need to justify my

actions, and I am certain that until the prayed-for metamorphosis has occurred I shall go on feeling just this need. Oh, how well I know that you would interrupt me at this point and warn me against expecting too much. So I shall say in lieu of metamorphosis, the prayed-for *improvement.* But until then I must justify myself every day. Perhaps you will get a letter every day. On some days the need to write lodges itself in my throat like a cry that must be uttered.

As for the Turkish problem, I am coming to it. You must understand that I am an admirer of Western civilization; that is, of the women who are members of this group. I feel myself that I fall short of being a member, that by some curious accident I was not born in Turkey but should have been. Because of my usual imprecision I cannot even tell how many countries belong to what we call Western Civilization, but I believe Turkey is the place where East meets West, isn't it? I can just about imagine the women there, from what I have heard about the country and the pictures I have seen of it. As for being troubled or obsessed by real Oriental women, I am not. (I refer to the Chinese, Japanese, Hindus, and so on.) Naturally I am less concerned with the Far Eastern women because there is no danger of my being like them. (The Turkish women are just near enough.) The Far Eastern ones are so very far away, at the opposite end of the earth, that they could easily be just as independent and masculine as the women of the Western world. The ones living in-between the two masculine areas would be soft and feminine. Naturally I don't believe this for a minute, but still, the real Orientals are so far away and such a mystery to me that it might as well be true. Whatever they are, it couldn't affect me. They look too different from the way I look. Whereas Turkish women don't. (Their figures are exactly like mine, alas!)

Now I shall come to the point. I know full well that you will consider the above discourse a kind of joke. Or if you don't, you will be irritated with me for making statements of such a sweeping and inaccurate nature. For surely you will consider the picture of the world that I present as inaccurate. I myself know that this concept of the women (all three sets—Western, Middle and Eastern) is a puerile one. It could even be called downright idiotic. Yet I assure you that I see things this way, if I relax even a little and look through my own eyes into what is really inside my head.

(Though because of my talent for mimicry I am able to simulate looking through the eyes of an educated person when I wish to.) Since I am giving you such a frank picture of myself, I may as well go the whole hog and admit to you that my secret picture of the world is grossly inaccurate. I have completely forgotten to include in it any of the Latin countries. (France, Italy, Spain.) For instance, I have jumped from the Anglo world to the semi-Oriental as if there were not countries in between at all. I know that these exist. (I have even lived in two of them.) But they do not fit into my scheme. I just don't think about the Latins very much, and this is less understandable than my not thinking about the Chinese or Javanese or Japanese women. You can see why without my having to explain it to you. I do know that the French women are more interested in sports than they used to be, and for all I know they may be indistinguishable from Anglo women by now. I haven't been to France recently so I can't be sure. But in any case the women of those countries don't enter into my picture of the world. Or shall I say that the fact of having forgotten utterly to consider them has not altered the way I visualize the division of the world's women? Incredible though it may seem to you, it hasn't altered anything. (My having forgotten all Latin countries, South America included.) I want you to know the whole truth about me. But don't imagine that I wouldn't be capable of concealing my ignorance from you if I wanted to. I am so wily and feminine that I could live by your side for a lifetime and deceive you afresh each day. But I will have no truck with feminine wiles. I know how they can absorb the hours of the day. Many women are delighted to sit around spinning their webs. It is an absorbing occupation, and the

Ilse Klapper

William Burroughs first met German Ilse Klapper née Hertzfeldt in the seaside town of Dubrovnik, Yugoslavia, in 1936. He was traveling after college and thought the efficient, no-nonsense Ilse, with her dry humor and her monocle at the ready, to be a competent guide and interesting host.

Bill left Dubrovnik to study medicine in Germany, but returned soon after when the winds of Nazism began to blow too strong. Ilse was terrified because her Yugoslavian visa was about to run out. For the young Burroughs the choice was obvious: wed Ilse and enable her to escape to the United States. Although his parents objected strongly, they did marry, Bill essentially saving her life. The two did not see much of one another in the States, but Bill never regretted his decision, saying, "She never asked me for a dime."

women feel they are getting somewhere. And so they are, but only for as long as the man is there to be deceived. And a wily woman alone is a pitiful sight to behold. Naturally.

I shall try to be honest with you so that I can live with you and yet won't be pitiful. Even if tossing my feminine tricks out the window means being left no better than an illiterate backwoodsman, or the bottom fish scraping along the ocean bed, I prefer to have it this way. Now I am too tired to write more. Though I don't feel that I have clarified enough or justified enough.

I shall write you soon about the effect the war has had upon me. I have spoken to you about it, but you have never seemed to take it very seriously. Perhaps seeing in black and white what I feel will affect your opinion of me. Perhaps you will leave me. I accept the challenge. My Hotel Henry experience includes this risk. I got drunk two nights ago. It's hard to believe that I am forty-seven, isn't it?

My love,
Emmy

Now that I have copied this letter into my journal (I had forgotten to make a carbon), I shall take my walk. My scheme included a few weeks of solitude at the Hotel Henry before attempting anything. I did not even intend to write in my journal as soon as I started to, but simply to sit about collecting my thoughts, waiting for the knots of habit to undo themselves. But after only a week here—two nights ago—I felt amazingly alone and disconnected from my past life, so I began my journal.

My first interesting contact was the salesman in the Blue Bonnet Room. I had heard about this eccentric through my in-laws, the Moores, before I ever came up here. My husband's cousin Laurence Moore told me about him when he heard I was coming. He said: "Take a walk through Grey and Bottle's Department Store, and you'll see a man with a lean red face and reddish hair selling materials by the bolt. That man has an income and is related to Hewitt Molain. He doesn't need to work. He was in my fraternity. Then he disappeared. The next I heard of him he was working at Grey and Bottle's. I stopped by and said hello to him. For a nut he seemed like a very decent chap. You might even have a drink with him. I think he's quite up to general conversation."

I did not mention Laurence Moore to the society salesman because I thought it might irritate him. I lied and pretended to have been here for months, when actually this is still only my second week at the Hotel Henry. I want everyone to think I have been here a long time. Surely it is not to impress them. Is there anything impressive about a lengthy stay at the Hotel Henry? Any sane person would be alarmed that I should even ask such a question. I ask it because deep in my heart I *do* think a lengthy stay at the Hotel Henry is impressive. Very easy to see that I would, and even sane of me to think it impressive, but not sane of me to expect anyone else to think so, particularly a stranger. Perhaps I simply like to hear myself telling it. I hope so. I shall write some more tomorrow, but now I must go out. I am going to buy a supply of cocoa. When I'm not drunk I like to have a cup of cocoa before going to sleep. My husband likes it too.

■■■

She could not stand the overheated room a second longer. With some difficulty she raised the window, and the cold wind blew in. Some loose sheets of paper went skimming off the top of the desk and flattened themselves against the bookcase. She shut the window and they fell to the floor. The cold air had changed her mood. She looked down at the sheets of paper. They were part of the letter she had just copied. She picked them up: *"I don't feel that I have clarified enough or justified enough,"* she read. She closed her eyes and shook her head. She had been so happy copying this letter into her journal, but now her heart was faint as she scanned its scattered pages. "I have said nothing," she muttered to herself in alarm. "I have said nothing at all. I have not clarified my reasons for being at the Hotel Henry. I have not justified myself."

Automatically she looked around the room. A bottle of whiskey stood on the floor beside one of the legs of the bureau. She stepped forward, picked it up by the neck and settled with it into her favorite wicker chair.

courtesy of Mary Greer

James Broughton, Madeline Gleason, and Robert Duncan in San Francisco. Photo taken by Jess.

Madeline Gleason
True Born Poet
(1903–1979)

"If I come into it personally, and I do, it's because Madeline Gleason in the first phases of the San Francisco scene was one of the prime members for me. In her own works, she created a transition from a passionate poetry close to Yeats as a master to an exuberant individual creation swinging in an ambit that could include Mother Goose and, long before 'Pop Art,' the voices of popular America."

—Robert Duncan, 1975

P oet, painter, and playwright Madeline Gleason played a vital role in revolutionizing modern poetry through the creation of the San Francisco poetry school of the late forties and early fifties. Born in Fargo, North Dakota, in 1903 as the only child of Irish Catholic parents, she found her way to poetry early. In the late twenties, as drought turned much of the Midwest into a dust bowl, she left Fargo, settling first in Arizona and then Oregon, paying her way as a singer and comic in a traveling minstrel show.

In 1935, she came to San Francisco, where she founded the San Francisco Poetry Guild, laying the foundation for the Beat poets to come. When Allen Ginsberg, Gary Snyder, Michael McClure, and other prime movers of the Beat Generation came to San Francisco with their wild new free verse, Madeline Gleason was already there, fascinating audiences with her singular style.

A seminal historical force amongst the West Coast literati, she initiated, with Robert Duncan and James Broughton, the Festival of Contemporary Poetry readings in 1947 at the Labaudt Gallery, which brought the first widespread recognition to Bay Area poets and established San Francisco as a major center of American poetry.

Madeline's first book, *Poems,* published in 1944, had a powerful effect on the emerging writing community of the time. Her musicality and mysticism caused Robert Duncan to claim that she "had a direct channel with God."

Initially a member of the Kenneth Rexroth poetry circle, Madeline focused on mythical themes that stood out in sharp contrast against the freely formed poetics of her contemporaries. Her elegiac poetry was more closely aligned with poet Mary Fabilli's husband, poet-priest William Everson, than with the more modern poets that came later. Powerfully combining the strict beat of music with the lucid motion of language, her poetry is magical, heavily woven with fairy tales, children's rhymes, and powerfully haunting rhythms, presenting lively parables. "Her subject is, like Emily Dickinson's, the sorrow in loving both God and his creatures," wrote James Broughton in the *San Francisco Chronicle.* "With her own homely juxtaposes of the secular and the celestial, the breezy and the woeful, she records the restless dismays of her heart."

Although Madeline did not introduce free verse or end stops, she did provide one of the first forums for the modern poetry reading. In April 1947, despite warnings of failure from naysayers, she organized the San Francisco Poetry Festival, the first such festival in the United States. Based upon the format of a music festival, readings were performed by the original authors, sometimes with the accompaniment of music. The feedback was so tremendously favorable that another festival was planned for the fall. It quickly became an institution, attracting East Coast poets, including early Beats. These festivals were the precursors to the more popular readings of the 1950s and 1960s, when poetry, music, and other media combined to form a spontaneous "bop" feeling.

With Robert Duncan, Madeline shared a common concern for spirituality, and he provided her with lifelong support and encouragement. He often said they were soul mates. She, in turn, was for him a source of inspiration, and he wrote a play about her called *Mrs. Noah.*

Immensely talented, Madeline could seemingly do anything she turned her hand to—painting, writing, singing. Her paintings are wildly colorful city scenes on backgrounds of pure black. She was fascinated by the chock-a-block development of San Francisco and the brilliant tangles of neon. North Beach, where she had her happiest moments, was her favorite subject for oil paintings.

Like her peer Helen Adam, Madeline worked as a runner for the stock exchange and financiers in San Francisco's downtown, rising at 5 A.M. to carry messages and money. In her North Beach flat, she held daily teas that became de facto literary salons with artists and poets dropping in and out. Madeline fondly remembered when the Beats came to town; Allen Ginsberg, Jack Kerouac, Neal Cassady, and the others made the rounds, paying their respects to the older, established poets.

In the late 1960s, toward the end of her life, Madeline moved from the North Beach scene to a hilly outer district of San Francisco. As she moved away from the lively center of poetry and art she so loved, she became very ill and depressed. Her lover and companion of twenty-five years, Mary Greer, remarked that "Madeline died of despair, what all poets die of."

Madeline and the other leaders of the San Francisco Renaissance were important precursors to the Beat poets. By making art and poetry the center of their lives, their life's work, they started an important shift in America's attitude about literature and the humanities. They took poetry out of the classrooms and out into the streets. They brought life, energy, and music into writing, setting free the muse and opening up a world of possibilities.

THE INTERIOR CASTLE

That invisible engine powered by words
runs fast, slow, haltingly, never rests,
collecting and dispersing as it goes
the soul's furnishings.

The insecurity of the poet
is his security.
His shambling mental movements
toward the moving machine
attract it to idle
at the threshold

of his unknowing:
the interior castle.
He enters, finds the great room bare.
There he summons forth that tree
of which the fruit is pearls, large as apples;
he approaches the tree,
plucks a pearl, and hums.

A good saint offers instruction
for his guidance,
and Beelzebub tutors
in the language of seduction.
Both bring their troops and trains,
a company of voices
rattling together,
celestial and uncelestial;
a crackling bonfire of words
rising in incense of golden smoke.
Saint and Beelzebub contend
for his allegiance.
During their contention
the poet makes of one wall
a mirror of invention
to see the child he is,
timing his wizardry
under the pearl tree.

The interior castle
where Theresa stayed
and all her spirit's lightnings played
to rigorous accompaniment
to that same place
the poet comes;
a place that by turns

is cold, warm,
pleasurable, intolerable.
With the influence of Venus in his heart
the influence of Saturn in his head,
the poet kills himself,
than rises from the dead,
climbs to the tree-top;
while around him
there, all there,
aboard the invisible engine
powered by words,
a company of voices.
In a fury he spins himself
turning upon the spit of his own burning rays,
and in a passion sings the room ablaze.

■ ■ ■

REBIRTH

The valley and the rolling hill
Become a landscape flat and stark
As any desert and as still.
He does not hear the meadowlark.

He does not see the squirrel bound,
The violet bank at sundown turn
Into a rippling purple mound
Moving upon a bed of fern.

Without a compass, dumb and blind,
Face downward in the field he lies,
Lost in the darkness of his mind,
The daisies pressed against his eyes.

He does not hear the wind that bends
The low bough towards him on the grass,
But only his world that cracks and ends
As his soul breaks its looking-glass.

■■■

LYRICS
To Teo

I
At Land's End the cold wind
Blew against my face,
I thought how we live between
The divine and the commonplace.

All extremes must meet,
And imagination take fire
From the innocent and the lewd,
From continence and desire.

The living must descend
And then ascend the slope,
Know joy, torment, despair;
The loss and return of hope.

All extremes must meet;
As some old poet has said:
Out of a little earth
And heaven, was Adam made.

■■■

THE POET IN THE WOOD

Peace hidden from him
And his nation
Like a star
In occulation,

The poet left the lazar-house
Of the world, where his friends,
Bankrupt in spirit, were encamped,
And pursued his own ends.

Days he walked wandering
In Muir Woods, forgot
What he had learned of the world
That was all merd and rot,

And drew peace to him
From ferns, delicate shoots,
Flourishing weeds,
Herbs, hedges and grass roots,

And having attained self-peace,
Was under the illusion
That the world was in order
And the wicked no longer in collusion.

He picked the leaves of a laurel,
With a wreath crowned him,
And considered
The small hills around him.

Before this poet
Whose laureateship
Commanded nothing
But boughs that dip,

Weighed down by wind,
A figure appeared and said:
"Return to those who fear,
Yet know not what they dread.

"Take off the laurel
and go home again,
Save those who live
In the lazar-house of pain.

"And tell those friends
About whom you forgot
That only half the world
Is merd and rot."

The figure fled.
And the poet stood
Alone, stunned
And shaken in the wood.

He turned to leave,
But turning thus,
Thought of that down-rolling rock
And helpless Sisyphus.

■ ■ ■

SOULGLASS

Who loves, yet is not dazed,
When in his own glass stirs
The image of that one
Who calls the soulglass hers.

No solemn shadow-land
Is this the mirror frames,
Where carefree as children
Elated at their games,

The trembling lovers look
Above them and below,
While sparks apocryphal,
Set the glass aglow.

Suddenly the mirror blazes
With fire through which they pass;
Light dazzles there as if
The sun rose from that glass.

■ ■ ■

I FORGOT YOUR NAME

I waited for you
to walk with me
towards heaven.
A long way,
longer ago
than being born.

Three tones
repeated themselves:
NEAR FAR NEVER
struck together
they sounded an agony.

Storms began in the mind
spread to the flesh
hurricaning with wrath.

I waited for you
bore with my unblessing.
I wanted to go at once,
start on the morning
of beginning,
but I had lost all sense
of direction.

My hair grizzled,
my joints stiffened,
my legs lamed.
Which way to heaven?
And where was love,
NEAR FAR NEVER
I forgot your name.

courtesy of Mary Greer

"Carnival Painting," circa 1954, by Madeline Gleason.

Josephine Miles
Mentor to a Revolution
(1911–1985)

"I don't like dualisms. I don't believe in things being split in two. But I think a lot of vital action is taken in rejection of things, and so you often get one mode fighting another and thriving just because it's fighting it. These really aren't dualisms, but they are leading trends and then minor oppositions coming in which they themselves grow."

—Josephine Miles on the birth of Beat

The great professor of English, Dr. Josephine Miles inspired more than just her students. Her impact upon the literary world was not bound by the walls of her classroom. It ranged from the board of directors at the National Endowment of the Arts to a struggling Beat poet searching for publication.

Her parents were childhood sweethearts in Chicago, who married after a twenty-year courtship. In June 1911, the first of their three children, Josephine, was born. A few months later, Josephine's father's insurance firm promoted him, and they moved to San Francisco. When Josephine was nine months old, her grandfather, Dr. Frederick Billing Miles, noticed that her hips were crooked. After corrective surgery, an intern accidentally cut her leg while casting it and did not dress the wound but instead covered it with a larger cast. An infection ensued; Josephine also later developed arthritis that racked her entire body for the remainder of her life.

Soon after, her father was again transferred, this time to Detroit. The combination of humidity and biting cold exacerbated Josephine's arthritis, and her body stiffened. With no other choice, the family moved to Palm Springs, California, where Josephine's health improved in the warmer climate. Confident that she had completely recovered, the Miles family moved back to Chicago just after her sixth birthday. But the bitter cold bent her body so badly that she underwent nearly six years of casts and drastic operations. The fierce winters finally forced her father to take a demotion and move to Los Angeles.

Josephine's first year in Los Angeles was spent in traction. Unable to sit or lie down, she could not attend school. During that year, she was home-schooled by her mother. Once she gained some mobility, she was moved to a wheelchair but was still not allowed to attend the local grammar school. Once Josephine moved past elementary skills, especially when learning to write, she required a tutor. The first teacher from the Los Angeles school system brought pine needles and raffia to make pine needle baskets. After six baskets and no other lessons, Josephine had enough and the teacher never returned. Josephine longed for real learning and spent countless hours reading in bed.

Other tutors came and went. It would not be until high school that she would be allowed to attend classes. But eventually, in 1928, Josephine enrolled in the University of California at Los Angeles to pursue an undergraduate degree. She entered school with few career plans. "All I remember is my dad would say, 'You must go somewhere to college where you get away from home and get some new experience, and somebody can help you besides your mother. The boys must go to Stanford.'"

She intended to concentrate on classic humanities, her passion while in high school. She changed her mind, however, after a class taught by a remarkably boring professor. She graduated with a bachelor's degree in English literature in 1932 and moved north for graduate studies.

Despite the damp and foggy climate of the Bay Area, the University of California at Berkeley provided the perfect environment for her literary pursuits. She received the Shelley Memorial Award for Poetry, and her Ph.D. three years later. The next year, she was named an American Association of University Women Research Fellow, which led to her appointment as an English professor at U.C. Berkeley in 1940.

Josephine soon found herself at the heart of the changing literary scene. With the arrival of the Beats just across the bay in San Francisco, students at Berkeley were exposed to a genre of poetry not taught in the classroom. They were excited about the changing face of poetry, bringing mimeographed copies of street poetry to their professors. Some teachers scoffed at its lack of structure, turning instead to the metered sounds of Yeats and Blake. Josephine, however, was intrigued by this new style and encouraged her students to develop their own voices. She mentored Robin Blaser and Jack Spicer, who went on to form the Spicer Circle with Kenneth Rexroth. The two eventually became part of the San Francisco Renaissance, which included Philip Lamantia, Madeline Gleason, and Robert Duncan.

Josephine even welcomed Allen Ginsberg's arrival to the Bay Area: "Allen Ginsberg came to town. This was a time when Allen was working for some business firm and had a pin-striped suit. He came to Berkeley to talk to Mark Schoer and me about whether he should be a graduate student at Berkeley.... He had this pin-striped suit and this big folder. So, he said, would I read these poems and tell him whether he should do graduate work. And it was quite a nice experience, you know, I mean, wow! He was rather unprepossessing looking, and to lay your eyes on something really full of energy was a real pleasure."

Josephine remained at the center of the Beat literary arena as mentor. At a poetry reading at a friend's home, she met a visiting poet and scholar from New York, Richard Eberhardt. He expressed an interest in the poetry scene in Berkeley, asking Josephine if she knew of any new writers. She mentioned Allen Ginsberg and gave Eberhardt her copy of his most recent work, "Howl." He was so impressed that he wrote an article for the *New York Times,* praising the new style—and the rest, as they say, is history.

The changing form of poetry beckoned Josephine. Writing about the influence of the scene around her, she noted, "I think my poetry has gotten looser and freer in form than it was. I think I don't write as many clear endings. I think I've been influenced." She never allied herself closely with any one school of poetry, but rather allowed herself to be touched by each one's style. "I've never been accepted as a soulmate by any of these groups," she once remarked.

She took her job as an educator very seriously and published many articles and books of literary criticism. She often worked late with her students. Poet Mary Fabilli remembers of those years, "When you went down the hall of Wheeler at six o'clock at night, all English department doors were open, and at every desk you saw a professor leaning over a desk with a student's paper before him and the student listening and asking questions about the paper." For Josephine, working with students was much like her poetry, structured but loose enough to include all trains of thought.

As the first female professor ever tenured at U.C. Berkeley, Josephine might be expected to be a women's liberation proponent. In general, however, she found more camaraderie among her male contemporaries than with women, with the exception of another strong-minded individualist—Pauline Kael—who became a close friend. Pauline later became a first-rate movie reviewer, turning her reviews into literature. Josephine's studies often brought her to New York, where she found the women aloof, leaving her no choice but to associate primarily with men. When approached by other women faculty members, she balked. "I simply liked working with men," she said.

During the sixties and seventies, her moderate politics clashed with those of her more hot-blooded colleagues. She had difficulty dealing with their rather radical methods, but she participated in mediation between the women's association and the male faculty and was instrumental in implementing a program designed to appoint one woman per year until some balance was achieved in the English department. The program was little more than an appeasement; as there were sixty male faculty members and only three women, parity wouldn't be achieved for many years.

She compiled and edited *American Poetry* in 1965 and *Berkeley Street Poems* in 1969. With the help of two other professors, she also started a quarterly of faculty essays, *Idea and Experiment,* to be sent to alumni. To Josephine's surprise, it was labeled communist by the alumni and discontinued after twelve issues.

Josephine was awarded the Blumenthal Award for Poetry in 1958. The National Foundation of Arts awarded her a Fellowship in 1965. In 1972, she became University of California at Berkeley's first female professor of English, and eight years later accepted a National Arts Endowment Senior Fellowship. She continued to write and live in Berkeley until her death on May 12, 1985.

CURTAIN

A picture window opening to the west
Is curtained in the morning; from the outside
It's a closed room. From the inside,
Gloom. The sun collaborates,
West gray in shade.
Now I must ask you whether a leaf of sun
Will gradually cast its tentative light within
Or whether you will proceed across the floor
Pull back the drapes and look into the day
As if you would renew it? From the outside
A scene of limitless shape, a chandelier
Bathed in reflection, each corner
Each morning
As if the furnished action had no fear
To act again.

■ ■ ■

TRAVELLERS

The little girl was travelling unattached, as they say,
Closed into her window-seat by a heavy
Business-man working on papers out of his briefcase.
From across the aisle another kept noticing
What help she needed, her travel-case latched,
Her doll righted, coloring-book straightened out,
And he kept leaning over across to assist her.
After a while the heavy-set man put away his papers,
Took out a small gameboard from his briefcase, and suggested,
How about a game of three-way parcheesi?

■ ■ ■

AT THE COUNTER

Give me a half sack of buttered popcorn, sweetie,
Would you like to hear some good news?
I'm a biochemist you know, even look like a biochemist they tell me,
Despite my rugged frame.
And today I discovered the cure for diabetes!
You may well exclaim.

You know what the cure is? An herb. It grows high
In the mountains of Mexico.
And my doctor tells me that my big chest.
Expanded from singing opera, will allow
My living as high as sixteen thousand feet
To cultivate the herb. What is its name?
I'll bet you'd like to know!

■ ■ ■

BUREAU

Skunks fight under the house and keep us
Wakeful, they are down from the hills in the drought.
Lots of colloquial remedies, mothballs, tomato juice
Leave them unmoved. Call the S.P.C.A.
Call the bureau of Health, Call the P G E where they rest
Past the meter box, call the Animal Shelter.
Call commercial exterminators; all reply
With a sigh, and a different number to call
Next month or next year when they're not so busy.
Asking around, getting the number finally
Of the chief health officer of the county.
Mr. Simms, his secretary answers,

What makes you think Mr. Simms will speak to you?
What makes you think Mr. Simms is interested in skunks?
As Mr. Simms is animal health officer of the county
His chief interest is wolves.

THE MUSES

© Allen Ginsberg/Fahey Klein Gallery

Joan Vollmer Adams Burroughs in New York City.

Reverse: Cowboy Neal at the wheel, with Ann Murphy, 1960.

Joan Vollmer Adams Burroughs
Calypso Stranded
(1924–1951)

**I went back to Mexico City
and saw Joan Burroughs leaning
forward in a garden chair, arms
on her knees....**
—Allen Ginsberg, "Dream Record," June 8, 1955

Joan Vollmer Adams Burroughs was seminal in the creation of the Beat revolution; indeed the fires that stoked the Beat engine were started with Joan as patron and muse. Her apartment in New York was a nucleus that attracted many of the characters who played a vital role in the formation of the Beat; those who gathered there included Bill Burroughs, Jack and Edie Kerouac, and Herbert Huncke. Brilliant and well versed in philosophy and literature, Joan was the whetstone against which the main Beat writers—Allen, Jack, and Bill—sharpened their intellect. Widely considered one of the most perceptive people in the group, her strong mind and independent nature helped bulldoze the Beats toward a new sensibility.

Joan paid dearly for her refusal to live within the boundaries of the social mores of forties' and fifties' America, ultimately dying in a horrible accident at the hand of her common-law husband, author William Burroughs. There is no denying, however, that Joan hastened the new consciousness that the Beats espoused in her short time with them. Joan was not an artist or writer, but Bill and others credit her with being a powerful inspiration for their work.

Joan Vollmer grew up in Loudonville, New York, a suburb of Albany. Her father,

David Vollmer, managed a large plant and worked hard to provide his family with the best of everything. Joan grew up in an economically privileged world, but wished for a sense of self that money could not buy. She fought with her mother constantly and chafed at the constraints of the household. As soon as she could, she eagerly departed the ritzy world of her family for New York City and Barnard College.

A handsome woman who constantly questioned the status quo, Joan read constantly and enjoyed discussing a wide range of topics, usually while in the bathtub. Her appetite for books was rivaled only by her appetite for men, and she married law student Paul Adams soon after arriving in New York, more an act of defiance than of love. After her marriage, Joan spent her evenings prowling bars like the West End, looking for the company of strangers; Paul had been drafted and was stationed in Tennessee.

Late one night, Joan met a kindred spirit, Edie Parker, during one of her rambles at the West End Bar and the two soon moved into an apartment at 421 West 118th Street. This was the first in a series of apartments that would provide an open forum for the exchange of new ideas and attitudes, with Joan at the center, a strong and magnetic presence.

Joan and Edie's apartment became a haven for a bunch of Columbia students who were disillusioned with all the starched-collar conservatism of the forties. Edie's boyfriend, Jack Kerouac, who had forsaken a football scholarship at Columbia to

Vickie Russell

Vickie Russell was a frequent guest at Joan's apartment salon, usually appearing with her good friend Herbert Huncke. The daughter of a Philadelphia magistrate, she changed her name from Priscilla Arminger to escape her wealthy suburban origins. She was gifted and gorgeous, a six-foot-tall redhead who fascinated men both straight and gay. Vickie kept herself in Benzedrine by working as a high-class call girl. She introduced the denizens of Joan's salon to the proper way to get pure Benzedrine from over-the-counter inhalers. Allen Ginsberg said she was "as attractive as any woman I know," while Jack Kerouac admired her ingenuity in Benzedrine extraction. Allen kept a portrait of Vickie on his mantel painted by Little Jack Melody, Vickie's boyfriend, who nursed her back to health when her addictions took their toll. Little Jack was a full foot shorter than Vickie and doted on her. Of Sicilian American descent, he made his living as a safe robber. Allen praised him for his gentle nature. Together, Allen, Little Jack, and Vickie once wrecked a stolen car, resulting in Allen's visit to Columbia Psychiatric Institution, where he met Carl Solomon, for whom he wrote "Howl." Vickie Russell dropped out of sight after the early New York Beat scene, resurfacing only in the memoirs of her friend Herbert Huncke.

pursue his writing, lived there when he was not shipping out with the merchant marines. One of Joan's lovers, a sixteen-year-old Columbia student named John Kingsland, also moved into the apartment, as did Hal Chase, a graduate student from Denver. The atmosphere was both intellectual and chaotic—a nonstop salon with both discourse and dalliance.

Columbia student Lucien Carr began coming around with his girlfriend, Celine Young. He also brought over a Columbia hallmate named Allen Ginsberg. Allen found the open exchange of ideas at Joan's place reassuring, for at the time he was grappling with his sexual identity.

Lucien decided that Allen's mind was ripe for an awakening and brought him downtown one day to meet a friend from St. Louis named William Burroughs. The heir to the Burroughs adding-machine fortune, William Burroughs had graduated from Harvard University in 1936. Allen was bowled over by the enigmatic Bill, a man who dressed in a suit, quoted Shakespeare in a nasal voice, and enjoyed skewering people with his dry wit. With a $200 monthly stipend from his parents, Bill enjoyed exploring the seedy Times Square area for kicks.

Bill started coming up to Joan's place and, although predominantly homosexual, he was intrigued by her quicksilver intellect and love of stirring people up. Joan was attracted to Bill for his brilliant mind, outrageous proclamations, and vaguely sinister air. Bill moved in and the two began their curious marriage of minds.

Bill brought with him a collection of hustlers, petty criminals, and drug dealers, and the uptown and downtown coalesced into an even stranger tableau. Joan and Jack were introduced to Benzedrine by a neighborhood prostitute named Vickie Russell, and Bill started his longtime addiction to heroin. Eventually, Bill and others were arrested for drug use, and Joan ended up in Bellevue, speed-addled and in need of help.

Bill arranged Joan's release from the hospital and they conceived a child soon after. Although never married in a ceremony, the two were never parted again. They moved to New Waverly, Texas, to escape the legal problems that had been plaguing them back in New York. Bill bought a farm—the plan was to make lots of money growing marijuana. Mostly though, they entertained guests, including their old New

York Beat crony Herbert Huncke, who came to "sharecrop," do drugs, and play with guns.

Joan and Bill had a special psychic connection which, friends said, seemed to transcend the normal—Joan had the uncanny ability to receive images that Bill sent to her telepathically. They would sit across the room from each other for hours, playing this psychic game and startling visitors with their amazing associative talent.

Later that year, Joan and Bill were caught in flagrante delicto by a notoriously vigilant sheriff, who charged Bill with drunk driving and public indecency. Rather than deal with more potential problems in the Lone Star state, they moved to New Orleans; Joan had plenty of Benzedrine to fuel her attempts to rake the lizards out of the trees in her new front yard. New Orleans was fine for a while, but once again a drug bust prompted another move. This time they moved to Mexico City to ensure that there would be no more reckoning with U.S. authorities.

Bill enjoyed Mexico because the boys and the heroin were cheap and plentiful; two hundred dollars went considerably farther than it had in the States. Also the *federales* were always willing to overlook a problem if there were some money in it for them. Joan could no longer get Benzedrine and made do with cheap tequila instead. She looked terrible and hinted to friends that her days were numbered.

On September 6, 1951, Joan and Bill were at a party. Everyone had been drinking gin for hours when Bill announced that it was time for the William Tell act. Joan

Helen Hinkle

Helen Hinkle, wife of Al Hinkle, went on the road with Neal Cassady and her new husband Al as their honeymoon trip, but "had started wanting to stay at motels at night and stopping for food and such nonsensical things as that," according to LuAnne Henderson Cassady. This conflict of traveling styles led to Neal and Al letting Helen out in Arizona. With Al's railroad pass, Helen made her way back to Joan's and William Burroughs' home in Algiers, Louisiana, where Helen awaited her husband's return on the loop back across the country. Her visit with the gun-crazed, lizard-infested Burroughs family was only slightly more comfortable and less surreal than the unheated car. Helen Hinkle remained close friends with Carolyn Cassady until Helen's death in 1995.

courtesy of Carolyn Cassady

Al and Helen Hinkle, Christmas 1949.

put a water glass on her head and turned her face, saying that she couldn't stand the sight of blood. Bill, a crack shot, took aim from about six feet away. She died instantly, not yet thirty years old.

Bill was able to keep himself out of too much trouble with the help of a good lawyer and spent only thirteen days in jail. But he would forever be haunted by Joan's ghost. He maintained years later that it was an accident, but has also said that there is no such thing as an accident. In either case, he has always maintained that it was Joan's death which has motivated him to write ever since.

Burroughs was not the only Beat to be inspired by Joan. Allen Ginsberg's opus "Howl" was written after a dream of Joan in 1957.

Herbert Huncke spent a lot of time with Joan and Bill during their life together. The following is a remembrance of Joan Burroughs from his autobiography.

from *Guilty of Everything*
by Herbert Huncke

Bill decided to move up into Joan's apartment not far from Columbia, where he was taking a course. Now, Joan had rented a large rambling apartment. I think there were actually three bedrooms and a gigantic bathroom with a tub in it. It was an old fashioned apartment that had been built about 1915, when that area was just beginning to be developed. It was right in back of Barnard there on 115th. She took this apartment at, I think, a very reasonable amount of money, by today's standards practically nothing. I think it was something like 75 dollars a month for this gigantic place. She kept the kitchen and the dining room and the living room for herself, and the three bedrooms she rented out to students from the university.

When she met Burroughs she immediately was attracted to him, and she saved her prize room for him. It was really a beautiful room, gigantic, in which he had his books and a desk and a bed for himself and the whole works. Then just a little bit beyond that was the bathroom and beyond that was Hal Chase's room. He was in one of the History classes and now teaches history, I think. There was some other young fellow that was just sort of in and out, not really a close member of the clique.

The clique consisted of Joan, Bill, Allen, who had a place of his own but spent a great deal of time there, myself, and later, Jack Kerouac. Then there were several Oscar Wilde types. I don't know what you'd call them. They were certainly effete, if I use the word correctly. They were very witty with a terrific bite, almost vitriolic with their sarcasm. They could carry on these extremely witty conversations. They were people that I didn't care much for, partly because I was intimidated by them. I couldn't always understand them, and it used to make me feel sort of humiliated because I obviously did not know what they were talking about, and I felt embarrassed.

Joan particularly fascinated me. I had never met a girl quite like Joan. As a young teenager, I had met several girls that I was attracted to, and one that I had sex with. I was primarily a homosexual at that time. In fact, I was going through many changes about my homosexuality. I didn't know whether I was purely homosexual, or bi-sexual. In fact, I didn't know if I could have sex with a woman for a long time. Well, I say for a long time. I was about 16 or 17 before I actually had sex with a chick, and then that was very quick and over with and done. After that, occasionally I'd ball with a girl, so I could have sex with women. That relieved a great deal of the personal problem that I had at that time but that was the Chicago period.

From *Literary Outlaw*
by Ted Morgan

Joan was five foot six, with a heart-shaped face, a small, turned-up nose, soft brown eyes that were set wide apart, and shoulder-length light brown hair with short bangs. She had a lovely complexion and a nice figure, with legs a little on the heavy side. When she walked her calves wiggled. Joan's beauty was more than the sum of its parts. She was soft and feminine, and wore silky clinging clothes and small bandannas tied close to her head. In her reserve, in her achievement of a personal style, she reminded Edie of Garbo.

"You should always cook eggs slowly," was Joan's advice in the kitchen on 118th Street. Joan did everything slowly, Edie reflected; she spoke, walked, dressed, and read slowly, as if savoring every moment. She read everything, every newspaper and magazine....

Edie thought Joan was the most intelligent girl she had ever met. She had an independent mind, always questioning what anyone said, including her teachers at Barnard. In one of her marginal notes in her copy of Marx's *Capital and Other Writings*, there are echoes of Burroughs' thinking: "Maybe Marxism is dynamic and optimistic, and Freudianism is not. Is one more serviceable than the other? Why does it always have to be either/or?"

Joan's idea of a good time was to go to Child's at 110th Street and Broadway and sip *kümmel* and have deep conversations about Plato and Kant while listening to classical music. Or she would spend the entire morning in the bathtub, with bubble-bath up to her chin, reading Proust. If you wanted to talk to her it had to be in the bathroom.

Following are two letters written by Joan Burroughs—one to Edie Parker Kerouac and another to Allen Ginsberg dated two years before her death. The letter from Joan to Edie in 1945 shows the transition her life was undergoing after Bill's arrest for forging prescriptions, Joan's hospitalization for amphetamine psychosis which, according to Carolyn Cassady, was the first such documented case, and their subsequent move to Texas.

"I've really had a mad year although now perhaps I've come to a resting point.... Huncke stayed around and made some money making parked cars for the luggage. After a while we began taking in desperate characters as boarders so before long I was running quite a pad. Everything in the damn place was hot, as were of course a couple of cars out front. Inevitably people kept going to jail, until finally, due to that and the ever present back rent we got tossed out.... I'd been taking so much benzedrine that I got way off the beam, with the result that I finally landed in the Bellevue psycho ward just before Whitey's trial. Anyways I was all clear in a couple of days but it took me a week to convince those stupid doctors that I wasn't completely mad. Everything was timed nicely though, because just before I got out at last Bill got back in town.

Although we're not married yet, Bill got a divorce, but I haven't yet. Make it to Mrs. W. S. Burroughs. New Waverly, Texas."

Mexico City, 1949

Dear Allen,

I was not much surprised to hear of your hospitalization, as I've been claiming for three years (today being my third anniversary from Bellevue) that anyone who doesn't blow his top once is no damn good. I'd had feared at one time that you'd never see the light, but when I saw you at Atlantic Beach I had some hope for you, when you asked Bill in a letter once to refer to me to Blake's sick rose, whose worm I'd been sharing for months, I had more hopes and lately they have been amply fulfilled. When I refer to it as top-blowing, I'm sure you know what I mean. No percentage in talking about visions or super-reality or any such lay-terms. Either you know now what I know (and don't ask me just what that is) or else I'm mistaken about you and off the beam somewhere—in which case you're just a dime-a-dozen neurotic and *I'm* nuts. However, it is a good luck in many ways, and don't let it get away altogether. And how is your invisible worm... I shant attempt to describe my suffering for three weeks, but with thyroid tablets, Reich and faith I made it. Wonder how poor Herbert managed.

> Yours,
>
> Joan

Carolyn Cassady
Karmic Grace
(1923–   )

"Dear Carolyn,

... Wouldn't it be wonderful for Neal, Allen, Bill, me and you to be all together talking at night; Bill and me with our wine, Allen with his upheld index finger, Neal with his oolong, and you with your pizza pies... and wine.

You are a golden angel and I'll always love you as I have & will..."

Jack

Wife, mother, writer, painter, breadwinner, and muse, Carolyn Cassady remains a pivotal figure in the turbulent world of the Beats. She spent fourteen years on and off with the legendary Neal Cassady, a man who exemplified the Beat lifestyle with his cross-country road adventures, voracious appetites and energy, and penchant for drugs. While Neal, as a contemporary Dionysus, provided Jack Kerouac, Allen Ginsberg, and, later, Ken Kesey, with a wealth of experiences to draw from, Carolyn provided Neal with the steady presence he needed when the party, inevitably, was over.

Indeed, Carolyn Cassady was the bedrock at the core of the great Beat trio of Jack Kerouac, Allen Ginsberg, and Neal Cassady. On the surface, it would seem that she was the closest to the fifties' ideal of a devoted wife and mother, "standing by her man." But Carolyn doesn't fit into any such convenient mold. An intensely creative person in her own right, she knew there was something very special about Jack, Allen, and Neal and chose to see them as not bound by the constraints of mere mortals. Carolyn Cassady is a great believer in the power of fate and she had the faith to recognize it.

Carolyn Robinson grew up in Nashville, Tennessee, where she was exposed early to the world of ideas. Both of her parents were educators and they raised her in an

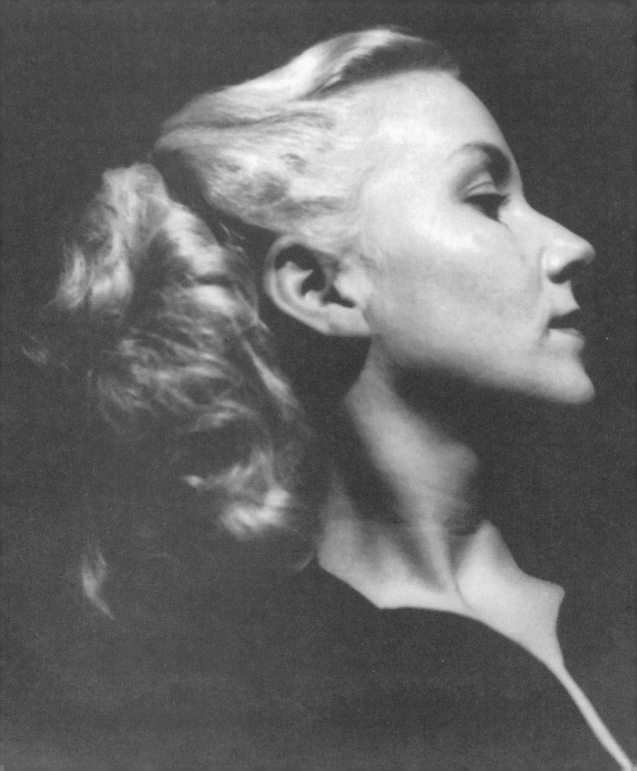

intellectual atmosphere that nurtured her curiosity and creativity. She was awarded a scholarship to Bennington College, at the time one of the most elite women's schools in the United States, where she trained in Stanislavsky's method acting and received a bachelor's degree in drama.

In her junior and senior years she ran the theater design department, because the teachers she studied with were fired without replacement. She also studied sculpture, ceramics, architecture, painting, and drawing, as well as dance with Martha Graham and psychology with Erich Fromm. In 1947, she moved to Colorado to pursue a master's degree in theater and fine arts at the University of Denver, where her all-American blonde good looks attracted many suitors, including the roguish Neal Cassady.

Neal was a human dynamo, his legs furiously pumping a mile a minute and his mouth blowing a verbal Dizzy Gillespie. Carolyn was immediately drawn to his piercing eyes, frenetic energy, and amazing ability to absorb everything happening around him and verbally weave it into a seemingly endless riff on everything from cars to Rimbaud. "He appeared caught up in observing everything and everybody on every side," she later wrote, looking at her "with those talking eyes."

Although Neal was married at the time to sixteen-year-old LuAnne Henderson, he convinced Carolyn that an annulment was imminent, and she was so taken with him that she bought the first of the many cons he would lay on her. "I'd never before experienced such solicitude, or such thoughtfulness and diligence in being agreeable. At this time, I accepted everything he told me as the truth." They began dating.

Neal, however, continued sleeping with LuAnne, and many others, while managing to hide his trysts from Carolyn. In Carolyn's eyes, Neal maintained "his open and innocent facade." Neal's infidelities were less an indictment of his love for Carolyn than a manifestation of his own insecurities. She became convinced that her relationship with Neal was a matter of predestination, her sense of which was enhanced by the fact that he was the first man she had fallen in love with "without romance or physical attraction being a dominant factor. A good sign," she decided. "Physically I felt the cogs mesh in the wheel of fate."

Facing page: portrait of Carolyn Cassady, 1946 (photo courtesy of Carolyn Cassady).

Neal told Carolyn about his great writer friends from New York—Jack Kerouac and Allen Ginsberg—whom he had met while on an extended honeymoon with LuAnne in New York City, intimating that he too was a part of this writing brotherhood and informing her that Allen was coming to Denver that June to stay for a while.

When Allen arrived, things between Neal and Carolyn were still fresh and exciting. Allen and Neal seemed to be old friends, and Carolyn respected their friendship as such. She had no reason to suspect that Neal and Allen were also having an affair. Neal's plate was quite full between Carolyn, LuAnne, Allen, and his job, but that did not stop him from proposing to Carolyn. Inevitably, it was just a matter of time before everything came crashing down.

Jack Kerouac came through town on his way to San Francisco, and Carolyn thought

LuAnne Henderson

LuAnne Henderson, once described by Jack Kerouac as a "nymph with waist-length dirty blond hair," was the sixteen-year-old bride of Neal Cassady whom he ultimately left for Carolyn. Neal had seen LuAnne's pretty blonde curls in a Walgreen's drugstore and announced, "That's the girl I'm going to marry." A month later, he did—in a terrible snowstorm shortly before Christmas. They decided to honeymoon on the road and set out for New York City in a stolen car with a few clothes, a volume of

courtesy of Carolyn Cassady

LuAnne Henderson in 1946.

Shakespeare, and Proust's *Remembrance of Things Past*.

LuAnne was as adventurous as Neal; the character of the girl in *On the Road* is based on her. With Neal at the wheel of the stolen Hudson, they raced at top speed on a spree of grifting: begging, borrowing, and stealing gas and food. She thrilled to every minute of the precarious journey now immortalized by Kerouac, "hocking all the way across" America. LuAnne wasn't just along for the ride, however; she was an equal participant, loving both Beats until the day Neal dumped her and Jack at the corner of O'Farrell and Grant in San Francisco with no money and nowhere to go. "Neal will leave you in the cold any time it's in his interest," LuAnne remarked to the bemused Jack Kerouac.

he was both handsome and polite. Jack had a habit of falling in love with his friend's girlfriends and one night he told Carolyn that it was too bad Neal had seen her first. This foreshadowed a romance that would later develop between Jack and Carolyn.

Meanwhile, Carolyn had finished school and decided to move to Hollywood to pursue a career as a costume designer. She hoped that Neal would follow her and they would eventually be married, but Neal had more immediate plans. He told her that Allen Ginsberg was in love with him and that he owed Allen some time. The two men were planning a trip to Texas to help Bill Burroughs, a friend of Allen's, harvest his crop of red-dirt marijuana. There was no reasoning with Neal, and Carolyn could only hope that he would eventually join her in California.

The morning she was to leave for the West Coast, Carolyn decided to pay Neal a surprise visit. She burst into his room to find Neal, Allen, and LuAnne naked in bed together. Neal attempted a lame explanation as Carolyn bolted in horror for Los Angeles.

While waiting for a costume design position she had been promised to open up in L.A., Carolyn moved to San Francisco. There Neal wrote to her, apologizing for his mistakes, begging her forgiveness, and asking for another chance. Carolyn was ecstatic and forgave him. Neal arrived in San Francisco on October 4, 1947, and their romance began anew. Shortly after Christmas, Carolyn became pregnant. Neal finally chiseled an annulment out of LuAnne, and Neal and Carolyn were married on April Fool's Day, 1948.

Cathy was born in August 1948, and life in the Cassady household began a prolonged cycle of ups and downs. There were plenty of good times when Neal was an excellent provider, a loving husband, and

courtesy of Carolyn Cassady

Carolyn and Neal in love. San Francisco, October, 1947.

61

a doting father. Neal had started working as a brakeman for the railroad, making good money, and they were able to save some with the hopes of eventually buying a ranch.

Ultimately, though, Neal was ruled by his compulsions, inevitably blowing the savings on a new car, a new girl, or some half-baked scheme. He would take off, leaving Carolyn to fend for herself and Cathy. While he cruised around the country, Carolyn held down a job as an office manager for a doctor for whom she also did medical illustrations and took care of her daughter. Although she swore again and again not to take him back, she could resist for only so long before Neal wore her down with his puckish charm.

Carolyn was pregnant for the second time, but Neal had once again taken off and was living in New York with a model named Diana Hansen. Diana called to let Carolyn know that she was also pregnant by Neal and that he wanted a divorce. Carolyn was so numb at this point that she agreed to start divorce proceedings. She gave birth to another daughter, Jami, in 1950, with Neal nowhere to be found. That June, the divorce was granted by an outraged judge and, although it would take a year to be final, that didn't stop Neal from talking Diana into believing that it already was. Neal married Diana Hansen on July 10, leaving her later that day to return to his railroad job and family in California. He bounced between his two wives for a few months, finally moving back in with Carolyn and the girls.

By September 1951, Carolyn gave birth to their third child, John Allen: Neal had named his son after his two best friends. Jack Kerouac himself had been through two marriages by this point, and in early 1952 came to San Francisco, where he took up residence in the attic of the Cassady home at 29 Russell Street. He was in the process of finishing *On the Road,* and Neal helped him get a job with the railroad.

Jack always credited Neal's "Joan Anderson Cherry Mary" letter, a 13,000-word, unpunctuated, handwritten piece as the inspiration for the bold new prose style that, ultimately, catapulted him to literary stardom. Much of the original letter that Neal wrote to Jack was lost, but a portion was published in *The First Third* by Lawrence Ferlinghetti's City Lights publishing house after Neal's death. Neal didn't take Allen Ginsberg's and Jack's enthusiasm for his writing too seriously, saying, "All the crazy folderol you two boys make over my big letter just thrills the gurgles out of me, but we still know I'm just a whiff and a dream."

Jack was always shy around Carolyn, but there was an attraction below the surface of their friendship. Neal, perhaps feeling some guilt over his past transgressions, even encouraged Jack and Carolyn to get together. Carolyn had endured Neal's philandering for so long that she decided to do it. The next few months were exhilarating for her as she now had the attentions of two men who were dear to her. Soon, however, tension arose between Neal and Jack, and the interlude ended with Carolyn choosing to stay with Neal.

The family moved to San Jose and then to Los Gatos. Being removed from San Francisco seemed to calm Neal down, and he roared up there only when the urge became too strong. The couple became interested in the work of Edgar Cayce, a psychic who preached a positive message of acceptance and reincarnation, and they spent time analyzing each other's thoughts and actions in light of Cayce's teachings. They became convinced that they had spent many lifetimes together with much "karma

to work out." Carolyn resumed her portrait painting and drawing around this time which she continues to this day.

In 1958, Neal was arrested for selling marijuana to undercover agents and spent two years in prison. Carolyn was as supportive as she could be, but Neal was unpredictable. Sometimes he was contrite and asked for forgiveness; other times he refused to see her. Carolyn was ready to escape abroad, but he convinced her to stay because he could not be released without a home to go to. Carolyn continued to support the family by working as a costume and makeup artist for Santa Clara University, the San Jose Light

Carolyn Cassady's portrait of Ellen Feldheym won "Best in Show" All California in 1968.

Opera Company, and a group called the Wagon Stages.

After prison, Neal continued to alternate between home and the road. Carolyn had finally come to terms with the relationship and although she would allow Neal to come home from time to time, she was free from the power he had held over her. She reflected later:

> As my attitude and responses slowly changed from possessiveness to detachment, I tried to work on the "loving" part of the formula and reviewed Neal's good qualities instead of concentrating on those I disliked. Thinking back on our first months together, I was ashamed how completely I'd buried my recognition of his many unusual virtues. Why, I wondered, did I feel it my duty to keep him informed of his vices? After all, everyone really knows within himself when he is doing something right or wrong; it isn't anyone else's business. This exercise allowed me to love Neal more, but in quite a different way, and in exchange for these tiny triumphs I traded in my original dream—the dream I'd fought so long to hold; the reason, I believed, for my living. I knew only greater pain would come from hanging on to a lost cause, and I also knew better than to forfeit the peace of mind I'd attained. It was an isolated and lonely peace at first. The bridge between Neal and me had fallen, and I looked at him now from the opposite bank, a gulf between us. Was this "loving indifference"?

During the sixties, Neal jumped the gap between the Beats and the hippies when he began hanging out with Ken Kesey and his group of psychedelic rangers, the Merry

© 1965 by Larry Keenan, Jr.

Neal Cassady and Ann Murphy.

Ann Murphy

Neal's steady girlfriend for the last years of his life, Ann Murphy had as good a handle on Neal's hurricane-force personality as any of them. She spent time with him during the Merry Pranksters hoo-ha at Ken Kesey's *casa* in La Honda, California. Ann was also part of the Prankster contingent that fled to Mexico after the staged Kesey suicide to avoid arrest.

Cassady had taken to flipping a four-pound sledgehammer and catching it while trying to get his ideas across to those who would listen, only dropping the hammer to get rid of bad vibrations in the room. Ann wanted Neal all to herself and had a hard time sharing him with other women. She liked to refer to him as "muscles, meat, and metaphysics."

Pranksters. He even piloted the day-glo bus, "Furthur," that they bombed around the country in. He was well known to these people as Dean Moriarity from *On the Road*, and he started doing massive doses of speed and LSD to bolster his superman image within the group. Kesey and the Pranksters nicknamed him Speed Limit, because of his incredible constitution and his ability to go days on end without rest. However, Neal's life on the road caught up to him in a small town in Mexico in 1968. He had left a party in the freezing cold and was found dead of hypothermia beside the railroad tracks the next morning.

For Carolyn, life after Neal consisted of raising their children and continuing to work as well as write and paint. She is the author of an excellent memoir about her time with Neal, *Off the Road*. It provides insight into what it was like to be a part of a roller-coaster ride of a marriage to a man immortalized in books, poems, and movies. An excerpt from *Off the Road* was published as *Heart Beat* without Carolyn's consent, but she did consult on casting and script for the movie version of *Heart Beat* in which she was played by Sissy Spacek and Neal was played by Nick Nolte.

Since 1984, Carolyn has made London her home and travels to California often to see her children and grandchildren. She is now working with a Hollywood production of "The Joan Anderson Letter" and a Francis Ford Coppola production of *On the Road* and continues to paint portraits and write. She lives, as always, by her credo, "You only have what you give away."

This excerpt from Carolyn Cassady's Off the Road *finds Carolyn, Neal, Jack, and the children leaving the house at 29 Russell Street in San Francisco in 1952. It's the only time Carolyn, Neal, and Jack were on the road together.*

Jack's sights turned more and more longingly to the peace and simplicity of Mexico.

In the light of the past months of comparative compatibility and serenity with Neal, I felt our married life was now built on a firmer foundation, and I let my thoughts return to plans for a family life based on the conventional patterns that had formed my own. Now seemed the time to solidify the tie with the grandparents, who had never seen our children but had shown a consistent interest in them. So, we decided to go to Tennessee and visit them, giving Neal a chance to see the farm as well. Neal, always ready to travel at any excuse, also thought it appropriate for me to accompany him on at least one "road"—after all I had had no vacation of any kind for five years or more. Neal also thought this a chance to look up his father.

There was now no doubt that the trip was an absolute necessity, not merely a pleasure. I plunged into plans. We could survive if Neal took a month off from the railroad. We'd take with us all of the baby food and most of our own, share the driving and keep the motels to a minimum. We'd drive Jack as far as Nogales across the Mexican border south of Tucson, to start him on his way.

Everything worked out beautifully. We took out the back seat of the "woody" and covered the floor with a cot mattress, putting John's small crib mattress across the back, which left enough room for the two girls to stretch out between it and the front seat. The sides were lined with our bags and boxes of food. There was a surprising amount of room.

Jack took a nostalgic farewell of his attic nook, leaving the bulk of his possessions in it, taking only his sea bag. He and I had no opportunity for a private talk before we left, and we all bravely minimized the impending separation by making happy plans for reuniting in Mexico in the nebulous future. It was accepted by all three of us that we would share a home somewhere for at least a part of each year.

Before pulling away from Russell Street, Neal took the girls into the front seat, and as we got underway he

courtesy of Carolyn Cassady

Carolyn and Cathy Cassady; Jack Kerouac and Jami Cassady on Russell Street in San Francisco.

enhanced their excitement with a constant patter about every passing scene. Jack and I had crawled into the back with John and sat crosswise, facing each other. The space was somewhat cramped for two adults, but this suited our melancholy mood. We lapsed into a silent reverie, realizing that time was growing short. We could make no overt move toward each other without feeling sorry for Neal, so communication had to consist only of longing looks and the occasional electric touch of knees. The tension was nearly unbearable by the time we reached Santa Barbara four hours later, but it was a romantic agony willingly suffered.

We spent the first night with Neal's younger sister and her husband, and the second in Los Angeles where Neal was able to locate two older half-sisters and two brothers. We visited from house to house, and they were all most cordial, in spite of this sudden arrival of three adults and three children. I seemed the only one concerned about this breach of manners, but my objections silenced, and at length I held my peace and relaxed on the floor next to Jack to watch television—the first I'd ever seen.

For all of the next day's drive I urged Jack to sit in front with Neal while the girls and I played games in back. I had to smile as I listened to the men, thinking what a different "road" this was from the others they'd shared. It didn't sound as though the family presence was dampening their pleasure in the least; in fact it seemed to add to it, especially when they passed a place remembered from a previous trip and would begin at once to tell me the stories attached to it.

While the children slept, we three adults sat in front and drove all night across the desert. The sky was deep and clear, and all of us were wistful, in tune with the knowledge it was our last night together. We listened to radio dramas, *First Nighter* and *The Whistler.* During the latter Neal became so emotionally involved that Jack and I had to laugh and remind him repeatedly that it was only a play. He probably was putting us on, but his absorption made me nervous.

Later, when there was only music for background, we peered into the vast panorama of glittering stars all around us and Neal astounded both Jack and me with a detailed discourse on the constellations and stars.

"Wherever did you learn all that?" we asked in unison. "I didn't know you knew anything about astronomy."

With a sigh Neal replied, "I know everything about everything—how many times do I have to tell you?"

The stars dissolved into the pearl gray dawn, and with it came a chill. The parting was near, and we grew silent. As if by accident, I let my head drop to touch Jack's shoulder, and he stroked my hair with his hand behind my head; it was the best we could do by way of farewell. Neal drove to the Mexican border and parked the car alongside a wire fence, but I didn't see any guards or customs, only dirt, weeds and trash. Everything was gray and dreary: the weather, the outskirts of the town, and now our mood. A few yards inside the gates was a white-walled café with chipping paint, and Jack said, "Aw, come on. Can't you have one last beer with me?" He stood forlornly beside the car with his sea bag over his shoulder.

"Sure, man," Neal condescended, and we got out.

It was no warmer inside the one big bare room that smelled of Lysol. A brown varnished bar lined one wall, and in front of it a few metal tables and chairs were scattered. Beer before breakfast was new to me, but this morning it was a good idea and helped calm me. Jack made a few stabs at cheery conversation, hopping from Mexico ahead to the adventures behind, but sensing only unrest on Neal's part, he too fell silent. I wondered if Neal's mood was less one of regret for Jack's departure than for not being in Jack's shoes, but all he said in the end was that in a few months maybe we'd all be living there together.

Neal was eager to get going, and I wanted the separation over, so we said corny goodbyes and ran back to the car, turning to wave until we'd lost sight of the sagging figure by the border fence. Later Jack wrote:

> … you could have come through with the car that morning… and we
> could have driven fifty miles around or anything at no charge (and bought
> stuff)… and seen a fiesta in the afternoon in the gay little city of Nogales.
> You have no idea what it is ten feet beyond that wire fence.

After the melancholy of the morning, we set out on the rest of the journey confident our former problems were the errors of youth. We had learned our limitations, and that gave us a new freedom. Now I could concentrate all my attention on my own little family.

We were together enjoying a shared experience; I didn't want to miss a minute of it.

Neal was all I could wish. He drove carefully and slowly—almost too slowly at times, I thought, but he had some notion about a "cruising speed" to preserve the car. Whatever it was, it dispelled my initial anxiety that we'd be bickering all over the country about his driving.

There was only one near-catastrophe on the way to Nashville: at a drawbridge near New Orleans, Neal drove under the barrier as it was descending to stop the traffic. I nearly died of fright to see the concrete highway rise up directly in front of the radiator. Somewhat hysterically, I began yelling at Neal, at which point a police officer rode up beside us and began doing likewise. I switched from scolding Neal to defending him, and in my terror inflicted the full power of my indignation on the officer. Neal wisely slid down in his seat between us, casting a hapless, henpecked look at the officer who, taken aback by my outburst, soon shot Neal a sympathetic look and rode off. My stability returned with the relief that we'd not received a ticket. "Ha, see there? It shows there's some advantage in having a shrewish wife, hunh, honey? Forgive me—you understand."

The two weeks with the grandparents went smoothly. Neal exhibited his good manners and thoughtfulness, also impressing my parents with his affection for and patience with the children. He listened with enthusiasm to my father's stories of the local folkways, crops and animals, and throughout our stay remained remarkably serene and agreeable, as pleased as the little girls with the horses, cattle, pigs, and lambs and the sight of tobacco growing. A cowboy he wasn't, and I couldn't get him on a horse, much to my surprise, but we took walks and played in the creek. I taught him to churn butter and we toured the historic battlefields and ghost-filled mansions of the Old South as well as my former Nashville haunts.

Neal was once again my ideal companion. The only problem I had with him wasn't between us; rather it was his failure to get the appropriate slant (for a white) on how to treat black people. He'd be naturally friendly and respectful to farmhand, coal man, or drugstore curb server, and they'd freeze in instant suspicion. I explained to him how I'd had to learn the techniques and attitudes of the Southern whites, although

I'd hated it and it had been a major cause of my leaving the South. "It's no use trying to reason with white Southerners—it isn't a matter of reason or intelligence. It's all emotional and ingrained. My parents and I have close friends who are wonderful people otherwise, but that is one subject we simply have to avoid. It took me a long time to comprehend." But Neal couldn't, and I was glad of it.

Then one afternoon shortly before our departure, I caught Neal smoking marijuana in our bedroom. I panicked, my confidence in him shaken. How could he risk any possibility that my folks would find out? I remained nervous and on edge until we were safely away.

In Kansas City we found Neal's brother Jim, against whom Neal bore no grudge for his childhood atrocities. We had a friendly visit for an hour or two, but Jim had no room for us to spend the night, so we went to a drive-in movie and slept as long as we could before continuing across the endless plains.

Whether it was being reminded of his childhood miseries by seeing Jim again, or a reaction against his recent submission to conventional behavior, or simply his psychological imbalance, I'll never know, but before we reached Denver, Neal reverted to his old self, escaping from us twice for many hours without explanation. I responded with the same old righteous martyrdom, more sadly now because everything had been going so well for so long, and I thought I had learned that lesson.

By the time we got to Denver I was attempting to collect the shattered pieces of our relationship again, and Neal behaved as though he wished to, too. It was a bitter pill to have to acknowledge that our differences had evidently been overcome only through circumstances, not through real change.

With some reluctance, but trying not to show it, I agreed to take the children to see Neal's father. Not that I didn't want to meet him or have him see the children, but he was living in a hotel in a neighborhood that made me uncomfortable, and I couldn't imagine what we would have to talk about. I knew I had to make the effort though— it meant so much to Neal. As it happened, all went well. Neal decided at the last minute to stay in the car with the children, letting them hang out the window to wave at their grandfather, while I went in alone. It was just as well; the poor dear really didn't know who I was, but as long as I kept mentioning his son, he was happy to see me. While I was there, a wonderful floozy of a women went in and out of his room, clucking and fussing over Neal, Sr., and I was glad to be able to reassure Neal that his father was being very well looked after. Afterwards Neal went up to see him on his own, while I stayed with the children. Neal's filial affection was appeased, and when his father died a few years later he was able to return to Denver with a clear conscience to arrange the burial.

We traveled the rest of the way home as fast as we could, resolving to return to Denver someday and review it properly—"when the children would be older and would appreciate it too."

We were both considerably depressed by the setbacks, but when we reached home we agreed to keep trying to find new angles. We promised each other we'd give analysis another, more attentive try. We also reached out for the hope that possibly a change of scene would help. I didn't really know how to raise children in a city—Neal had just seen the wide open spaces I'd been accustomed to—and although a city boy himself, he concurred it might be better for us all if we moved to a more rural area. It gave us something else to look forward to, more plans to make, and as we settled into our own bed again, dim hope recycled once more.

Two letters awaited us, plus one addressed to Jack—the first word we'd had from Allen for three months. In the letter he'd written first, he said he'd found a missing chapter of *On The Road* which he was forwarding to Jack, apparently unaware of our trip, writing "Jeepers, where is Jack?" The other letter said he'd just received a 'monumental letter from Jack in Mexico' and that we were to send back the twenty-three opening pages, while Jack was sending him the rest.

> Jack says your mad at him or tired of him, Neal, is that true?…I'm afraid for him in Mexico, it is a kind of lostness…he's smoking with Mexicans in mudhuts…He says you are busy and obsessed with "complete all-the-way-down-the-line materialistic money and stealing groceries Anxieties," etc., etc. Also said he was happy there…are you in Frisco, even? What's going on around there anyway?

Back in harness, Neal became depressed again. In those days I didn't understand his need for change and excitement, still judging others by my own standards. He wrote Allen a nice note, saying "You're the same great wonderful guy and I'm more of a bum than ever..." and ending with "Why don't you come out here? Nice place if one likes it. Be brakie and make lots of money. Or write in attic and make love to wife and me."

Much to my delight and surprise Allen wrote a letter to me, breaking the ice of five years:

Dear Mrs. Cassady:
How is you, after all... as I see things now I think maybe you been through the mill bad, always been sorry I contributed to the privation... Too bitter to forgive? Hope not. Take care of the children (that means Jack and Neal too) as everybody will ultimately be saved, including you... I plan no imminent invasion of Frisco but would like to someday and hope I will be welcome to you and we can be friends. You always seem all right to me. Jack likes you but is afraid of you. (you know?) I wonder how you feel about him.
Yours,
Allen The Stranger

I answered him cordially, and he wrote Neal "Maybe a change of scene would be good. I may come out there yet." He also replied to my letter and sealed our friendship.

Much thanks for your letter. Didn't expect to be so well received either. So that dispenses that cloud. Was Jack's tip too; he not so dumb, with other peoples' female notions... Would be interested know your process of changes of love and thought. Don't realize too much of yr. interior of last years except by conjecture. Thank you for child name. Never got the idea from W.C. Fields that you had anything to do with it, but now that you mention it does sound sort of inevitable that you might have had some hand in naming yr. own children. Yipe! Consider my letters henceforth addressed to you, too. Would it be possible to have my epistles (like St. Paul) read in state at dinner table in front of the children of the Church? Constantinople here needs me so can't get to Rome temporarily, and waiting for a Word, Understood your letter. Thanks. Shy.
Allen

Immediately, I jumped at the offer to share my thoughts by pouring them out to him and requesting his comments and advice only position with Neal and Jack. He further gratified me by setting down a thoughtful and thorough analysis of all our relationships:

> Jack's attitude: a) as I haven't got all his letters here, I'll send on an anthology of statements apropos his relations with Neal when I assemble them. What *I* think about it is, Jack loves Neal platonically (which I think is a pity, but maybe about sex I'm 'projecting' as the analysts say) and Neal loves Jack, too. The fact is that Jack is very inhibited, however. However, also, sex doesn't define the whole thing.
>
> b) Jack still loves Neal none the less than ever.
>
> c) Jack ran into a blank wall which everyone understands and respects in Neal, including Jack and Neal. It upset and dispirited Jack, made him feel lonely and rejected and like a little brother whose questions the older brother wouldn't answer.
>
> d) Jack loves Carolyn also, though obviously not with the same intensity and power as he loves Neal, and this is acceptable and obvious considering all parties involved, their history together, how much they knew each other and how often they lived through the same years and crises. Jack is full of Carolyn's praises and nominates her to replace Joan Burroughs as Ideal Mother Image, Madwoman, chick and ignu. The last word means a special honorary type post hip intellectual. Its main root is ignoramus, from the mythology of W.C. Fields. Jack also says Carolyn beats Ellie [a girl in New York] for mind.
>
> e) Jack said nothing about sleeping with you in his letters.
>
> f) Jack thinks Neal is indifferent to him, however only in a special way, as he realizes how good Neal has been to him and that Neal really loves him; but they

courtesy of Carolyn Cassady

Blakean portrait of Allen Ginsberg by Carolyn Cassady.

Allen, the sage, a portrait by Carolyn Cassady.

couldn't communicate I guess. However, he would love to live altogether with everybody in Mexico, I believe. He would claim right to treat Neal as a human being and hit him on the breast with balloons. I will transmit all messages immediately.

g) I did not think (even dream) from Neal's note he is bitter. I was surprised to get his invitation to visit, and thought it showed great gentility in the writing and the proposal which I accept with rocky belly for sometime in the future. Had I money I would fly out immediately for weekends by plane.

h) Perhaps Neal wants to feel like a crestfallen cuckold because he wants to be beat on the breast with balloons. I well imagine him in that position. Neal's last confession is perhaps yet to be made, tho his salvation is already assured... however nobody seems to take seriously the confession he has made already and continues to do so, which have always had ring of innocency and childlike completeness and have been all he knows which is more (about himself) than anybody else knows anyway. I believe Neal.

I include his preoccupation and blankness (preoccupation with R.R. household moneying, etc.,) as final confessions of great merit and value, representing truth to him.

What further sweetness and juiciness issues therefrom no one knows, even him; there is no forcing anything... that will be fate. Neal has already unnecessary guilt (He does not know?) He is already on top of the world. What to do with world is next problem.

Jack probably feels no remorse, just compassion for Neal.

... Mexico may be a good idea for all of us when become properly solidified... what we must make plans to do is all meet somewhere where it is practically possible to live, under our various pressures, when the practical time comes. Shall we not then keep it in mind to try to arrange for a total grand reunion somewhere for as long as it can last?... I am definitely interested in going to bed with everybody and making love ... P.S. Neal, write me a letter about sex. A.

Allen's attitude about sex always managed to raise my Puritan hackles, and I suspect he knew it. It certainly pricked my romantic bubbles, but in other respects his thoughts were reassuring, and I felt accepted, thinking that if we all lived together, pressures could be siphoned off in small doses in a variety of ways. Deep in my heart I still yearned for a monogamous arrangement with Neal, but if it wasn't possible, perhaps the arrangement held possibilities hitherto unknown in conventional patterns. My ability to analyze it ended there.

courtesy of Carolyn Cassady

Carolyn and Neal Cassady with son, John Allen, in the Summer of 1955.

Edie Parker Kerouac
First Mate
(1923–1992)

"And this is something Edie knows, most likely—an unarticulated sadness. That Jack, despite her dreams of marriage and 'Oh, we'll have our Bohemian period and then we'll settle down and he'll write his books and we'll love each other forever,' is unpossessable. Edie's got her resourceful spirit, though. She's even had her own adventures, working as a longshoreman while Jack's at sea, and as a cigarette girl on Forty-second Street. You can weave such an exciting ambiance around a man he'll hardly know he's being held by it."

—Joyce Johnson

As Joyce Johnson notes, Edie Parker Kerouac was no fifties' housewife. Indeed, along with Joan Burroughs, Edie was at the very center of the intellectual and creative vortex that produced the new consciousness of the Beats. Edie was involved with the group for a relatively short time, but it was an intense period of growth for all of the people involved and set the stage for all that would follow.

Edie Parker grew up in the wealthy suburb of Grosse Pointe, Michigan. Life there was full of fancy people and elegant parties, and she was a dark-haired beauty with an adventurous enthusiasm that charmed those around her. In 1941, her parents sent her to Columbia University with the expectation that she would find a suitable young gentleman to marry. Edie had very different ideas; she was interested in leaving her sheltered existence behind in favor of a wide variety of new ideas, people, and experiences. At first, she attended evening classes while living in an apartment near the campus with her grandparents. But she preferred night life to school and spent most of her time investigating the neighborhood hangouts. She became an expert at sneaking out of her grandparents' apartment to rendezvous with her boyfriend du jour.

Edie's most lasting attachment to anybody from this period was to Jack Kerouac. She was introduced to Jack by her boyfriend at the time, Henry Cru. Henry was an old friend of Jack's and they were both merchant seamen. When Henry shipped out, he told Jack to keep an eye on Edie. Jack did more than that, and they were soon involved in a love affair. When Jack was sent to sea as well, Edie discovered that she was pregnant; she had no idea whether the father was Jack or Henry. Although she decided not to have the child, Edie resolved to inform the two friends about the situation.

When Henry returned to New York, he proposed to Edie and she promptly told him about Jack and the baby. Jack returned soon after and was met at the West End Bar by Henry and Edie. When Jack was apprised of the facts, he stormed away in shock and anger. Jack's Catholic guilt got the best of him, however, and he appeared at her door later that night and told her that they should live together.

It was just about this time that Edie met Joan Vollmer Adams, and they moved into an apartment together on 118th Street. This apartment-cum-salon provided the freedom that they both had been seeking, and it wasn't long before Allen Ginsberg, Lucien Carr, and Bill Burroughs were regular visitors. Jack moved in with Edie, and the two of them began a mercurial, nonmonogamous relationship. Edie would quickly replace Jack whenever he shipped out, and Jack did not hide his attraction to other girls. Nobody stayed mad for too long, and these intragroup dalliances only strengthened the bonds between them all. The free and easy attitude that they were all playing with came to a disastrous climax with the death of Dave Kammerer.

Dave was part of a group of friends from St. Louis that included Lucien Carr and Bill Burroughs. Dave had been obsessed with the sharp-featured Lucien since Lucien was a boy, and had been following him around ever since. Lucien was not interested in Dave, but did nothing to discourage his attentions. In fact, Lucien seemed to enjoy the whole drama of the situation. Things got progressively worse, however, and the group tried unsuccessfully to get Dave to disengage.

It was the evening of August 13, 1944. Lucien went out drinking with Allen and Jack at the West End. Dave dropped by, and he and Lucien closed the bar at around four that morning. The two then went to Riverside Park where Dave finally pushed too hard; he made a play for Lucien, who stabbed him with his Boy Scout knife, killing him. Lucien weighted down the body and rolled it into the Hudson River. He went to see Burroughs, who gave him some money and advised him to obtain counsel and plead self-defense. Lucien then went to see Jack and Edie. The three of them discussed various plans while Edie made breakfast. Jack and Lucien disposed of the knife and Dave's glasses. Lucien surrendered to the police two days later.

Jack and Bill were picked up as material witnesses in the case. While Bill's parents reached into their deep pockets to bail him out, Jack's father decided to let Jack rot in jail. A few days behind bars were enough for Jack, and he came up with a solution to his problems: Edie. Edie had been interested in marrying Jack, while he was unwilling to commit to something so final. But married life with Edie was looking a whole lot better when compared to prison life, and Jack consented to marry Edie if she would bail him out. They were married at City Hall on August 22, 1944, with a detective standing in as best man and Celine Young as the maid of honor.

The marriage was short-lived. Jack and Edie went to Grosse Pointe, Michigan, after the honeymoon. Edie's parents were wealthy Protestants who had no understanding of Jack's working-class, French Canadian, Catholic background. Nor could they appreciate his attempts to become a writer. Edie tried her best to make Jack feel at home in this suburban world. Her father got Jack a job in a factory, but Jack worked only long enough to pay back Edie's father for the bail money. He left Grosse

Stella Sampas

In November 1966, Jack Kerouac married Stella Sampas, the older sister of his best friend from childhood, Alex. Stella was his wife during the most difficult part of his life, when he claimed that being famous was preventing his being able to write. By this time, his alcohol intake was interfering with every aspect of his life, and he would wander the streets of Lowell, Massachusetts, in a stupor. Stella tried to stop his nightly ramblings by hiding his shoes, but he went out to the bars anyway, downing a fifth of Johnny Walker Red a day and washing that down with Falstaff beer and Colt 45 malt liquor. With his success after *On the Road*, he finally had money enough to support his mother and buy her the house she'd always dreamed of, where all three of them lived. But their domestic bliss was curtailed when his mother had a stroke. From that point on, Stella was essentially a caretaker for the two Kerouacs. Upon his death, though they were separated at the time, Stella claimed rights to Jack's estate, a literary legacy that is being contested by Jan Kerouac's estate.

Pointe after just a few weeks to ship out to sea from a New York port.

In December, Jack and Edie reconciled in New York and moved back in with Joan in an apartment on 115th Street. Allen had also moved into the apartment, and Bill Burroughs took the remaining room. The reunion between Jack and Edie was very brief; they were young and marriage overwhelmed them. Soon after this attempt at reconciliation, Edie was back in Grosse Pointe and applied for an annulment within a year.

There was no malice in the breakup, and Jack would continue to write to her or drop into Grosse Pointe to see her when he was on the road with Neal Cassady. Years later, Jack wrote to her to complain about his fame and yearn for simpler times.

When the *New York Times*' rave review of *On the Road* appeared, thirteen years after their divorce, Jack received bags of fan mail, including a letter from Edie asking to reconcile and go on a "world tour." Edie's subsequent marriage to a midwestern small businessman couldn't match the excitement of life with the hero of the Beat Generation. But the reunion was not meant to be.

Edie married a total of four times before her death in 1992. She was bitterly disappointed when her writing remained unpublished, unable to understand why the world wasn't eager to hear about her great love affair with Jack Kerouac. At Jack's funeral in October 1969, Edie ran toward the casket screaming, "I'm the wife of Jack Kerouac—the *only* wife of Jack Kerouac!"

What follows is an account by Edie of one of those times when Jack and Neal dropped by. It comes from You'll be Okay, *Edie's unpublished autobiography.*

Jack and Neal came to visit me in September, 1947, following their first road trip. They stayed with me and my girlfriend Virginia Tyson at her parents' home in Grosse Pointe. The Tysons were out of town, visiting Nova Scotia.

Virginia's father Ty Tyson, was Detroit's Number One radio announcer, famous for his Detroit Tigers baseball broadcasts and popular interview shows. Jack loved the grand piano in Virginia's sunken living room, and Neal was attracted to Virginia.

Ed White, who was staying in Dearborn that summer, had received a letter from

Jack telling him to advise me of his pending visit! The two lane roads were quite primitive then, like the Mexican roads today, and the boys needed a rest. Of course I would put them up, but I could not do it at my house due to my mother.

Virginia planned a big party with the Tigers because the house was hers. Her brother Bill was at home, but he was no problem; he had his own crazy group of friends. Virginia decided to have the party catered, so we went shopping and spent everything on booze and big roasts. Thank God for her charges, or Virginia would have dined on cookies for the next two months (the house was stocked with all her father's advertising products including beer).

Jack and Neal were coming from Denver; Jack's letter to Ed White had come from Marin City, California, where he had stayed with Henry Cru. Jack and I had not conventionally "split up" in our own minds anyway; in a manner of thinking, we never really did. We were just caught up in the "excitement" of our lives, of what we were doing from day to day, enjoying the freedom of finally having become "adults." Our parents left us pretty much alone, as they had during the war, our living together, Jack's shipping out, and getting married.

My mother was pleased that I was back in Grosse Pointe, out of New York for good, and thought that Jack was out of our lives. She could not have been further from the truth. We met whenever we could, and this was one of the times in the late '40s and early '50s.

This time, Jack and Neal arrived by Greyhound, coming from Chicago in the middle of the day. We stuck their canvas luggage in the trunk and off we went, Neal in the drivers seat with his blond, and Jack and I holding hands tightly in the backseat. We loved each other, and I could see he was happy travelling. "Go" as John Clellon Holmes' book says. The top was down on the big white Lincoln convertible, the radio was blaring, and we were all talking at the same time. The wind was in our sails, whoo-whee!

We stopped at the Rustic Cabin Saloon for drinks. Virginia drank V.O. and ginger ale so we all did. It was thirty five cents per drink, and we had a tough time rounding it up between us. Funny thing about Grosse Pointers: the people have everything except cash! Jack got up and went to the men's room then came back grinning. He ordered another round, and came up with a rumpled "ten spot." Neal was shocked. "Where did you get that gold?" he asked. Jack never answered. Neal didn't know Jack as well as I did. He gave Neal a quarter for the "great" juke box. Pete Ouelette, the "French Canuck" owner, loved Frank Sinatra. He played six of Frank's songs for two bits and we had to sit through all of them.

We got to Virginia's about four; Billy was playing baseball in their big front yard. Jack and Neal joined right in with the gang; Neal pitching, Jack catching. Bob Jackson, a friend of Billy's, came over and helped Virginia and I with the luggage. Neal was in the room with the double bed, and Jack in the twin-bedded master bedroom. The house had four bedrooms with four huge bathrooms. The grand piano was downstairs, the real reason Jack wanted to stay here, instead of the Saverine Hotel with the Detroit Tigers. When they wanted to stay at the Saverine, Virginia got them in with food and lodging for a very low price, which she and I later split.

Virginia and I unpacked their luggage for her maid Maggie to do the laundry. Maggie and her daughter were downstairs in the kitchen, preparing dinner. Some great smells were drifting through the house. Hams, turkeys, potato salad, and garlic meat sauce for spaghetti!

The Tysons had a tradition of "silver and candle light sit-down dinners," served at 7:00 P.M. in the dining room by Maggie. Jack was expecting this as we had the same custom at my mother's house. Suddenly the piano came alive, and Jack was playing loud jazz music. Neal wanted a beer, which was through the kitchen and outside. As I showed him the "ins and outs" of the house, he beamed at all the young, tanned help. They were great and lived in the house. I was concerned about their welfare around "jail educated" Neal. The cupboards were full of Altes beer, Wheaties, cookies, and Chuckles.

Ty Tyson had a live broadcast, "Man of the Street," where he talked to people "and pronto!" in front of the Michigan Central Railroad Station every day at noon, five days a week, for station WWJ. He eventually became president of the station. Ty always wore a black French "tam," which was placed on his casket at the Verheyden Funeral Home when he died; even his pallbearers wore them. And I also wore one— as a hostess—for that memorable event. All the Detroit sports and political "big shots" came to the house for Ty's wake, the same kind of wonderful party we gave for Jack and Neal.

Virginia was nervous so she kept the silver locked away in drawers. She need not have worried, for Neal never would have done anything to discredit Jack. If Neal had been alone, however, she would have had more than silver to worry about! As seven o'clock approached, Jack went upstairs to take his customary shower and shave. He came back downstairs wearing one of Billy's clean white shirts, no tie. Jack scowled at Neal, so he went to wash up and comb his hair.

We went in for dinner and the phone started ringing. Virginia took it off the hook, and we started passing the dishes for our feast. Maggie and her daughter ate in the kitchen, where we brought our plates after dinner, rinsing them and setting them in the sink. Then Virginia served coffee, apple pie, and Sander's vanilla ice cream. This was Jack's favorite dessert, and he was pleased. Neal wanted to know whose birthday it was! He was always making corny remarks.

We got up and went into the living room, with Jack and I on the floor, stretched out by the fire. He wanted to know who was coming to the party we had planned for the next day. We said we didn't know what to do about the music, either to play the radio or our own records on the Victrola. Jack and Neal said to leave it to them. Then we all went to bed, after a long day. Jack and I were anxious to be together again behind closed doors.

The next day flew. Jack, Billy, and Neal went out for fresh bread and to the Saverine to see about a band. I was so excited about Jack's return that I started drinking too much, too soon. When the guests arrived, I was well on my way.

We held the party in the Tyson's rathskeller, a finished basement with a bar serving Altes tap beer. We had a large assortment of food on a covered ping-pong table. Jack and Neal had found a black, three-piece band, where I'll never know. They were great, with Jack and Neal taking turns on the drums. There was an upright piano which they also took turns playing. We drank and danced until very late in the night; it was wonderful. But I'd had it about midnight, and went to bed. I woke up once to hear the party still going, and Jack finally came to bed when it was light. He crawled into my twin bed, I heard the musicians laughing and leaving in a cab, and I fell back to sleep.

I got up before the rest of the crowd and put on my pajamas. I went to the bathroom, flushed the toilet, and it started to gurgle! I was too sleepy to give it any thought, so I started cleaning up, picking up glasses as I worked my way downstairs. The Tyson's wonderful old school clock in the kitchen said 6:00 A.M. The place was half picked up, so I made some coffee. They had so much coffee, I wondered if they got that free, too. I took my coffee into the living room, which was filled with sleeping bodies! I started the fire up, and sat down to enjoy my thoughts of Jack's visit. I should have had a hangover but I felt pretty good. I was still in love with Jack, which kept my adrenalin flowing.

One of the guests, a nurse, got up with her boyfriend as she had to go to work. He reported that the toilets were stopped up! So I phoned the plumber for emergency repairs. I woke Jack up at 7:00 A.M.; I was never happier to be with him, then or ever. The plumbers arrived in two trucks, I suspect to partake of the party! They were all over the house with electric snakes and all their paraphernalia. It took a half a day to discover the problem; they reminded me of doctors. They were continuously consulting about the four bathrooms. There was a blockage of some kind in the pipes, and they decided they would have to dig up the lawn outside. In the meantime, some of the guests were still partying, particularly Neal. I wondered who he'd slept with. I woke up Virginia and told her about the plumbing situation; she put me in charge and went right back to sleep.

The plumbers dug up the front yard and several of us stood around the hole, watching. This took at least an hour. It looked like they were digging a grave; the hole was big enough for a casket! Then one of the plumbers jumped in with his hip boots on and pulled the pipes apart. Out floated, with you-know-what, a pair of men's shorts! The plumber, Dean, grabbed them, rinsed them with dirty water and put them on display on the grass. We were spellbound; they were white with big red polka dots! We became hysterical with laughter. Fortunately, no one claimed them.

The plumbers mended everything just as before except for the new "bump" in the lawn, looking like someone was buried there. When Virginia got the bill for the damages, it was more than the cost of the entire party, and boy! was she furious, wanting to know whose shorts they were. She was hoping someone would help pay.

Well, the party went on for another three days, then everything ran out: beer, food, patience, hospitality. Jack and Neal moved to the Saverine, and later, in a lost letter, Jack told me the shorts belonged to Neal. He had recognized them but never let on. They really didn't have any money anyway. So they enjoyed the rest of their stay with the Tigers at the Saverine, with fun players like Roy Cullenbine, Barney Markowsky, and Dick Wakefield.

Jack and Neal later visited my friend Lee Donnelly's future husband Clotaire DeMueleemeister's bar on the east side of Detroit. Clot's mother Emma was always there. Clot was John Wayne's tall double. At Emma's house there was always plenty to eat, and the basement bar had a walk-in refrigerator. Their bars were fully stocked, with beer on tap, pool tables, rifle range games and "one arm bandits," which were legal then and I loved to play them, in our homes and other far away places. The speakeasy atmosphere of the twenties and early thirties still hung around such places, with a hint of illegality and gangsters. We were all drinking and driving at the age of 14, and no one enforced the laws in Grosse Pointe society.

Emma, Clot's mother, was something else. Clot had his bar on the same avenue as his father, up till the late 1970s and Emma worked with him to "get the kid ahead in the bar business." It was across from Motor Products. Clot had married Lee while in the service. One late night, two hold-up "artists" came in (the bar cashed checks, so was known to have a lot of money), stuck big guns in Emma's neck, and told her to open the register. Emma snapped back, "the hell I will, you'll have to shoot me to get it." These boys were astonished! They ran out of the bar, but were arrested, one of whom turned out to be a future Detroit Tigers player. He was discovered when they sent him to Jackson Prison. But Clot said he wouldn't endanger his family and closed the bar, and Motor Products followed. The whole east side of Detroit was by then in depression, and could not cope with the growing crime, taxes, city government, and unions; moving their business south and out of the country.

Lee lived on Mount Vernon Street in Grosse Pointe. Her mother Marie and her husband Kelly also lived there, and her Aunt Jean. Clot's uncle Tyne, a poor relation, lived in Emma's large home on Jefferson beyond Grosse Pointe, as did a number of Belgian immigrants. Uncle Tyne maintained a large bathtub in the backyard, which was continually running over with water supplied by an ugly black hose. He kept an assortment of fish in it, ready for the frying pan; he had fresh trout for every lunch.

Emma's huge mansion was covered with ankle-deep oriental rugs, silk upholstery, the most expensive glass, and porcelains, with Belgian masterpiece paintings on the wall. There was a huge American flag on the wall over the couch, as the focal point of the living room, where the double Tiffany glass doors were always locked, and all you could do was peek into this exquisite gallery. Never being allowed in made it even more extraordinary.

Jack and Neal visited this house one afternoon. They were drinking beer, and then we started to have Courvoisier brandy; this is when Lee and I discovered Manhattans made with this brandy. Boy! it was delicious. Then Clot, Neal, Jack, Tyne, and a few others started playing baseball, this time with Jack as right fielder, Neal as pitcher, Clot on second base, Tyne as catcher, Lee on third, and me on first! It was hilarious, none of us "feeling any pain," and the game did not last long. Then Tyne said, "Let's eat," and we ate on Emma's wonderful porch, looking out on beautiful Lake St. Clair. Jack wrote about this, but his editor Malcolm Cowley cut out most of his Detroit visits, changing Lake St. Clair to Lake Michigan, clear across the state from Grosse Pointe.

courtesy of John Bowers on behalf of JanKerouac's estate

Joan Haverty Kerouac

Joan Haverty Kerouac
Nobody's Wife
(1931–1990)

"She really knows how to write from instinct & innocence. Few women can do this. Joan Kerouac… a new writer on this old horizon. I see me & her cutting around the world in tweeds, yass… Mierschom [sic] pipes with youknowwhat in them, he he."

—Jack Kerouac

Joan Virginia Haverty grew up with her younger brother and her somewhat domineering single mother in the thirties and forties in Albany County, New York. Notorious for constantly challenging her teachers and elders, Joan was persistent in asking difficult questions and never satisfied with rote answers.

Visiting an artists colony in Provincetown, Massachusetts, at the age of nineteen, Joan fell in with Bill Cannastra, a troubled, sexually adventurous New York attorney vacationing as a scallop-boat fisherman. She followed Bill to Manhattan at the end of the summer of 1949, and there she hung on to a precarious but happy existence, reveling in her seamstress job, window-peeping at night with Bill on the streets of New York, and deferring her mother's frequent requests that she return home. Bill tried to engineer a romantic meeting between Joan and another friend, Jack Kerouac, but before it could be arranged, Bill suffered a grisly and senseless death while trying to climb out the window of a moving subway car.

Joan and Jack finally did meet in a providential accident, related tenderly at the end of *On the Road,* when Jack, lost and looking for a party, called up to Joan's window from the street. Jack was instantly enchanted with Joan, and he proposed to her that night. They were married two weeks later, and Jack began his teletype-roll manuscript of *On the Road* in their newlywed home in Bill Burroughs' old loft. Jack encouraged

Joan to write and noted in the introduction to *Dharma Bums* how naturally "Beat" her writing was.

Fearless in marrying this near-stranger, Joan also accepted the final rupture of the marriage eight months later, resolutely rejecting Jack's demands that she abort their unplanned child. Forced to choose between Jack and the baby, Joan embraced her own future without hesitation, and the marriage dissolved in mutual bitterness in the spring of 1952. Daughter Jan Kerouac would not meet her father until she was ten.

During the fifties, Joan moved restlessly around the country, married again, and gave birth to twins. Although she wrote constantly and tirelessly throughout her life, Joan destroyed most of it, for she viewed writing as something private, a way she worked things out for herself. Only once did she write for publication—an article in the tell-all style for *Confidential* magazine in 1961: "My Ex-Husband, Jack Kerouac, Is an Ingrate." Jack had demonstrated the aptness of the article's lurid headline with his court battles to avoid paying child support and his public claims that Jan was not his daughter (claims he withdrew after he finally met her).

Joan made homes in San Francisco, Oregon, and Washington. A fourth child was born in 1965. Her children affectionately recall her idiosyncratic gardening style, her

Gabrielle "Mèmére" Kerouac

Gabrielle Kerouac, Jack's mother, was a French Canadian immigrant who moved to the United States with her husband, Leo. A devout Catholic with a strong personality, Gabrielle had a particularly forceful hold on Jack and purposely discouraged his relationships with others so as to have him all to herself. According to the women in his life, Jack never truly freed himself from his mother's powerful hold, and when he was not on the road he could usually be found with Mèmère.

Her attachment to Jack is evident in this excerpt from a letter she wrote to him after he married Edie Parker and moved to Grosse Pointe:

> Honey, I'm still not able to realize that you have left me for good. I keep searching the Boulevard looking out the window for hours thinking I'll see you come walking and waving to me. I dare say I miss you a lot now and more so now that I know you don't belong to me anymore but that's life and sooner or later I'll get used to the idea. I hope you will be very happy, Honey, and that nothing will ever stop you from being a great 'Man.' With the help of your new Mother and a good Wife you should become a great 'writer.'

Gabrielle got her wish—and lived long enough after Jack died to see him become an American icon.

habit of dismantling walls wherever they lived, and her inability to feel physical pain. Throughout her life, Joan rejected anesthetics and often injured herself without realizing it until blood appeared.

At the beginning of the eighties, several factors combined to bring Joan around to the idea of writing her own memoirs for publication. Her daughter Jan Kerouac had had notable success writing about her own life in her first novel, *Baby Driver*. A lover from the pre-Jack Manhattan days reappeared in Joan's life and then, suddenly and unexpectedly, died of a heart attack. And the first biographies of Jack seemed to her to be hero-worshipping and inaccurate. Finally, in 1982, Joan was diagnosed with breast cancer and given only a few months to live.

In characteristically stubborn style, Joan disdained the doctors' projections, writing in her own medical history: "I feel that I have a long time if I can just avoid infection." In fact, Joan hung on for eight years, during which she produced thousands of relentlessly written manuscript pages about her life, her views, and the real personalities of the famous literary figures she had known. She titled her manuscript *Nobody's Wife* and focused most closely on the whirlwind events of the two years that passed between her introduction to Bill Cannastra and the angry breakup with Jack Kerouac.

Joan worked over these sections in revision after revision. She died in 1990 with her cherished work incomplete. Jan found the beginning under Joan's bed; other pieces were found hidden in walls. It took six years for her children and friends to complete the work of organizing these manuscript fragments into the powerfully personal and radical retelling of literary history that Joan envisioned.

To date, sections of *Nobody's Wife* have been seen only by a few biographers and scholars. This anthology contains the first published excerpt.

What follows are two pieces from Nobody's Wife: *the introduction by Jan Kerouac and chapter 12. Chapter 12 is the story of Joan's first meeting with Jack's mother, Gabrielle, and the rest of the Kerouac family.*

Introduction

by Jan Kerouac

During the last ten years of my mother's life, her constant preoccupation, aside from the garden, was to write this book.

I remember watching her, her bony frame in her favorite antique turquoise sweatshirt, shuffling over to sit down at her typewriter. It was an ancient machine, covered with tobacco dust. She would sit down every evening, or whenever she got a chance, and between intermittent gulps of coffee, and drags on her hand-rolled Bugler-tobacco cigarettes, she would tap away with one finger on each hand.

She started writing the book in 1980, just after she was diagnosed with breast cancer. The doctors told her she had a year or so to live. But she was determined to hang on, to prove them wrong, to last until she could get the book on paper. She went through periods of remission and illness, had a double mastectomy, and still kept writing.

She could get going really fast with only her two index fingers, because she was telling her stories, the stories of her young adulthood. Often I was there with her in her little wooden house in Eugene, Oregon, listening to the squealing brakes from the hump yard nearby. There was a family of possums living under the house, and they'd be bumping around. My mother would come into the living room, where I was, and we'd talk and talk, and then we'd talk some more. She was my greatest friend and confidant.

I watched my mother, over and over again, trying to get the first sentence of the book right. She was such a perfectionist. In fact, I don't think she would have ever finished this book if she had lived, because she used to write the first sentence over and over again, and she was never satisfied with it. It's fortunate that she did spend some time writing all the other sentences.

She died in 1990. When it came time to clean out the worn little house, my brother David and I flipped a coin to see who would do the fridge and who would clean underneath the bed. I lost the toss and had to face that mountain of paper under the bed. I was sneezing and coughing because there was so much tobacco dust in among the papers. We knew the book wasn't finished, so I just put all the crumbling paper-clipped pieces into a box, and David put the box into his attic, and it stayed there for three years.

Then a very special fellow came along to put all those pages in order—David's brother-in-law, John Bowers. John read through the pieces my mother had written, became very excited about its potential, and asked David and my sisters and me for permission to organize it and weave it together and edit it for publication. He ended up working on it for almost two years, and I think he's done an exceptional job. He had to put everything together like a puzzle, all the fragments of chapters. I know my mother's voice so well, and I know John has done a fabulous job, keeping that voice intact on every page.

Reading it reminds me of listening to her telling me stories. She was a great storyteller, as you'll see when you read this. I knew that any time of day or night, I could go up to her and say "Mommy? What happened on that night in 1950, when Jack yelled to you from the street and you threw down the key to your loft?" And she would clear her throat, take a gulp of coffee, and launch into the whole fascinating story. I really miss that.

In fact, one thing I realized a few years ago is that the stories of my childhood perished along with my mother. No one else knew me when I was a baby—just her. So with her died all the knowledge and all the memories of me as a baby. I'm sorry she didn't write all those years as part of her book. It's a hard thing for an adult child to come to terms with—that never again will you be able to ask someone what color dress you were wearing in Central Park that day in 1953, or whether you had tantrums, or whether you got along well with other children. I have to be content now with just remembering what I remember, and I miss being able to listen to her memories.

As my mother worked on this book, she had various titles in mind. One of them was *Smart Alecky Basketweaver*. In 1979, she briefly got back together with her lover, Herb Lashinsky, whom she hadn't seen in 29 years. The first time she first met my father Jack, she'd been with Herb in her loft, as you'll read here. Sometime in those intervening years, Herb sent her a card with an ugly cartoon picture of an Indian weaving a basket, and the caption said "One thing I can't stand is a smart-alecky basketweaver."

That was how Herb felt about her, that she was a primitive and didn't really know anything. She was a woman, she was uneducated. Yet she had ideas, these incongruous abstract scientific ideas. It infuriated Herb, who was a scientist, that she had no credentials but would still attack these weighty topics in genetics, philosophy, anything that attracted her attention.

My mother had high hopes that she and Herb would finally get together after that reunion meeting, but within just a few months, Herb died unexpectedly. Then, right after that, she received the blow of her cancer diagnosis. She started writing then, and at first the whole book was supposed to be about her relationship with Herb, but as she went on, she came to realize that the stories she really wanted to tell were about Jack Kerouac and Bill Cannastra and Neal Cassady, too.

Herb, and sometimes Bill and Jack too, reminded her of her mother. Anybody who scoffed at her or told her she couldn't do something the way she wanted, reminded her of her mother. Maybe that was the key to her very fiercely independent personality that made her do so many rebellious things in her life. My mother spent most of the days of her life trying to prove to people that she could do anything she set her mind to.

One day I was sitting in the front yard in Eugene, watching her pace back and forth along the street, carrying a shovel. A guy from down the block came walking by, and he looked at her, and he said "What are you doing?"

And she said, "I'm planting tomatoes." She started shoveling, right then and there, in the front driveway.

He looked at her like she was crazy and said, "You can't plant tomatoes in the driveway!"

She stared right back at him and answered defiantly, "Oh, no? You'll see. Just watch me. I'm going to plant tomatoes here, and you'll be envying them all summer."

In fact, he did envy them. She added a whole pile of compost to the driveway and planted the tomatoes in that, and throughout the summer she tended those plants. They were succulent and delicious, and she made sure the neighbor knew it.

And now, as she looks down from wherever she is, she can see that her biggest project is finally finished. She struggled for ten years to tell her story, and at last that dream has come true. She's glad for it, I know, and she knows that it turned out really well.

And finally, she can say to the world, "See? Here it is. I told you I'd do it."

Chapter 12

The house was in a row of duplexes on a quiet, orderly street. Jack cut across the frozen lawn and I followed him, asking, "Is your mom expecting us?"

"Sure." He held the front door for me and the warm smell of Sunday cooking enveloped us. "Up here," he said, leading me up the stairs. "The apartment's on the second floor. She doesn't know we're coming *today*, but I told her I'd bring you to meet her soon."

"Jack! You should have called her to ask if today was all right."

"It'll be all right." He opened the apartment door without knocking and we found his mother sitting in an overstuffed chair, darning socks in front of the TV set, the room darkened by drawn shades. After the brilliant sunlight, I had difficulty adjusting my eyes, and I didn't know how she could darn in that light. She must have done it by feel, since she was watching television at the same time.

"Ma, this is Joan." He propelled me toward her chair. "Remember? The girl I told you about?"

"Yes." She looked away from her program briefly to smile at me and indicate the chair next to hers with a nod of her head. "You sit here."

Jack took my coat and I sat down.

"I'm glad to meet you, Mrs. Kerouac." I didn't extend my hand. She would have had to put down her darning to shake it.

"You call me Gabe," she said. The 'beeg bloo eyes' Jack had described were sparkling.

"That's what all her friends call her," Jack explained. "It's short for Gabrielle. See? She likes you already!" He reassured himself more than me, speaking as though his mother weren't present, but then he turned to her and spoke about me the same way.

"She's a seamstress, Ma. Sews, makes dresses, you know?"

She answered him with a barrage of French only slightly resembling any I remembered from high school. He laughed and translated.

"She says she knows what a seamstress is."

"You like cheeken?" she asked me.

"Oh, yes!"

"Good! You stay for dinner."

Jack stood by her chair overseeing our meeting, looking from one of us to the other, beaming hopefully. Or, perhaps, apprehensively?

"I bought her that TV set," he told me proudly. "With money from my book."

"You go get Ti-Nin," Gabe ordered him. "Tell her *she's* here."

"Ti-Nin!" he exclaimed. "What's she doing her?" Aside to me he said, "That's my sister."

Another stream of French from Gabe, answered by Jack's "aah, oh," made me feel that this was family business. I hoped we hadn't chosen the wrong time for a visit.

"Go now," she insisted, and as soon as he was out of the room she whispered to me, smiling secretively, knowingly.

"He's a good boy."

I smiled back, not knowing what remark was expected. My eyes were becoming accustomed to the dim room, and I saw that the furniture had been arranged for TV viewing. The chairs we sat in, large pieces with faded wine-colored upholstery, were almost directly in front of the matching sofa. Horsehairs protruded here and there, placing the date of their manufacture in the twenties or before. I imagined they had been transported from Quebec to Lowell and finally to New York. Jack's oak roll-top desk was beside the set, but his swivel chair could easily be moved back in line with the others to a comfortable viewing position. A variety of small tables were covered with doilies, knick-knacks, photos and souvenirs which Gabe must have dusted daily, for everything gleamed, spotlessly clean. This was the room Jack had described as homey and cozy. I found it oppressively crowded and close, but then I remembered Bill had accused me of exaggerating the importance of space.

Jack returned with a pretty brown-haired girl, looking younger than her thirty years. She was thin but her hip structure promised the eventual pear shape of her mother's figure. He introduced her as I extricated myself from the deep comfort of the chair.

"My sister, Caroline. She was putting my nephew down for his nap."

Then to Caroline he said, "This is Joan. She's going to be your sister-in-law."

"Oh really? How nice!" she exclaimed. "When..."

"Jack," I broke in, "I never said..."

"Never mind!" he cut me off. "You'll see. Next week we'll get the license."

Gabe had gone into the kitchen to put dinner on the table and she called to Caroline to help her. I went in too, to see if I could do something, and Jack followed, not wishing to be left alone. The television continued to blare without an audience.

Caroline removed a yellow oilcloth table cover, shook it out and folded it. Escaping wafts of oilcloth odor floated in the steamy room, reminding me of upstate farm kitchens. Now Gabe replaced it with a white plastic cloth embossed to look like lace. I helped set the table in the midst of the joshing and jostling and the good-natured insults, all in a language I couldn't understand, of this close, loving family. They had a bond and a humor born of kinship, shared values and shared experiences. My own family, though no less loving, seemed reserved and constrained by comparison.

Dinner was chicken-in-the-pot with vegetables, and it was superbly flavored. An unexpected guest made no difference in the portions served at this table, for Gabe had prepared a prodigious amount.

"So much!" I remarked to Jack.

"She always cooks a lot on Sundays so I'll have something to eat while she's at work." We spoke in English while Gabe and Caroline continued to converse in French.

"Your mom works?" I had thought he supported her.

"Yeah. She's a leather skiver at a shoe factory. She uses a little tool that scrapes the leather and thins the edges so they can be rolled and stitched."

Our conversation turned to other subjects and though we spoke softly, the mention of Allen's name did not escape Gabe's notice.

"You know Geensbairg?" she asked me, almost accusingly.

"Yes," I admitted.

"Communist Jew!" she spat out.

"Now, Ma," Jack began.

"You know what zay do!" Gabe continued.

"No Ma, please! Not now!" Caroline tried to stop her, but Gabe overruled both of them.

"Put poison een ze water! Een ze reservoir zay put. Poison!"

"Who?" I asked.

"Communists! Foreigners!" she cried venomously.

I wondered what Gabe's definition of that might be, so I asked her, "What's a foreigner?"

"Don't." Jack shook his head and warned me. "You'll just get her started."

"She's already started," I said. "I want to know what she thinks."

While Jack stared out the window in annoyance and Caroline gazed at the ceiling, Gabe attempted to explain.

"Anybody zat doan have... Eef ze grandparents..." She gave up and turned the job over to Jack. "Jackie, *you* tell her!"

"Anybody whose grandparents weren't born in the U.S.A.," he imparted reluctantly.

"*Ou* Canada!" she prompted.

"Or Canada," he obliged.

Gabe nodded her head in satisfaction and Caroline availed herself of the opportunity to change the subject.

"Does your family live in New York, Joan?"

"They live upstate," I told her. "In a small town near Albany. But we're from Forest Hills, originally. I was born in the Jamaica Hospital, as a matter of fact."

"Oh! That's just a stone's throw from here. You must feel right at home."

"I was very young when we left. We moved to California during the depression, so I don't remember anything about Forest Hills."

"I remember the depression very well," Caroline said. "How old are you now?"

When I answered that I was twenty, Gabe clucked her disapproval.

"Too young!" she objected. "Too young to be away from ze mother!"

"Oh, Ma," Caroline sighed, "lots of girls live alone nowadays."

"It's all right," Jack said. "She won't be alone much longer."

It was my turn to change the direction of the conversation.

"How old is your little boy, Caroline?"

"Little Paul is two," she said. "He's named after his father."

"And you live in South Carolina?"

"In North Carolina. We came up by train last night and Little Paul hardly slept. He'll have a good long nap." She got up to clear the table while Gabe served us warm apple pie and coffee.

"Joan says she can't make a good pie crust, Ma," Jack told his mother as she and Caroline sat down.

"Ees no very hard," Gabe said to me. "I show you."

"I knew she'd say that!" Jack laughed.

"I'd love to be able to make a pie like this, Gabe," I told her. "This is delicious!"

"I make for Jackie, apple. He like eet best."

"But you should taste her *cherry* pie, Joan," Caroline said. "Ma makes the best…" She rolled her eyes as she was interrupted by a call from her son.

"What happened to that long nap?" Jack asked.

"Oh, well," she said, getting up, "I guess it was just wishful thinking." Jack followed her to the bedroom and Gabe and I did the dishes.

"Why you come to New York?" Gabe asked me.

"There are better jobs here," I evaded.

"I've been looking for a roommate."

"Much better you have husband. One girl, two girl, no make deeference. Ees no safe!"

I busied myself looking in a cupboard for the glasses, not willing to say it aloud, but ready to agree with her.

"Thees one." Gabe opened the cupboard over the sink. "I tell you, Jeanne," she said, converting my name to the French, "Jackie bee good husband. He love ze cheeldren and no chase ze girls. Some day he make good money. You see. He's a good boy and you're a good girl. I like to have you my daughter."

"Thank you, Gabe." I didn't take this compliment lightly, after all I'd heard about her rejection of Jack's friends.

Jack came into the kitchen with a sunny-faced little boy in tow. His blond hair fell down over his brow and his blue eyes were the duplicate of his grandmother's.

"Give Mèmére a kiss," Jack said.

"Mere kiss!" he cried happily and ran to her. She dried her hands and gathered him up in her arms, kissing his round little cheek and speaking to him in French.

"French will only confuse him, Ma," Caroline cautioned. "We want him to learn English first."

Gabe put him down, saying something to the effect that she never thought she'd see the day when a grandchild of hers would not speak French.

"It will be easier for him when he goes to school," Jack agreed. He would know. He had told me how difficult it had been to have to learn to read and write in a language he could barely understand.

"Let's take Little Paul out to the park," Jack said to me. He turned to his sister. "Okay, Nin? Can we do that?"

"If you don't keep him out too long," she answered. "He's not used to the cold."

"Dress him warm," Jack advised her. "And we'll take his ball. If he's active he won't be cold." He went with Caroline to help dress Little Paul.

As I got my coat from the hall closet I heard her say to him, "Don't you dare go off and get married and leave Ma alone again, Jack! She'll come and stay with us, and believe me, our marriage is too shaky right now to survive that kind of strain."

"Aw, don't worry about it!" Jack replied. "Ma wants me to get married anyway."

He came out carrying his nephew on his shoulders, ducking under the doorway. "This is Joan, Ti-Paul. Can you say Aunt Joan?"

"Antome," Paul obliged.

"Hey! That's pretty good," Jack said. "He calls me 'Untadat.'"

We made our way downstairs slowly, Jack ducking where necessary, and once outside, Paul cried "Horsie! Horsie!" Jack complied by breaking into a trot and giving a convincing whinny.

"Hey, don't pull my hair, you little bugger!" He put up his hands for Paul to use as reins, and slowed down to a walk.

"Listen," he said to me. "Don't pay any attention to my mom when she gets going like she did about the Jews. She's just very narrow-minded on this score. Always has been. Best thing is not to let her get started."

"It's not her fault," I said. "Hasn't her exposure to the world been pretty limited?"

"Well, I don't know. She's been working for years. It isn't as if she's been sheltered or isolated."

"But who does she work with? Not Jews, I bet!"

"No," he chuckled. "A Jew owns the factory. That only adds to the prejudice she already had. The women she works with are mostly Italian, Irish, and Spanish, with a few scattered Poles and French. And just about all Catholic, I guess."

"And they probably share her view of the world. You would too, if you hadn't gotten out of Lowell and gone to school. If you hadn't examined the world for yourself, you'd have nothing to counteract her prejudice with."

"Yeah? Maybe."

"I think you should bring more people home, and take her to town with you once in a while. Give her a chance to see what the world is like outside the shoe factory. *She's* the one who's being short-changed."

"Nah, nah. You don't know her. She doesn't even like half the people she works with. They're 'foreigners.' And in Lowell we lived among Greeks and she didn't like them. She's hopeless. But she's very good and sweet in her own way. In her own innocent, ignorant way."

"Horsie! Horsie!" Paul was impatient with our talk. Jack gave a little jump to make him laugh.

"Anyway, I'm glad you don't hold her narrow-mindedness against her," Jack concluded, as he trotted into the park and deposited the little boy on a huge flat rock. The sun was bright and the rock was warm in spite of the chilly air. I sat on it and watched them play with the ball till Jack threw it across the field and asked Paul to get it.

"He's the one who needs the activity," Jack said, sitting down beside me. "Not me."

But Paul, seeing us sitting idly, abandoned the ball and ran back to climb up onto the rock and join us.

"Where ball?" Jack asked him. "Paul get ball. Give to Jack."

Paul looked at Jack and laughed.

"Why do you talk to him that way?" I asked. "You're teaching him baby talk."

"But he's a baby. Gotta keep it simple."

"If you don't want him to wait for school to learn English, why should he have to wait till then to know how sentences are constructed?"

"But that's too much to expect of a little kid," Jack objected.

"Too much to say, maybe, but not too much to understand. Look." I put my arm around Little Paul. "Paul, will you please get the ball and bring it to me?" He jumped down, ran to get the ball, and ran back to place it in my lap. "Thank you, Little Paul." I lifted him onto my lap and hugged him. "Thank you for not proving me wrong."

"Well, how do you like that!" Jack said. "Where'd you learn so much about kids?"

I smiled. "I spent half my childhood baby-sitting. And I was a kid myself. Don't you remember listening to adults make fools of themselves talking down to you?"

"No, I don't remember anything like that, but maybe that's because of the language difference. When I was little my mom spoke even less English than she does now. So her attempts to teach me were pretty simple." He stood up and bounced the ball absently, looking at me shyly, like a schoolboy. I was seeing the Jack I liked best today, straight and sober, showing no trace of the gloom he often conveyed, and exhibiting none of the irritability and false confidence I found annoying. "I want to have eight kids like Old Man Martin in my book," he said, throwing the ball into the air. "There's no nicer sound than the sound of kids yelling and playing in the yard. And when I'm old I'll put my feet up on the oven door of the wood stove and listen to my grown children tell me about the world as they see it."

Little Paul was pulling at Jack to get him to come and play.

"And in the evening of our life together, you'll read stories to our grandchildren," he finished, and then he gave his attention to his nephew.

"Okay, Ti-Paul. What do you want to do?"

"Run!" Paul shouted and took off across the park. The little boy had no fear of falling. He bounced along unsteadily but weightlessly, and Jack followed close behind, pretending he was having difficulty keeping up, allowing Paul to stay just out of reach. Paul laughed happily as he ran and screamed excitedly when Jack reached out to almost tag him. Finally Jack caught him up and swung him around. The laughter of the man and the boy reached me from across the park and made an imprint upon some blank unfulfilled space within me, and I heard myself thinking *that's what I want.* But at the same time I suspected that I was a victim of subliminal advertising.

Was it so simple? Just to put away doubts and take the necessary practical steps to make the farm house and the children a reality? Was that all there was to it? Maybe I was beginning to abandon a vision, paring down the dream to a realizable, manageable size.

Between us there was not even a physical attraction we might have mistaken for love or magic. We would never share the miracle of a sunrise while singing silent hymns of praise. Nor would we know the solemn commitment of standing hand in hand in the Fifth Avenue Presbyterian Church, listening to Handel's Messiah. There was no weakness in the knees, no trembling, no sigh, none of the catching in the throat I had felt with Herb. That magic was memory. I knew better than to make any attempt to duplicate it. If an attempt like that succeeded, it would result in pain, need and subjectivity. If it failed, there would only be subsequent attempts, a jaded appetite, a blasphemy of the memory itself.

I was a candidate for a hermitage, except for my determination to have children. I knew my children now, before they were born, especially the daughter who would be first, who had spoken to me in a dream, and I anticipated her birth as the manifestation of an idea. Not my idea, but the largest idea, the idea that predated all life.

For me, Jack's appeal lay more in what he was not than in what he was. He was not sexually aggressive, not intellectually curious concerning me, not anxious for me to achieve goals or improve myself, and he was neither critical nor demanding except in regard to domestic matters.

I was being wooed because our meeting coincided with Jack's decision to marry, because Bill, before his death, had expected our relationship to be propitious, and because I was acceptable to his mother. It helped that I could cook and that I was no threat to him, would not upstage him. And it was convenient that we shared a dream of children. His reasons may have been more complicated, and his feelings may have been deeper, but this was all I saw, all I wanted to see.

My view of the situation was that we could be, for each other, a means to an end. On this bright November day, it seemed suddenly a workable solution to a number of problems. It was the least of many evils.

Eileen Kaufman
Keeper of the Flame
(1922–   )

"I knew all the Beat writers and artists. Bob was so gregarious that he had friends everywhere. We were like an extended family from coast to coast and all thru Europe and certain grapevine isles and countries throughout the world. It was a joyful time of communication with kindred souls that only was extended when the hippie movement came in. We were precursors of that community, and we were happy to have influenced their loving feeling."

—Eileen Kaufman

As the wife of San Francisco poet Bob Kaufman, Eileen Kaufman passionately took on the role of lover, wife, muse, mother, and personal archivist, a position she maintains to this day. Eileen was an up-and-coming journalist, heading to the top of her profession when she dropped everything to fully embrace the Beat philosophy, poetics, and lifestyle—a decision that changed and still informs her writing.

Revered in Europe as the "black Rimbaud," Bob Kaufman was a shamanic figure, a street bard, and an anarchist. Eileen married him in 1958. "In those early days," she recalls, "I'd accompany Bob and Jack Kerouac to those infamous Blabbermouth Nights in North Beach. There was a bottle of champagne for the winner—the best poet to stand up and improvise—and since either Bob or Jack always won, I always knew I'd be drinking champagne that night."

When Allen Ginsberg, Gregory Corso, Jack Kerouac, Philip Whalen, and Gary Snyder eventually all departed San Francisco, Bob Kaufman remained, becoming the guiding light of the North Beach Beat scene. In the spring of 1959, Eileen, Bob, and

photo by Alix, courtesy of Eileen Kaufman

Eileen and Bob Kaufman in Fairfax, California, Spring 1974.

Allen founded *Beatitude,* a magazine devoted to unpublished poets, which lasted a year but had a tremendous impact on the poetry community. City Lights first published Bob in a broadside, "Abomunist Manifesto" in 1959, and in 1965 New Directions published his first collection of poems, *Solitudes Crowded With Loneliness.* But more than his writing, it was the force of Bob's presence that had such an impact on the San Francisco poetry scene. A true street poet, Bob was the Diogenes who vigilantly moved through the North Beach corridor seeking fakes to expose and spouting poetry. And Eileen was right by his side, transcribing his oral poems into written form.

By the time his first book appeared, however, Bob had little to do with it. In 1963, in the wake of the Kennedy assassination, he took a vow of silence that lasted ten years, during which time he was sometimes referred to as "the silent guardian of the center." Eileen left with their four-year-old son, Parker, for Mexico, where she prepared *Solitudes* for publication.

Upon her return, Eileen started writing for the *Los Angeles Free Press,* covering the Monterey Pop and Jazz Festivals, and was instrumental in drawing attention to Janis Joplin, Jimi Hendrix, the Doors, and the Grateful Dead. Her articles on the rock-and-roll revolution appeared in the Los Angeles *Oracle, Billboard* magazine, and *Music World Countdown.*

With the election of Richard Nixon, she once again left the country with her son, this time for Europe, where she stayed for four years before returning to San Francisco. In 1973, Bob emerged from his prolonged silence, New Directions published his book *The Ancient Rain,* and in 1976 he and Eileen reunited in a ceremony on Mt. Tamalpais in Marin County.

Ultimately, the Kaufmans separated again. Bob remained in San Francisco, and Eileen left with Parker for Los Angeles, where she worked for a time as a copywriter. In 1980, she moved back to San Francisco, and Bob began his courtship anew. They remained together, on and off, for the next five years.

In 1985, Eileen flew to Paris, where she presented Bob Kaufman's body of work up to 1980 to the Bibliotec Archives at the Sorbonne; the rest of Bob's work that Eileen transcribed is in the Mugar Museum and Library of the Letters section of

Boston University. In January 1986, Bob Kaufman died of emphysema. In 1987, Mayor Dianne Feinstein proclaimed "Bob Kaufman Day," and a small street in San Francisco, Harwood Alley, is now called Bob Kaufman Street. Eileen remains, in her words, "the keeper of the flame," traveling the world for Bob Kaufman celebrations, reading both his work and her own.

Included here are "Jazz Chick," a poem that Bob wrote for Eileen, and an excerpt from Eileen's unpublished autobiography entitled Who Wouldn't Walk with Tigers? *It provides an intimate window into the San Francisco Beat scene.*

JAZZ CHICK

Music from her breast vibrating
Soundseared into burnished velvet.
Silent hips deceiving fools.
Rivulets of trickling ecstasy
From the alabaster pools of Jazz
Where music cools hot souls.
Eyes more articulately silent
Than Medusa's thousand tongues.
A bridge of eyes, consenting smiles
Reveal her presence singing
Of cool remembrance, happy balls
Wrapped in swinging
Jazz
Her music...
Jazz.

For Eileen
By Bob Kaufman

courtesy of Eileen Kaufman

Eileen Kaufman at the first Human Be-In, 1967, in San Francisco.

from *Who Wouldn't Walk with Tigers?*

Mark Green had been cluing me that there was really nothing going on in North Beach at the moment, but when Jack Kerouac, Allen Ginsberg, Bob Kaufman and Neal Cassady came back, there really would be something happening.

The third week in May, Mark seemed unduly excited. He whispered to me, "That one there—in the red beret—that's Bob Kaufman."

I looked over. I saw a small, lithe brown man/boy in sandals...wearing a red corduroy jacket, some nondescript pants and striped t-shirt. A wine colored beret was cocked at a precarious angle on a mop of black curly hair...and he was spouting poetry. A policeman came in and told Bob to cool it. He stopped—only until the cop left. Then once more, he began. This time, he jumped up on the nearest table in the Bagel Shop. "Hipsters, Flipsters, and finger-poppin' daddies, knock me your lobes." He was quoting one of his idols, Lord Buckley.

Next, he began to shout some of his own poetry. Everyone was laughing, listening to this poet. When he left the Bagel Shop, everyone within hearing seemed to leave with him. We all wandered over across the street to what was then Miss Smith's Tea Room. And Bob proceeded to hold court at a large round table like a latter day François Villon.

Flashing black eyes dancing as he spoke, gesticulating as a European does. I couldn't believe this. It all seemed to me like a scene from one of my favorite operas that I had sung the year before.

Rudolfo from "La Boheme" must have appeared like this bard...even down to the black goatee. And watching Bob hold court down in the Tea Room at the huge table filled with artist friends and admirers, generally leaving the bill for the enthralled tourist...it seemed very much that scene from Boheme wherein Musetta joins Marcello, Mimi, Rudolfo and their artist friends, leaving her wealthy escort to pay the outrageous bill.

I think I began to play Mimi subconsciously—in the hope that this dynamic Rudolfo would notice me. No luck that evening, but a few nights later, still recuperating from my first head spinning peyote trip, instead of going off to Sacramento to write copy—I remained in the pad which my friend with the MGA and I maintained for weekends. We sublet it to Joe Overstreet, a painter, during the week.

There were four rooms with a long hall connecting them. One in back—a store room—a small kitchen, a bathroom, a tiny living room, and the bedroom which Joe used.

Lucky for me that I kept the apartment and used it. For it was on this night that Skippy, Bob Kaufman's old lady, chanced to throw him out.

I was still asleep beside Mark Green when I heard the voice I recognized from the Bagel Shop.

"Let me in. I need a cuppa' coffee... you know?"

That voice was hoarse and low. If you ever heard it, you could never mistake it for another. After ten minutes of Bob's pleading, Joe Overstreet came in and said, "For Gods sake, somebody, get Bob Kaufman a cup of coffee so we can all get some sleep."

I got up, curious to see the small brown bard again. I went to the window. Mark was visibly annoyed. I padded over and opened the door. "Just a minute, o.k?"

Suddenly I was looking into the deepest brown eyes I had ever seen—a well I was to explore for many years. I asked him in. Bob never stopped his monolog.

"Hey, man... my old lady, she threw me out... and I need a cuppa' coffee... can you give me a cup, huh? I don't even have a dime..." and on... and on, while I slipped on my poncho over black leotards and t-shirt.

We walked down Kearny, crossing Broadway over to the original old Hot Dog Palace on Columbus, where El Cid now sprawls on the triangle. Bob sat on a stool near the door. It was such a tiny place that anywhere you sat it was near the door.

I paid for three cups of coffee for Bob while I drank hot chocolate. All the time we were there, he was charming everyone within earshot with his poetry, his quotations of great poetry of the ages, and his extraordinary insights. I was so completely overwhelmed by this young poet that I lost all sense of time, forgot my surroundings... everything banal.

Bob was teaching. Money was not important... a fact that I was fast coming to believe... Living was. Awareness is all. High on Life.

Time drifted by in the Hot Dog Palace. Bob was rapping on every subject known to Man... giving us all a show... expounding on history, literature, politics, painting, music… He kept repeating after every heavy subject that his lady had thrown him out… truly confused that such a thing could be.

We finally left the stand. We walked in the damp San Francisco fog up the Kearny Steps. It might have been the Steppes of Central Asia. It might have been Hawaii. I was neither hot nor cold. I could only hear that hoarse, low voice.

When we got to the flat, I asked Mark for the key to his apartment on Telegraph Hill. I didn't want to disturb Joe further. We three walked to Mark's pad below Coit Tower.

Bob kept up a running conversation, and Mark went to the kitchen to look for food and tea. We just couldn't talk to each other enough. There were so many things we had to find out about each other all at once. Bob had seen a poem of mine which Mark had pinned on the Bagel Shop wall, without my knowledge.

Then Bob quoted one of his poems to me, "An African Dream."

> In black core of Night, it explodes
> Silvery thunder, rolling back my brain,
> Bursting copper screens, memory worlds
> Deep in star-fed beds of time,
> Seducing my soul to diamond fires of night.
> Faint outline, a ship—momentary fright,
> Lifted on waves of color,
> Sunk in pits of light,
> Drummed back through time,
> Hummed back through mind,
> Drumming, cracking the night,
> Strange forest songs, skin sounds
> Crashing through—no longer strange,
> Incestuous yellow flowers tearing
> Magic from the earth,
> Moon-dipped rituals, led
> By a scarlet god.
> Caressed by ebony maidens

With daylight eyes,
Purple garments,
Noses that twitch,
Singing young girl songs
Of an ancient love
In dark, sunless places
Where memories are sealed,
Burned in eyes of tigers.

Suddenly wise, I fight the dream.
Green screams enfold my night.

I was overwhelmed. Here was a real poet. He reminded me of Coleridge, my childhood favorite. Bob was not one of those schlock artists who write just to be doing
something. This man was real, a genuine poet with that calling.

I thrilled every time I looked into his dark, serious eyes. It wasn't hypnotism,
because I was fully conscious. But the dynamic glance and depth of the poet's eyes was
too much to bear for seven hours. This is how long we talked. We had to get through
to each other immediately. I knew that I had suddenly fallen in love with a poet. I had
been entranced—from the moment Bob began to talk...running down the hill, hand
in hand, to the Hot Dog Palace.

We left Mark at his pad (I can't really say that I considered his feelings. I was too
mad about Bob Kaufman). My Rudolfo and I wandered back to my flat hand in
hand. Joe slept on—unaware of the changes I was experiencing. We sat down on a
mattress in the back room and talked softly.

"You are my woman, you know," said Bob. I just gazed at him with newly opened
eyes, now wide in disbelief.

He whispered, "You don't believe me now...but you'll see."

His arm was around my shoulders. I was standing next to him. I swayed a little
then, and he caught me in his arms, broke my balance, and together—we fell laughing onto the bare mattress. He was laughing at me, and I was laughing because, well,
I was a little scared and kind of high from our meeting and subsequent conversation.

Suddenly, I sat up straight and leaned over Bob, letting my hair fall into his face. He took hold of my long, loose hair with one hand and pulled me down to him. Then he kissed me. Except for holding hands or casually putting his arm about my shoulder, that was the first actual physical contact with him.

I shivered, and he pulled my hair a little harder, and consequently me closer. How did I feel? Like sunsets and dawns and balmy midnights and ocean voyages. My pulse was dancing a wild Gypsy rhythm, and I felt alive! We searched each other's mouths for a time. Then, as if we had found an answer there...without a word we broke apart...and each began to undress the other.

It was a simple task for me, because Bob wore only trousers, t-shirt and sandals. I was eager to feel his strong brown body. It seemed a long time until I was in his arms and stroking that sensual body. This man—with the body of Michelangelo's David—wanted me—and yes, oh yes, I certainly wanted him—for as long as he would have me.

When you find your soul mate, there can be no question, no hesitation, no games. You have been lovers before in many other lives, so you are attuned to each other immediately.

Why else is there love at first sight? Hollywood is often chided for its use of music coming out of nowhere in a big love scene. Believe me, there is music then—music from the spheres.

Without the slightest formal introduction on my part to Eastern eroticism, Bob and I became Tantric lovers spontaneously that morning. That was my second psychedelic trip in two weeks in North Beach.

It is true that your soul leaves your body during a very passionate love embrace. It happened to me just that way. And I suspect that Bob experienced a bit of magic too... as he held me throughout the entire tidal wave.

When I caught my breath, I looked at him and smiled. I noticed that he was lying beside me drenched and spent. He said it again, "You see? You are my woman. You have absolutely no choice in the matter."

For the first time, I began to think. How can you ponder what is happening in a vortex...at the eye of the hurricane...in a whirlpool? You can only swing with it and hope that you don't go under permanently. Was I going under? Up to this point I hadn't even cared.

But now I leaned on one elbow and looked down into Bob's smiling eyes. I said it as well as I could. "It's just all too overwhelming for me, Bob Kaufman. Go away please and leave me for a few hours...till maybe 6 tonight, ok? I really have to think about everything that's happened last night and this morning."

Bob's smile faded.

"But hold me now. We can talk later," I added.

He brightened and seemed to understand. He turned on his side, folded me back into his arms, and went to sleep. I may have slept, but I heard him when he got up to dress. I opened my eyes and said sleepily... "See you around 6 tonight...on Grant."

Bob said, "Then you'll be my old lady. You have no..."

I put my fingers over his mouth lightly. "Tell you then. I really have to be alone all day to think it out. Bye."

Bob kissed me lightly on the mouth and vanished. He was gone as suddenly as he had arrived.

I danced the rest of the day through in a hazy kind of mist. I wasn't high on peyote any longer. I was high on Bob Kaufman. Maybe contact high—maybe more, since he had all kinds of dope available to him...and he has never been known to turn down any of it!

I dressed slowly, brushing my hair overtime, taking a little more care with the black eyeliner...too excited to eat anything, I threw on my poncho and ran out the front door. We didn't have a clock in the pad, and I wasn't going to be late for this important decision.

I ran down Green Street, turned the corner at Grant. Walking down past the Bagel Shop, I saw Bob on the opposite side of the street. He stared at me intently and clenched his teeth, as he has a way of doing when asking a silent question. I just nodded. He came bounding across the street. I said, "You're right. *I'm your woman.*" And he hugged me tightly in answer.

We started to the Bagel Shop. Bob read a few victory poems there, drank a few beers and laughed a lot. He told everyone, "Meet Eileen, my old lady."

That very night, I got my first taste of life with a poet. And that taste has since stayed in my mouth. I could never love a lesser man than an artist.

Bob began to hold court in the Coffee Gallery about 7:30 in the evenings, and for several hours while the locals and the tourists brought him beer, wine, champagne—anything, he, in turn, would speak spontaneously on any subject, quote great poetry by Lorca, T. S. Eliot, ee cummings, or himself. I would just sit adoringly at his side.

I wish I had been able to tape every conversation, every fragment, because each time Bob speaks it is a gem in a crown of oratory. His wit... Cities should be built on one side of the Street... His one-liners... Laughter sounds orange at Night... and his prophecies—all are astounding. Bob's entire monologue is like a long vine of poetry which continually erupts into flowers.

In the late '50s the Coffee Gallery was arranged differently. After the management took over from Miss Smith, the Gallery became the "other" place in the 1300 block on Grant.

There was no partition for the entertainment section, and jazz was played throughout the place any time the musicians fell by. Spontaneity was the key word in our life style in North Beach. This is what made it "the scene," for one never knew in advance just who might show to read a poem, dance, play some jazz, or put on a complete play.

The tourists were delighted to buy a pitcher of beer, bottle of champagne, or anything we wanted—just to be a part of the Life emanating from our table. The Life was, for the most part, Bob, and his hilarious monologues, sparkling wit and funky comments. Even the "Mr Jones" who didn't know what was happening in the late '50s knew that *something* groovy was going on, and he would *buy* his way into it, by God, if he couldn't get in any other way! That's where we accumulated our camp followers, hangers-on and groupies.

Some nights Bob would really get it on. In the early evening he would be writing on note paper, napkins, finally toilet paper, just to get his speeding thoughts down. I began to keep these valuable fragments for him so that he could finish the poems when he got home.

In the early morning, Bob would wander out and take one of his dawn-morning walks—harking back to walks with his great-grandmother. Sometimes I would go with him. Other days I would sleep in. Bob and I would begin our Grant Avenue odyssey around three or four each afternoon. And whatever happened would happen. We would run down the hill, laughing, and brighten the lives of the tourists, adding to the disorder of the day. We proceeded to urge on any musical activity in Washington Square. (New Yorkers, please note: We have our own in North Beach.) Bob might recite a poem or write a new one in the Bagel Shop...or we might drink wine or smoke grass at someone's subterranean pad. We spent a lot of time on the rooftops smoking hash.

When I met Bob Kaufman, King of North Beach, my values changed overnight. I had been a greedy, mercenary career girl whose only object was to get it while you can. But the very night I met Bob, I could see these values totally changing. When Bob read "African Dream" to me, I knew I had met a genius.

And so I knew at once what my life would be: Tempestuous, Adventurous, Passionate, but always new experiences. I reached out for Bob Kaufman, the man and his poetry. And he made my life a shambles. It was not as though I didn't ask for it. I knew at a glance and after one night that this man could create my life or destroy it. The life I had known was in ashes, and like the Phoenix, my new life had begun. It was to be everything I had seen in the flash of an African Dream...and more. Suddenly wise, I did not fight the Dream.

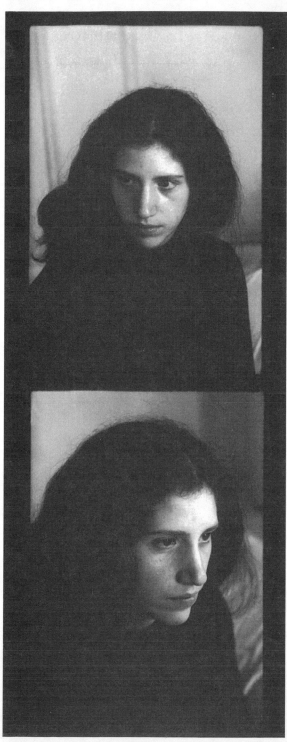

© James O. Mitchell

THE
WRITERS

courtesy of Ann Charters

Poet Mary Fabilli at home.

Reverse: Portrait of a Beatnik, Diane di Prima, circa 1957.

Mary Fabilli
Farmer's Daughter
(1914–)

And I do wonder what he is
going to say
about the long lost poets in
San Francisco . . .

—Mary Fabilli, July 1989

Mary Fabilli is a quiet voice amid the howls, raps, and roars of the Beat Generation. She wrote poetry but never read publicly during the heyday of the Beats, although the purity of her work inspired such well-known poets as Robert Duncan, who was a great supporter.

The daughter of an immigrant Italian farmer, Mary Fabilli found poetry by instinct, for her education did little to inspire her. When Mary was young, she tried to imitate her older sister Josephine's writing by copying her poems. Then, at age sixteen, she purchased *Palgraves' The Golden Treasury* and from studying the poems, she learned how to write poetry. Her favorites, she recalls, included "Emily Dickinson. I like English lyric poets, as well. Shelley, Keats, Byron."

Mary was born on February 16, 1914, in the small company town of Gardiner, New Mexico. Her parents came from Pacentro, Italy, a small town in the mountains east of Rome, to work in Rockefeller's New Mexican coal mines and coke ovens. Eventually, the family moved to Colorado and then to Pennsylvania, where she began grammar school.

While Mary was in elementary school, her father decided the family should return to Pacentro for a visit. Once back in his homeland, her father wanted to stay. Her mother, however, reasoned that the education system in such a small Italian village could not compare to the public school system in America. Although Mary's father knew he would miss his homeland, they returned to the United States.

The visit to Italy rekindled more than a love for his country. He decided to return to his job as a farmer and purchased a twelve-acre farm ten miles outside of Delano, California. Transplanted once again, Mary and her three sisters and one brother enrolled in yet another new school.

After high school, she took a job at the Tulare County Free Library in Visalia to save money for college. When her younger sister, Lillian, went to U.C. Berkeley and got a room-and-board job, Mary followed with her last month's pay of $62 and also enrolled at Berkeley.

Mary's first job in the San Francisco Bay Area was with the National Youth Administration, a government-funded project founded by President Roosevelt. She also took art classes at the University of California. Living in Berkeley led to many friendships, including one with a young painter, Virginia Admiral, with whom she eventually roomed. She also met a young poet, Robert Duncan, who introduced her to the San Francisco Renaissance and Beat scenes.

Because of the Depression, Mary was forced to drop out of college for a while. She got a job working on a WPA Art Project in Oakland for a year and a half until she had enough money to go back to school. She finally graduated from U.C. Berkeley in 1941 with a bachelor's degree in art and a minor in English. She took only one poetry course, taught by Beat mentor Dr. Josephine Miles, who was very encouraging. "She was very nice," remembers Mary, "a good teacher. She had to be carried into and out of class, she was so crippled by that time."

Then World War II broke out. For two and a half years, Mary worked swing shift in Richmond at the Kaiser shipyards as a steel checker. She explains her job as pattern making, as if for a dress. Her job consisted of locating parts on the ships such as peaks and double bottoms for heister drivers and riggers. She would indicate where they were stored in the shipyards. It was hard work, standing in the bitter cold, directing machinery, trying to keep the piles of steel separated.

After the war ended, Mary visited Virginia Admiral in New York for a while. When she returned to the Bay Area, she taught seventh-grade art at the Bentley School in Berkeley and to adults at the YWCA in Oakland. Then she began working at the *East Bay Labor Journal,* compiling their mailing list.

Mary's next job became a lasting career. After passing an exam, she was offered a job at the Oakland Museum on 14th Street by Lake Merritt. She worked as a teacher and lecturer, teaching art to children and adults in the summer. During the school year, she gave lectures on Colonial history in the eastern United States as well as California history. She even demonstrated how to weave on a loom and load a musket.

When the new museum opened, she was transferred there to work as associate curator in the history department, specializing in California's Mexican and Spanish periods and twentieth-century labor and politics, where she remained until retirement in 1977. Although it enabled her to unite her interest in both art and literature, her work never affected her love of poetry. "Poetry was always important to me. I love poetry, but I had to make a living." She never measured success by the number of publications she had. "My poetry isn't politically correct," she claims.

Even so, she published relatively frequently. Her largest work was her 1981 anthology entitled *Poems: 1976–1981.* It included short, blank verse as well as her more developed, *Aurora Bligh* storytelling poems. She also published a number of works for *Oyez,* founded by Robert and Dorothea Hawley, which included *Go Now, Lightfooted Into Danger, Aurora Bligh,* and *The Animal Kingdom.* Besides self-publishing her poetry in mimeographed pamphlets, such as the collection of poems entitled *The Old Ones,* her strongly descriptive poems were published in Duncan's literary magazine, *Epitaph.*

Her closest association with the San Francisco Beat scene came during her marriage to William Everson, a local Beat poet. William encouraged Mary to write, and her linoleum-block art accompanied two of his poems, "Triptych for the Living" and "Heavenly City, Earthly City." A devout Catholic, Mary gave Everson a copy of St. Augustine's *Confessions,* and he became so enthralled with the Roman Catholic Church that he converted to Catholicism, had their marriage annulled, and joined the Dominican Friars as Brother Antoninus. He left the Order in 1969 and died in 1984.

After retiring from the library museum in 1977, Mary devoted herself more fully to art and writing. She continues to publish her work in retrospectives featured in literary magazines such as *Talisman*. Poetry continues to be her form of choice. At one point in her early writing career, she began a novel, but after three chapters she set it aside and never picked it up again. Her latest prose poem has been published in *Sierra Journal '96* and is entitled "A Letter to Aurora Bligh."

Her work is characterized by a strong tie to the Roman Catholic Church. Many of the religious aspects are subtle but always present. "You may have to search," she claims, "but you will always find my love for God in my work."

Interestingly, Mary Fabilli's work has much more in common with that of her close friend Robert Duncan than her husband, William Everson. Her poetry evokes a dark intimacy that Duncan called an "ecstatic pessimism."

Included in the following selection of Mary's work is "Letter to Robert," her tribute to Robert Duncan.

LETTER TO ROBERT

We who devour our unclean dead are now arisen
we are walking in the corridors under the vaulted stairs
from our shady pockets the sun has never risen
these   our vested interests   our noble heirs
in derision we have warned them
exploring with our fingers   sensing the fragile bone
who will atone for our deception?
who will consume the marrow breaking through with a stone
listen and you will hear them the liars   the deceivers
running furtively to be alone in the shady corners
trailing their unclean fingers as they flutter up the stairs
We who devour our dead have left their prison
we have forgotten the twilight swaying about their beds
the twilight   the fiery pebbles   the livid eyes on the stairs
but they have resumed our wisdom
liars all & believers   they   boneless bodies dead

they have heard us groan in the corridors
they have barred the doors with threads
we who are dead have devoured us & have gathered to watch these children
playing games with our stones
with the polished bones of the dead
(This is what I think of the international situation—very lucid, it is not).

■ ■ ■

ADVENT

Rain yesterday and today,
rain and music.
The Hopi Indian said,
"I will be lonely tomorrow . . . . .
"Don't ask me to sing anymore,
there's too much rain!"

"Can't you sing any other songs?" we asked

"I can sing of the snow."

Snow falling on Christmas trees
deep in the forests of Arizona,
and falling fast in Zion,
while the angels sing in a strange land,
peace and companionship—
the child that is born to us—
sing songs of him in all the mesas
after two thousand years.

■ ■ ■

DECEMBER EVENING

Fog tonight
and rain
and a vinyl Christmas tree

at the neighbor's window.
The Argentine tango
weaves through my rooms
a voluble python
civilized
non-venomous.

Fog and music
rain and swish of tires
and then a floundering airplane
reverberating thunder . . . . . .

(this afternoon a troubled cat
stretched cautious legs across the winter grass).

■ ■ ■

THE ROLLICKING ROSES

The rollicking roses
of the past
were of a compulsive nature
inscribed in her memory
in isometric perfection . . . . .
Then, frankly forgotten.

Venus and Eros conspired
but Pallas Athena complained.

Jove in his wisdom
from a mass of components
manufactured a monkeywrench.

The past was notoriously
wrecked and
no longer noteworthy.

Diane di Prima
Poet Priestess
(1934–   )

"I think the poet is the last person who is still speaking the truth when no one else dares to. I think the poet is the first person to begin the shaping and visioning of the new forms and the new consciousness when no one else has begun to sense it; I think these are two of the most essential human functions"

—Diane di Prima

R aised in Brooklyn, Diane was close to her maternal grandfather, Domenico Mallozi. Very political and a diehard freethinker, he counted prominent anarchist Carlo Tresca as a close friend. Diane began writing poetry at the age of seven. At thirteen, she entered Hunter High School in Manhattan and since then has written constantly. After nearly two years of studying physics at Swarthmore College, she moved to the Lower East Side—well before the arrival of any "scene." There she pursued her writing and her passion for knowledge full-time, working in bookstores so she could read as much as possible, often all day and into the night.

In the early fifties, before the Beats became known, Diane di Prima became friends with the "new bohemians." Her various "pads" were centers of lively discussion and activity, filled with friends who often slept together. "Out of this fact," she wrote in *Memoirs of a Beatnik,* "grew nuances of relationship most delicate in their shading."

In 1953, she started what was to be a very influential relationship with Ezra Pound. They corresponded and Diane went to visit Pound at St. Elizabeth's, a psychiatric hospital in Washington, D.C., and spent time with him there. During this same period, her thirst for discourse and the desire to connect with other strong minds led

© 1978 by Ed Buryn

Diane di Prima and Michael McClure at the 1978 Tribal Stomp in Berkeley, California.

her to a literary correspondence with several other poets—including Kenneth Patchen, Lawrence Ferlinghetti, and Allen Ginsberg.

Diane went out of her way to learn from writers she respected. In an interview with Anne Waldman in the 1980s, she reflected:

> Don't forget, however great your visioning and your inspiration, you need the techniques of the craft and there's nowhere, really, to get them because these are not passed on in schools. They are passed on person to person, and back then the male naturally passed them on to the male. I think maybe I was one of the first women to break through that in having deep conversations with Charles Olson and Frank O'Hara.

An equally important spiritual aspect of Diane's life also started in these years and continued well past her "beatness." In 1953, she met the teacher and choreographer James Waring and began a serious study of Zen and meditative composition that paved the way for her lifelong practice of Buddhism. The Waring/di Prima creative partnership also involved Diane's stage management of the Monday night series for the Living Theatre.

In 1957, Diane finally met Allen Ginsberg and his companions Jack Kerouac, Peter Orlovsky, and Gregory Corso in New York. This meeting of mind and body is most famously depicted in her written-for-hire erotic autobiography, *Memoirs of a Beatnik.* In it, she describes a Beat orgy involving Ginsberg, Kerouac, herself, and two others as being "warm and friendly and very unsexy—like being in a bathtub with four other people."

That same year, Diane's first daughter, Jeanne, was born, followed a few months later by the publication of her first book, *This Kind of Bird Flies Backward.* Three years later, her first book of prose, *Dinners and Nightmares,* was published by Corinth Press.

Diane modeled for artists and worked at various jobs. She also helped her friends Hettie and LeRoi Jones publish the literary journal *Yugen.* LeRoi and Diane had a daughter together and founded a mimeographed subscription newsletter, *The Floating Bear.* Here they published the work of many Beat writers, both those who became legendary and those who have slipped into obscurity.

Barbara Guest

In the 1950s, Barbara Guest was a frequent contributor to *Yugen* and *The Floating Bear.* Both Hettie Jones and Diane di Prima were impressed by the newcomer, whose poems were strikingly original with a clarity and intelligence well matched to the brand-new Beats. Greatly influenced by both the writers and the abstract expressionist painters who were coming to the fore at that time, Barbara names as her greatest inspiration French poet Anne Marie Albiach and said in an interview, "I drag my coattails in the dust of the Russian poets Akamatova and Mandelstam."

She was also fascinated by the Imagists and spent five years writing the biography of the original Imagist poet, HD (Hilda Doolittle). *Herself Defined: The Poet H.D. and Her World* was a critical success, but Guest's subsequent novel *Seeking Air,* an experimental collage, nearly escaped attention. Undaunted, Barbara continued to take risks with language and break new ground, including "Tuerler Losses," a twenty-two-page epic about the loss of two wristwatches. In a 1988 interview, Barbara Guest stated that she believes "women poets to be writing the finest poetry today."

At the same time, Diane was very involved in other creative pursuits and, along with Fred Herko, LeRoi Jones, Alan Marlowe, John Herbert MacDowell, and James Waring, founded the New York Poets Theatre, producing four seasons of one-act plays by poets, with fine-art sets by artists from both coasts. In 1961, she traveled to the West Coast to meet the San Francisco Bay Area avant garde—Robert Duncan, Helen Adam, Michael McClure, Kirby Doyle, Wallace Berman, and Jay DeFeo.

LeRoi Jones and she were arrested by the FBI in late 1961 for the so-called obscenity of the ninth issue of *The Floating Bear.* LeRoi defended them before a grand jury on the precedent set by the cases of *Ulysses* and *Lady Chatterly's Lover,* and the case was thrown out. This was not to be the end of legal hassles, however, and Diane learned to "look for trouble from all directions."

This stance would come in handy when the New York Poets Theatre was brought up on charges of obscenity for showing Jean Genet's film *Chant d'Amour.* Diane and her partners fought and eventually won a long civil rights suit. Meanwhile, two years after the first issue of *The Floating Bear,* LeRoi resigned as co-editor because of Diane's marriage to Alan Marlowe. With Alan, Diane founded Poets Press, which published the poetic works of Audre Lorde, Clive Matson, Herbert Huncke, David Henderson, and many others.

The last half of the sixties saw Diane very much on the move—living at an upstate New York ashram; staying at Timothy Leary's experimental, psychedelic community at Millbrook; and traveling on an epic 20,000-mile journey, kids in tow, across America in a Volkswagen bus, reading poetry at dance halls, bars, storefronts, colleges, and galleries. She finally settled in San Francisco. In 1968, Diane joined the Diggers, the now-infamous political troupe. Along with other members such as Peter Coyote, Lenore Kandel, and Emmet Grogan, she distributed free food and staged political events. During this time, her *Revolutionary Letters* was published widely through the underground press. She divorced Alan Marlowe in 1969.

The dawn of the seventies saw Diane shift from activist to contemplative, when she began to devote more time to studying and practicing zen. After all the years of perfecting her craft, Diane finally felt she was ready to teach. She embarked on her long poem "Loba," gave classes for the NEA's poetry-in-the-schools program (teach-

© 1978 by Ed Buryn

Diane di Prima at microphone with (from L to R) Allen Ginsberg, Lenore Kandel, Michael McClure and Wavy Gravy at the Tribal Stomp 1978, Greek Theatre, Berkeley, California.

ing at reform schools, reservations, and prisons), as well as offering writing, visualization, and dream workshops in San Francisco. At the same time, she also managed to raise three daughters and two sons. In 1972, Diane married Grant Fisher. In 1977, two years after her divorce from Fisher, she met her life partner, fellow Buddhist Sheppard Powell, with whom she shares an affinity in spirituality, healing, and the arts.

Later she taught at the Masters Program in Poetics she helped found in 1980 at the New College of California in San Francisco with Robert Duncan, David Meltzer, Duncan McNaughton, and Louis Patler. There she taught occult and Hermetic traditions in poetry for seven years. Diane di Prima's expertise also includes healing work and magical practice, which she taught through her San Francisco Institute of

Magical and Healing Arts. In 1983, after over twenty years of practicing zen, Diane embraced Tibetan Buddhism, becoming a student of Chogyam Trungpa Rinpoche.

Diane di Prima's body of work spans fifty years, including over thirty books and thousands of poems in addition to her epic, "Loba." More than any other woman of the Beat, di Prima has taken her place alongside the men as the epitome of Beat brilliance.

What follows are poems from various stages in Diane di Prima's career and an excerpt from Memoirs of a Beatnik:

RANT

You cannot write a single line w/out a cosmology
a cosmogony
laid out, before all eyes

there is no part of yourself you can separate out
saying, this is memory, this is sensation
this is the work I care about, this is how I
make a living

it is whole, it is a whole, it always was whole
you do not "make" it so
there is nothing to integrate, you are a presence
you are an appendage of the work, the work stems from
hangs from the heaven you create

every man / every woman carries a firmament inside
& the stars in it are not the stars in the sky

w/out imagination there is no memory
w/out imagination there is no sensation
w/out imagination there is no will, desire

history is a living weapon in yr hand
& you have imagined it, it is thus that you
"find out for yourself"
history is the dream of what can be, it is
the relation between things in a continuum

of imagination
what you find out for yourself is what you select
out of an infinite sea of possibility
no one can inhabit yr world

yet it is not lonely,
the ground of imagination is fearlessness
discourse is video tape of a movie of a shadow play
but the puppets are in yr hand
your counters in a multidimensional chess
which is divination
               & strategy

the war that matters is the war against the imagination
all other wars are subsumed in it.

the ultimate famine is the starvation
of the imagination

it is death to be sure, but the undead
seek to inhabit someone else's world

the ultimate claustrophobia is the syllogism
the ultimate claustrophobia is "it all adds up"
nothing adds up & nothing stands in for
anything else

THE ONLY WAR THAT MATTERS IS THE WAR AGAINST
                            THE IMAGINATION

THE ONLY WAR THAT MATTERS IS THE WAR AGAINST
THE IMAGINATION
THE ONLY WAR THAT MATTERS IS THE WAR AGAINST
THE IMAGINATION

ALL OTHER WARS ARE SUBSUMED IN IT

There is no way out of the spiritual battle
There is no way you can avoid taking sides
There is no way you can *not* have a poetics
no matter what you do: plumber, baker, teacher

you do it in the consciousness of making
or not making yr world
you have a poetics: you step into the world
like a suit of readymade clothes

or you etch in light
your firmament spills into the shape of your room
the shape of the poem, of yr body, of yr loves

A woman's life / a man's life is an allegory

Dig it

There is no way out of the spiritual battle
the war is the war against the imagination
you can't sign up as a conscientious objector

the war of the worlds hangs here, right now, in the balance
it is a war for this world, to keep it
a vale of soul-making

the taste in all our mouths is the taste of our power
and it is bitter as death

bring yr self home to yrself, enter the garden
the guy at the gate w/ the flaming sword is yrself

the war is the war for the human imagination
and no one can fight it but you/ & no one can fight it for you

The imagination is not only holy, it is precise
it is not only fierce, it is practical
men die everyday for the lack of it,
it is vast & elegant

intellectus means "light of the mind"
it is not discourse it is not even language
the inner sun

the *polis* is constellated around the sun
the fire is central

■ ■ ■

FOR PIGPEN
Velvet at the edge of the tongue,
at the edge of the brain, it was
velvet. At the edge of history.

Sound was light. Like tracing
ancient letters w/yr toe on the
floor of the ballroom.
They came & went, hotel guests
like the Great Gatsby.
And wondered at the music.
            Sound was light.

jagged sweeps of discordant
Light. Aurora borealis over
some cemetery. A bark. A howl.

At the edge of history & there was
    no time

shouts. trace circles
of breath. All futures. Time
was this light & sound
spilled out of it.

        Flickered
& fell under blue windows. False dawn.
And too much wind.

        We come round.
Make circles. Blank as a clock.
Spill velvet damage on the edge
of history.

■ ■ ■

MY LOVER'S EYES ARE NOTHING LIKE THE SUN
for Sheppard

These eyes are amber, they
have no pupils, they are filled
w/a blue light (fire).
They are the eyes of gods
the eyes of insects, straying
godmen of the galaxy, metallic
wings.
        Those eyes were green
are still, sea green, or grey
their light
less defined. These sea-green
eyes spin dreams on the

palpable air. They are not yrs
or mine. It is as if the dead
saw thru our eyes, others for a moment
borrowed these windows, gazing.
We keep still. It is as if these windows
filled for a minute w/a different
light.

Not blue, not amber. But the curtain drawn
over our daily gaze is drawn aside.
Who are you, really. I have seen it
often enough, the naked
gaze of power. We "charge"
the other with it /   the leap
into non-betrayal, a wind
w/ out sound we live in. Where
are we, really, climbing
the sides of buildings to peer in
like spiderman, at windows
not our own

■■■

THE DOCTRINE OF SIGNATURES

There are knowable numbers too
As when the primrose reveals the six in its heart
But the number imprinted on my heart
Is a darker business.

Say this: the pulse of pain
is a cycle of five.

                    And you have not said
all. The mighty wind

                    blows from the 8 to the 7
thru the Tower called God's house
                    What signature
shapes the vector of the breath
                    flowing outward?

There is a smoke that arises from the heart
a pillar of cloud of the Will
                    & we move toward the Good
like the stars, like young rams,   like a god
who yearns to be himself
                    & frighten no one.

                    ■ ■ ■

NO PROBLEM PARTY POEM

first glass broken on patio no problem
forgotten sour cream for vegetables no problem
Lewis MacAdam's tough lower jaw no problem
cops arriving to watch bellydancer no problem
plastic bags of melted ice no problem
wine on antique tablecloth no problem
scratchy stereo no problem
neighbor's dog no problem
interviewer from Berkeley Barb no problem
absence of more beer no problem
too little dope no problem
leering Naropans no problem
cigarette butts on the altars no problem
Marilyn vomiting in planter box no problem
Phoebe renouncing love no problem
Lewis renouncing Phoebe no problem
hungry ghosts no problem

absence of children no problem
heat no problem
dark no problem
arnica scattered in nylon rug no problem
ashes in bowl of bleached bone & juniper berries no problem
lost Satie tape no problem
loss of temper no problem
arrogance no problem
boxes of empty beer cans & wine bottles no problem
thousands of styrofoam cups no problem
Gregory Corso no problem
Allen Ginsberg no problem
Diane di Prima no problem
Anne Waldman's veins no problem
Dick Gallup's birthday no problem
Joanne Kyger's peyote & rum no problem
wine no problem
coca-cola no problem
getting it on in the wet grass no problem
running out of toilet paper no problem
decimation of pennyroyal no problem
destruction of hair clasp no problem
paranoia no problem
claustrophobia no problem
growing up on Brooklyn streets no problem
growing up in Tibet no problem
growing up in Chicano Texas no problem
bellydancing certainly no problem
figuring it all out no problem
giving it all up no problem
giving it all away no problem
devouring everything in sight no problem

what else in Allen's refrigerator?
what else in Anne's cupboard?
what do you know that you
        haven't told me yet?
no problem.   no problem.   no problem.

staying another day no problem
getting out of town no problem
telling the truth, almost no problem
            easy to stay awake
            easy to go to sleep
            easy to sing the blues
            easy to chant sutras
what's all the fuss about?

it decomposes—no problem
we pack it in boxes—no problem
we swallow it with water, lock it in the trunk,
    make a quick getaway.   NO PROBLEM.

■ ■ ■

THE LOBA ADDRESSES THE GODDESS / OR
THE POET AS PRIESTESS ADDRESSES THE LOBA-GODDESS

Is it not in yr service that I wear myself out
running ragged among these hills, driving children
to forgotten movies? In yr service
broom & pen. The monstrous feasts
we serve the others on the outer porch
(within the house there is only rice & salt)
And we wear exhaustion like a painted robe
I & my sisters
            wresting the goods from the niggardly
            dying fathers
healing each other w/water & bitter herbs

that when we stand naked in the circle of lamps
(beside the small water, in the inner grove)
we show
no blemish, but also no superfluous beauty.
It has burned off in watches of the night.
O Nut, O mantle of stars, we catch at you
      lean   mournful
      ragged   triumphant
               shaggy as grass
our skins ache of emergence / dark o' the moon

■ ■ ■

photos by Sheppard Powell

Diane di Prima in 1979, and 1989 (inset).

from *Memoirs of a Beatnik:*
Chapter 10
Summer

You never do get to go *back* to anything, but it really takes a long time to learn that....

When I stepped off the bus at 40th Street and Eighth Avenue, it was like arriving at a foreign port. The city, steaming and tropical, resounded with music: guitars, harmonicas, an occasional horn, radios blaring, children playing in the dark, women talking together on the sidewalks or stoops, or calling to each other from the windows. The night was pregnant with lust and violence, and the small, dark men stalked softly. It was a universe away from my world of home-fries and roadwork that I had left only an hour and a half earlier, and yet it was the same, exactly the same—crowded together and seen in the dark.

Downtown the streets were filled with youngsters who had made their way to the Village over the summer months. You could hear their drumming blocks from Washington Square, and when you stepped into the crowd around the fountain, you saw the young men barefoot and naked to the waist, and the young women, their skirts held high, stomping and dancing together in the heavy night.

I had no luggage and I had no pad. The apartment had been lost for non-payment of rent while I was away, and O'Reilley had moved my "stuff"—mostly books— to a West Tenth Street apartment where a little street-hustler-ballet-dancer named René Strauss lived. I joined the kids at the fountain, chanting and clapping, greeting friends and acquaintances, hearing the news. Finally the crowd thinned, the musicians all went home, and I wandered over to René's and fell out.

I spent the next few days casing the scene. The city was really crowded; there were, simply, no pads to be had, and rather than hassle I took to sleeping in the park.

At that time no laws had been passed limiting a citizen's right to access to the public parks, no curfews were in effect. By two o'clock in the morning Washington Square was usually clear of its usual crowd: folksingers, faggots, and little girls from New Jersey on the make, and I would stretch out on the steps by the fountain and sleep peacefully until just after dawn, when a Park Department man with a big broom would come by and wake me. He swept my bed and went away again, and I and the half-dozen other people, all complete strangers, who shared these quarters, would exchange dazed greetings and go back to sleep till ten or so, when people started to arrive.

There was a regular crew of about eight of us who slept there, four to six of the eight being there on any given night, and we all got to know each other pretty well, as far as moods and habits and aura went, but we never spoke. Something about the intimacy of our shared space and the code of coolness in effect at that time would have made it unseemly for us to know each other by name, or have anything more to say to each other than the minimum morning greeting. It would have been intrusion, filling each other's turf and head with rattling chatter and conversation, and the inevitable unfolding of our emotional lives would have destroyed the space that the indifference of the city gave each and every one as her most precious gift.

At ten I would get up, stretch, look around me, and read for an hour or so till I was thoroughly awake. Then, stuffing all my accoutrements into the attaché case that served as my portable home and contained a raincoat, a toothbrush, notebooks, pens, and a change of underwear, I would pick it up and set off for the Chinese laundry on Waverly Place. I kept all my clothes there on separate tickets: one pair of slacks and one shirt on each ticket. I would take out a ticket's worth, and, carrying now attaché case and laundry package, I'd amble to Rienzi's, which opened at eleven, and order a breakfast, usually some kind of sweet and espresso coffee, though occasionally I'd splurge and treat myself to eggs and English muffins, or even some sausages or bacon. While the order was making, I'd find my way to the bathroom which was hidden away downstairs; down a rank, damp staircase with oozing walls, and along a corridor straight out of the *Count of Monte Cristo* to a tiny, cramped room, fortunately vaguely cleaned, where I would wash my face and feet and hands, brush my teeth, and change clothes, stuffing the dirty ones into a paper bag I carried in the attaché case for that purpose. Would then pull a brush through my hair and tie it up, and, feeling vaguely human, would grope my way up the stairs and to my breakfast.

Great pleasure it is to sit in an unhurried, uncrowded shop, drinking good, strong coffee and reading while your friends come in and out and the morning draws to a close and you write stray words in a notebook. I would linger as long as I could, usually a couple of hours, leaving finally to go to my afternoon's "work." The man to whom Duncan Sinclair had been selling his pictures, a real porn tycoon named Nelson Swan, had been busted, and that market was dead for the moment, but I had found it simpler and pleasanter, though much less lucrative, to work for some of the older painters on the scene—painters who were one or two generations older than the abstract expressionists, and still used models.

They were gentle, friendly folk who had come of age during the depression and were given to painting what in the thirties had been known as "Social Realism"— people with a sad, haunting sense that the world had changed since their "day," and a persistent kindly determination to discover of what the change consisted. Most of them were within walking distance of Washington Square, and I would walk up to the studio where I was expected, stopping along the way to drop off the bag with my yesterday's clothes at the Chinese laundry. I would perch on a high stool, or recline on a couch, in Moses Soyer's studio, while his wife rattled in and out chattering and Moses told me the gossip about his other models: who was going to have a baby, who was leaving for San Francisco, and almost one could believe oneself in that haunting and haunted world of nineteeth-century Paris, would catch the bold and flashy faces from *La Bohème* out of the corner of one's eyes. The money I got for two hours modeling was enough to buy me dinner and next morning's breakfast and to take another outfit out of the laundry, and, as I had no other needs, I thought myself quite rich.

After a while a certain number of luxuries attached themselves to this routine: I met Victor Romero, a young photographer with a job and an apartment, and he gave me a key to his place, which had a shower; and occasionally I would work two jobs in one day and take René or O'Reilley out to dinner; and I got a card at the New York Public Library, which varied my reading considerably....

Elise Cowen
Beat Alice
(1933–1962)

"[A] woman from the audience asks: 'Why are there so few women on this panel? Why are there so few women in this whole week's program? Why were there so few women among the Beat writers?' and [Gregory] Corso, suddenly utterly serious, leans forward and says: 'There were women, they were there, I knew them, their families put them in institutions, they were given electric shock. In the '50s if you were male you could be a rebel, but if you were female your families had you locked up. There were cases, I knew them, someday someone will write about them.'"

—from Stephen Scobie's account of the Naropa Institute tribute to Ginsberg, July 1994

Elise Cowen, though dead more than a quarter century, is in many ways more tangible than many of the other Beat women. She is alive in the pages of Joyce Johnson's *Minor Characters* and in the memories of many of the survivors of the Beat Generation whom she marked forever with her generous friendship. Janine Pommy Vega, with whom Elise lived for a time, says, "I still think about her every day. She was the smartest person I knew."

Elise was born to a wealthy family on Long Island who were given to high-strung histrionics interspersed with brittle attempts at normalcy. Her parents had achieved the American Dream with the perfect house in the perfect neighborhood and the perfect job. More than anything, they wanted the perfect daughter to complete the ensemble, and Elise became the focus of their rages.

Although Elise didn't make good grades, she was extremely bright and read extensively. Poetry, especially the works of Ezra Pound and T.S. Eliot, were particular favorites, and she could quote them at will, just at the right moments. She favored the darker poetry most of all, suggesting a shadow side to the good-friend persona she kept on display.

She attended Barnard in accordance with her family's plans, but didn't flourish in the ways they had hoped. Instead, she met Joyce Johnson and Leo Skir, among other Beat players, and got involved with her philosophy professor, Alex Greer. Elise doted on Alex, who led an exciting life and had a child but no apparent wife. He also had lots of friends traipsing in and out of his messy apartment while Elise cleaned up and baby-sat for his two-year-old son.

Alex proved the portal to Elise's future; when his friend Allen Ginsberg arrived on the scene, Elise recognized a twin soul. (Joyce Johnson mentions how they even looked alike during that time.) They dated for a while, but when Allen moved on, Elise was never quite able to let go. Ironically, Allen and Elise both met Carl Solomon (for whom Allen would eventually write "Howl") in separate stays at mental hospitals, which Elise took as a sign that they should be together. Allen went to a psychiatric ward instead of jail after the infamous wreck in the stolen car with Herbert Huncke, Vickie Russell, and Little Jack Melody. Elise was in Bellevue Hospital during one of her episodes of depression. When Allen became lovers with Peter Orlovsky, Elise took a woman lover named Sheila and, at one point, the two couples even shared an apartment.

After her graduation from Barnard, Elise became depressed more often and was never completely free of the shadows. She took a job as a typist and had a dismal career, typing at night, drinking red wine, and writing poetry in secret. After being fired from her job, she ran away to San Francisco, disappearing from view. The Elise that returned to New York a year later was changed: thinner and quieter, she seemed even more haunted than before.

Elise was admitted to Bellevue and released a few days later into her parents' care. Their intention was to take her to Miami, for rest and recuperation. Elise never made the trip. On February 1, 1962, she jumped out of the window of her parents' living room in Washington Heights. She died instantly. The police noted that the window was still locked—Elise had jumped through a closed window.

None of her poetry was published in her lifetime, but eighty-three poems have rested in a box in her friend Leo Skir's basement in Minneapolis; her remaining poems and journals were destroyed by her family after her death. Over the years, Leo, a still-loyal friend, has sent some of Elise's poems to *Evergreen Review* and several small literary magazines. For this book, Leo provided Elise's never-before-published poems from the box in his basement.

Elise might never have found much happiness or success in her short life. But judging by Leo's memoir, she had a rare gift for friendship.

from the collection of Leo Skir

Elise Cowen: A Brief Memoir of the Fifties
by Leo Skir

Allen Ginsberg and Elise Cowen.

I was working in the Welfare office.

Someone called me to the phone. I can't remember who.

"Hello. Leo?" the voice on the telephone said.

"Yes," I said. "What is it, Sheila?"*

"Have you heard about Elise?" she said.

"You mean that she's not going to Florida?"

"No," said Sheila, "she jumped out the window. From her parents' apartment. The seventh story."

"Is she dead?" I said.

"She was killed instantly," said Sheila.

There was more talk. Then the conversation ended. I hung up and tried to go back to work....

*Pseudonym

Elise was dead.

Allen was in Bombay.

I wrote him that night, getting a reply about a week later: He wrote:

Allen Ginsberg
Express
Naoroji Rd
Am   aia

Leo Skir
P.O. Box 154
Cathedral Station
   York 25, N.Y.

Dear Leo:
         Thanks for your letter, I received it and
Irving's the same day, & was a little emptied for
a few days to hear about Elise, I just answered
Irving, & reread yours, & think, if it's alright,
with Irving, & you want to make book, use the letter
I wrote Irving, of which I don't have a copy. There's
not much about Elise in it but there are some remedies for nightmares. I don't think I could write
well intentionally for an occasion, no matter how
strange the occasion, as this, except by accident in
such as letter. Hope you are well, you sound cheerfu
& your letter did find me both happy & in good health
& Peter says Hello. How are Elise's parents? They must
have been --god knows what. If you are in touch
with them give them my respects & best wishes. I hop
everybody is not scared or plunged further into
painful dreams by Elise's hints. None of the dream
systems is real, not even death's. The Self that
sees all the plots is   worth attention, not the
plots. That's as far as I know.   Good luck--Allen
                                             Allen

I had met her in 1949 at Hechalutz Hatzair's Zionist training farm in Poughkeepsie. It was Thanksgiving and already very cold in upstate New York. I was seventeen and a Columbia Freshman. Being seventeen was pretty old in our Youth Movement whose members usually went to Israel not to college. I was Movement leader. I had hung behind in America out of fear and asthma.

I was asthmatic that day, wheezing in the cold downstairs room at the farmhouse. The cold was seeping in through the windows. Almost everyone but me was out picking corn or throwing fertilizer on the earth.

I looked out the window at the workers. I was eating a piece of bread spread with colorless margarine.

Then she was there. Elise. Looking like so many of our Jewish girls, the sallow complexion, black lusterless hair bound with a rubber band, a diffident sulky air.

I introduced myself. She was not a Movement member.

"Why not?" I asked.

"I don't want to go to Israel," she said.

"Is there a place for you in America?" I said.

"No," she said.

"Is there some other country you are planning to go to?"

She smiled, embarrassed, the smile half-dissolving behind the thick lenses of her glasses. She pushed her finger nervously against the bridge of the glasses.

"Not yet," she said.

I didn't see her again at any Movement meetings or when I came back to the city.

I didn't see her again until my Senior year at college. I was a member of the Players and we were producing *Henry IV: Part I*. I was Peto. I had only one good line. *"No, no. They were not bound."*

There was a girl who assisted in the dressing

Allen Ginsberg and Elise Cowen.

room. She told me she knew someone who knew me.

"Who?" I said.

"Elise Cowen," she said.

"I don't remember her," I said.

"She's a friend of a friend of yours," she said.

"I have no friends," I said. "There are no friends." (A quote from Aristotle.)

Later that evening I visited my friend Pittsburgh John, a rich gentile son of a Pittsburgh manufacturer. John was in deep analysis. He was not at home, but a girl was there.

It was Elise.

She was very nice, very shy, soft-spoken. She didn't ask me why I wasn't in Israel, or if I would be going. I was no longer a Zionist. I was a neurotic Columbia student. So was Pittsburgh John. So was Elise. Being neurotic together.

She had brought over her Woodie Guthrie records, 78 shellacs. She had brought them from her parents' home in Washington Heights, to her little furnished room across the street from Pittsburgh John's. Her room had no phonograph but Pittsburgh John's did.

Pittsburgh John and Elise and I had many pleasant evenings together. When I was with Pittsburgh John he would talk about his *relationship* with Elise, and Elise would talk about her *relationship* with Pittsburgh John. Apparently it wasn't much of a relationship. They would talk about what they dreamt and what they said to their analyst and what the analyst said to them. Then they would go out to eat. They smoked a lot. Pall Mall. They didn't drink much. We all went to movies a lot and classes very little.

Pittsburgh John got A's and B pluses. Elise and I got C's and D's and F's and WD (withdrawn) and NC (no credit).

One day, toward evening, I saw Elise wandering through the street.

She didn't seem to see me.

I called to her.

She was carrying the Woodie Guthrie record albums, 10 inch shellac 78's.

She told me Pittsburgh John had asked her to take the records and not visit for the next few weeks. His girlfriend from Pittsburgh would be in the city. She wouldn't understand.

Elise was broken. She talked to me about their *relationship,* how she wasn't really heartbroken since it wasn't a full adult love-relationship but only a dependency relationship.

She talked on and on.

"Am I boring you?" she asked.

"It's OK," I said.

"Please stay with me tonight," she said. "I don't want to be alone."

I went with her to her room. It was a small furnished room on the top story of a private house, one of those rooms that in "better days" had been the maid's.

"The janitor hasn't given me clean sheets for two weeks," she said. "I haven't paid the rent, so I can't talk to him."

We sat around and talked. I looked at her books. *The Oxford Anthology of Greek Poetry.*

"I stole it from the library," she said.

The Poems of Dylan Thomas.

"I bought it once when I was almost broke," she said. "Whenever I'm almost broke I buy an expensive book."

The Pisan Cantos of Pound.

"I stole that," she said. "I think that's the only moral way to get books."

She talked about her friends. I had thought she knew only Sheila and Pittsburgh John. She was part of a circle of poets and psychology students around Columbia. They were all having breakdowns.

She had tried to commit suicide the night before. There were scratches on her wrists. She had also turned on the gas ring for a while.

It was very late.

"Let's get to sleep," I said.

She covered the window with a blanket (she had no shades) and undressed, getting into little-girl pajamas. She washed out her underwear and gargled with an oxygenating rinse. She had trench mouth.

"I'll sleep in the chair." she said. "You can have the bed."

"Shit," I said, "Come on in."

She turned out the light, took the blankets off the window and came to bed.

The next day she got a statement from her analyst that she had to leave Barnard for a while and went back to her parents' home in Washington Heights.

I didn't see her again that term or that summer.

Before the term's end I had had my nervous breakdown and my analyst, a Horneyian on Park Avenue, had given me a note to Columbia telling them I needed a second Senior year. By the time my second Senior year had begun I'd split with my friend Clay and was onto a second nervous breakdown.

This while working in the juice-pouring and fried egg counter of the Lion's Den in John Jay basement at Columbia.

I was having a nervous breakdown, reading Shakespeare, frying eggs.

One morning (I worked from 8 A.M. to 10 A.M.) I looked up. There was only one person in the Lion's Den tables.

It was Elise.

I came over to her.

She was reading Freud (the red-covered Perma-Book edition of the *Introductory Lectures*) and drinking black coffee. She had returned to school. She was studying French. She wanted to read Rimbaud in the original.

She had met, slept with, was in love with a poet. She had worn a red dress the night she met him, had been speechless. He had thought her very deep. Slept with her.

Now she was afraid he would think she was deep.

Where was he now? He was in California with his friend Peter.

I told her about Clay's defection.

"I'll be getting a room around Columbia," she said. "If things get too bad you can stay with me."

I can only remember one night at her room. It was a furnished room in the private apartment of a Russian woman. The room next to Elise was occupied by a Czech actress called Vera Fusek.

That evening I was terribly depressed over Clay.

"I think I'm going to commit suicide," I said.

"What's stopping you?" said Elise. She was reading Rimbaud.

"If I wasn't a Catholic I would have committed suicide long ago," said Vera.

The next morning we woke up late and the Russian landlady was already up. Before I left the room Elise made me wear a babushka. I had been wearing blue jeans, a leather jacket, and moccasins. Elise put on her blue jeans (rivets on her fly), her leather jacket, and combat boots. We nodded at the landlady as we left. I, a little conscious of my morning beard.

We got out of Columbia. We all managed somehow. Or we dropped out and went to another school. But we got through. We weren't the type to attend graduation ceremonies and shake hands and pick up diplomas. I can remember finding mine one afternoon, while on my way to the psychiatrist. It was rolled up and in my mailbox at the student dorm. It was dated October 15th. I thought that no one else graduated October 15th. It didn't make me feel boo hoo or ha ha.

Then we were out and drifting in the world.

We began trying to make homes for ourselves. I had the top floor of the house of the sculptor Chaim Gross. It was on West 105th Street. I was moving downtown from Columbia.

Elise had an apartment with Sheila. One night I went to visit them.

A tall James Dean looking boy was there. His name was Peter. Elise bare-chested was ironing clothes. Sheila was reading *Candide* in the

from the collection of Leo Skir

Allen Ginsberg and Peter Orlovsky.

bedroom. Peter was telling us of his first sexual experience, with a Spanish whore.

"Excuse me," he said to me, "I hope you don't mind my asking, but are you homosexual?"

"I don't know yet," I said. "I'm in the middle of my analysis."

"Would you like to sleep with me?" he said.

"Of course." I said. "But it makes me a little nervous to sleep with strangers. I have to go now."

"I hope I haven't offended you," said Peter.

"I'm complimented," I said. "But I have to get up early to go to work."

I left.

I didn't visit Sheila and Elise's apartment for a long time after that but I would call, speaking sometimes to Sheila, sometimes to Elise, once to Allen who had moved in with them.

"Howl" had come out. Allen was famous. New York was closing in on him. For a while he and Peter stayed with Sheila and Elise. He was getting ready to go to Europe.

I went out with them all one night. We were going to a movie theater on 42nd Street to see *Vitelloni*. It was the first time I met Allen.

"I went to Columbia," I told him. "After you."

He looked at me. "Columbia ruined a lot of people," he said.

In the movie theater I was seated beside Peter's brother, Lafcadio.

Vitelloni was on. I saw the city wasn't Rome.

"What city is that?" I asked Laf.

"New York," he said confidently.

Sheila and Elise split up right after Allen left for Europe.

I went over to stay with Sheila.

She fed me chicken cacciatore. She bought chickens used in the cancer experiments at the Payne Whitney Clinic. They cost only 14 cents each.

She was looking for a new job. She had no job. Her father was in the hospital dying.

"I lost all respect for her," said Sheila.

"Why?" I said.

"When Allen came in she changed completely," said Sheila.

"How?" I said.

"Everything she read, said, did, changed." said Sheila. "Everything was Allen."

"Don't you like him?" I said.

"He's a slob," she said. "Peter is worth ten of him. Peter is wonderful, so clean, so considerate."

"OK," I said. "I get the picture. Let's get to sleep."

"I am so happy that she's gone!" said Sheila.

"OK," I said. "Let's sleep."

In the morning the telephone woke us. It was Sheila's stepmother. Sheila's father had died.

Sheila and I got dressed. We went downstairs.

"Are you going home?" I said.

"I'm going to look for a job," she said.

"But your father just died," I said.

"I still don't have a job," she said.

Her bus came.

Elise had moved to the lower East Side, she and her cat. She suspected the cat of insanity. Elise had been hanging out in a tough lesbian bar. She had an all-night job typing up scripts in a special projection machine for ABC. I had somehow gotten in touch with her. We made a date to meet one evening at the Mariner's Gate, on Central Park West in the Eighties. The Mariner's Gate is one of the entrances to the Park.

She was there and on time. One of the few times she was on time.

She had been kicked out of her job at ABC, literally kicked out. On Friday when she was paid there was a note saying she was suspended. There had been no other notice.

"It's true," she told me. "I was a bad worker. I came in late and often drunk and made many mistakes. But they shouldn't dismiss me with a note. They should come to me personally and say 'Miss Cowen. You stink. Get your ass out of here.' *That* I would have taken."

"What did you do?" I asked.

"I came back Monday and sat at the typing machine. Everyone stared at me. Finally the boss came over. He looked very frightened. He said, 'Miss Cowen, will you leave?' Until then he had always said Elise. If he had even spoken to me in a human way, or called me Elise I would have left. I said, 'I was fired without explanation or discussion. I think I have a right to that. I want to speak to Mr. Lomax, or someone in charge.' He went away. A few minutes later the police came. They grabbed me by the arms and began to pull me away. They didn't even give me a chance to walk normally. When they got me in the door one of the policemen hit me in the stomach, while the others held me. When I got to the police station I called my father. He got in touch with my uncle. They both came down. My father said to me, 'If your mother ever hears of this it will kill her.'"

"Did they lock you up?" I said.

"No," she said. "They let me go. No charges pressed."

"What are you going to do now?"

"I was planning on going to San Francisco," she said. "I'm going to go Wednesday."

We made a date to meet for lunch Tuesday afternoon at the Italian restaurant near my Welfare Training Station on Avenue B and East 3rd Street.

I had gotten a job as Social Investigator for the Welfare Department. I was in training.

But she didn't show up. By Tuesday she had left for California.

There was a real beat scene out on the West Coast; I got letters from Elise. She was living with a drunk Irish artist in a cheap rooming house.

One night, lonely for her, I called her. The rooming house said she might be in a bar called The Place. I called The Place. She was there.

"I'm pregnant," she said.

"Can you afford an abortion?"

"They're easier to get out here," she said. "I'll write you from the hospital."

Early in January she wrote me from the hospital. By the time she had qualified for a psychiatric abortion the doctors were all away on Christmas vacation. By the time they returned, after New Years (she had looked out the window, seen their skis strapped to the auto tops) the fetus had grown too large for a simple D&C. She had to have a hysterotomy.

I sent her a copy of Stendhal's *De l'amour* (in French) to read in the hospital.

"I hope she can get hold of a dictionary," I thought.

Meanwhile time passed. I was working in Welfare, getting a little extra money.

I had made up with Clay when Columbia ended. He had been in the Navy; now he was out, up in Harvard, getting his Master's.

One weekend I packed to go visit him. As I was about to leave the phone rang.

It was Elise, calling from San Francisco.

"I want back," she said. "Can you send me the money by telegraph?"

"Sure," I said.

I telegraphed the money from Cambridge, Mass.

When she came back to New York City she came to live with me. I was still living in Chaim Gross's house.

We didn't get along.

We had different ideas about what life should be.

I didn't push her to go back to work and Elise was more than a little inhibited about going back, so three months passed. She felt guilty about not getting a job and she made me feel guilty about making her feel guilty. It was very sad.

The whole beat thing seemed sad to me. I didn't mind being poor. But I couldn't stand her idleness, sleeping all day and being so grumpy and saying "and like, and like, and like" all the time and using Negro slang when she was, after all, no Negro at all but a Jewish girl graduated from Barnard.

Peter was back from Europe. He came for dinner one evening with Lafcadio.

I put curry and fried onions into some chopped meat and served it over rice.

We talked about Welfare.

"The Welfare Department wants me to support my mother," said Peter. "Isn't it more important that I save money to go to Japan to worship the Buddha at the Nara Shrine?"

"That's a difficult question," I said.

One evening I told Elise that Clay would be coming in from Cambridge for the next weekend.

"I'll go to Joyce's," she said.

"You can stay."

"No," she said. "Three's a crowd."

She packed and left.

She called the next Tuesday. She was going to California with Keith Gibbs. She would be by to pick up her belongings and return my hula hoop.

She came by that evening. Keith was waiting downstairs. I helped her bring her things down. She gave me a Marianne Moore record she had stolen from the public library.

We kissed.

"Don't get caught stealing from foreign libraries," I said. "They might send you to the foreign legion with all those Germans."

She went down the stairs.

I heard the car go, made circles with my hula hoop.

I phoned Joyce, talked to her. Joyce said she felt the thing with Keith was *real,* that her love for/with Allen was a dream.

"I don't know," I said.

There were letters from Elise, letters also from Sheila. Sheila had left for France after her father died. She had a small income. In Paris she had met an Algerian. She was working for Berlitz and the FLN.

I was still working for Welfare. I saved money. I went to Mexico on vacation. I wrote a book, *Leo in Mexico.*

Then Elise was back.

One day the doorbell rang and there she was, holding a bag, just like the movies.

"Don't worry," she said. "I'm not staying. I just wanted to wash up before going to my parents' house."

Sheila had come back from France. The three of us had a party together. I read sections of *Leo in Mexico;* Sheila said there would have to be another French Revolution. "Blood has to flow in the streets," she said. She was very pretty. She was wearing a basic black. "What this country needs is a lot of good cheap heroin," said Elise.

Allen had come back. He had moved into 170 East Second Street. He got an apartment for Elise a floor above him. I gave her some of my furniture, furniture my parents had given me, the last of my childhood: cherry-maple furniture. For her house-warming she served peyote buttons and Cosanyl. She wouldn't take the peyote. She had gone too far out the last time. Allen had come in with Peter, talked, left. The man who had helped us move, a young paranoid from California, took one peyote and was AWAY. I ate two. Didn't feel anything.

Elise and I went out walking.

"I'm hungry," I said.

She bought me a plate of spaghetti at Bruno's.

"You're not supposed to be hungry after peyote," she said.

But I was hungry.

From then until the time she died, her world was Allen. When he was interested in Zen, so was she. When he became interested in Chassidism, so did she. Did he drink mocha coffee? So drank she. When he went down to Peru there was Peter, left behind downstairs, still there to be with. Peter loved a girl from New Jersey. Elise loved the New Jersey girl. When Allen came back, the New Jersey girl moved in with Elise.

New Jersey! New Jersey! I can understand all human passions but how can one love someone from New Jersey!

Then Allen was going to leave again. He was going to India. With Peter. Without Elise.

She came to see me, bringing a salami. Could she stay for a week?

"What happened to your apartment?" I said.

She had given it up.

She was no longer able to do things. She wouldn't/couldn't keep a job, pay rent, electricity. It was too much.

She had been staying at the apartment of Irving Rosenthal but she wanted out. I lent her $50.

That night she stayed at Sheila's new apartment.

She came back the next day, very depressed. Sheila had gone rich-girl, was waiting for the Revolution in Sutton Place, sharing an apartment with her Aunt. Carpets, over-stuffed furniture, Chinese porcelain.

"I feel she's dead," said Elise.

The next morning she packed her bags to go look for a job. She was wearing toreador pants.

"I don't think you should wear toreador pants for a job interview," I said.

"I'll change in the ladies' room in the subway," she said.

A few days later I got a post card from her. She had gotten a post office box instead of a room. She didn't say where she was living.

I was hospitalized.

The day I got out I went to my post office box. There was my last letter to Elise marked: "Moved. Address unknown."

I called her parents' house.

Elise was in Bellevue. She had gone in with hepatitis (serum), then become psychotic.

"Leo," her mother said, "I want you to be truthful with me. Did Elise ever take drugs?"

"Not to my knowledge," I said.

"Her father looked through her writings while she was in the hospital," she said. "He says they're filthy. She seems to have been mixed up with a lot of homosexuals. Did you notice any among her friends?"

"None," I said. "Can I visit her?"

"She doesn't want any visitors now," Mrs. Cowen said. "Maybe when she gets home."

Sheila and I went to see her at her parents' home. Her parents had had her transferred out of Bellevue to a private sanitarium, then signed her out against doctor's orders.

She looked fine, better than we had ever seen her, neat, clean. But she was mad, quite mad. Paranoid. She felt the City (New York City) had machines trained on her, could hear all her thoughts and also that she could hear them, the New York City workers, foolish, bored, boring, mean-souled people. She described to me in detail the four people, two men, two women, assigned to her.

"Elise," I said, "you're paranoid."

"No," she said, "I'm not."

She had become a complete phobic. Always fearful, she couldn't go out any longer without one of her parents.

A child again, and at home.

She had read Joyce's novel *Come and Join the Dance* in which she is given the name of Kay.

"It's *The Group* laid in Barnard," she joked.

She had a review of *The Group* in front of her. I glanced through it. There was a Kay in *The Group*. She became paranoid, had been interned in Bellevue, finally fallen out the window, looking for enemy planes.

"Where are your machines?" I said. "The ones that tap your brain?"

"They plant them outside the window," she said.

Mrs. Cowen had prepared us a supper of slices of tongue heated in the roto broiler. On the side, green peppers and tomatoes she had pickled herself.

We left after supper. I walked with Sheila along Overlook Terrace to the subway.

"What do you think?" I said.

Sheila sat beside me in the subway. She was distracted. She looked away. I noticed that she wore gloves. Of course. A lady always wears gloves in the street.

Sheila sighed in exasperation.

"Leo," she said, "that life seems so far beyond me now. It's unreal. It doesn't make me feel anything."

When we came to her subway stop she got off. "I'll call you," she said.

I wondered why she would call, our worlds now so far apart....

I was working in the Welfare office.
Someone called me to the phone.

■■■

A SKIN . . .
A skin full of screams
I think
"Bludgeon"
"Roselle under the bludgeon"
Red Queen of back-of-the office
Who stares at space into me
Roselle de Bono

Then
For Roselle?
For me?
A confusion of tears over the Royal typewriter
Nutritious Roselle.

■■■

SITTING
Sitting with you in the kitchen
Talking of anything
Drinking tea
I love you
"The" is a beautiful, regal, perfect word
Oh I wish you body here
With or without bearded poems

■■■

TEACHER—YOUR BODY MY KABBALAH . . .

Teacher—your body my Kabbalah

> Rahamim—Compassion
> Tiferete—Beauty

The aroma of Mr. Rochesters cigars
among the flowers
> Bursting through
> I am trying to choke you
> Delicate thought
> Posed
> Frankenstein of delicate grace
> > posed by my fear
> And you
> Graciously
> Take me by the throat

The body hungers before the soul
> And after thrusts for its own memory

Why not afraid to hurt elig—
> couldn't hurt me except in wit, in funny
> I couldn't, wouldn't arm in relation
> but with a rose or rather skunk cabbage

Just—Mere come I break through grey paper
> room
> > Your
> > Frankenstein

What is the word from	Deberoux Babtiste
the Funambule	I
Desnuelu (who's he?)	to choke you
Duhamel	and you

159

De brouille
Deberaux
Decraux
Barrault
Deberaux
Delicate
French logic
Black daisy chain of nuns
Nous sommes tous assasins
Keith's jumping old man in the waves
   methadrine
  morning dance of delicacy
  "I want you to pick me up
   when I fall down"
     I wouldn't and fell
      not even death
     I waited for
      stinking
      with the room
      like cat shit
      would take me
Donald's first bed wherein this fantasy
  shame changing him to you
  And you talking of plum blossom scrolls
  and green automobiles
Shame making body thought
  a game
Cat's cradle & imaginary
 lattices of knowledge & Bach
  system
Fearing making guilt making shame
  making fantasy & logic & game &
  elegance of covering splendour
  emptying memory of the event

Graciously
Take me by the throat

covering splendour with mere elegance
covering
sneer between the angels
Wouldn't couldn't
Fear of the killer
dwarf with the bag of tricks & the colonels picture
To do my killing for me
God *is* hidden
And not for picture postcards.

■■■

EMILY . . .

Emily white witch of Amherst
The shy white witch of Amherst
Killed her teachers
With her love
I'll rather mine entomb
my mind
Or best that soft grey dove.

■■■

WHO WILL SLAP . . .

Who will slap
my backside
When I am born
again

Who will close my eyes
when
In death
They see

■■■

DEATH . . .

Death I'm coming
Wait for me
I know you'll be
at the subway station
loaded with galoshes, raincoat, umbrella, babushka
And your single simple answer
to every meaning
incorruptible institution
Listen to what she said
"There's a passage through the white cabbages"
High and laughing through 3 hours

        Faithful paranoid
        It's all One to you
            isn't it
        Real, that is,
        Literal
        enough
To find a snoozing place among thick visions
      till she'll stumble
      over you
Or wait till rot down
      with the
      majesty orange
      she stuck on
        her finger

Real as the worn green
hideabed I brood on
Never hearing clearly enough
to remember

Or openarmed at the passage end

The homeless
Who lights in her/from her/is
(Her moving human perfection)
Waits for no one
Not even you

■ ■ ■

DID I GO MAD . . .
Did I go mad in my mother's womb

Waiting
to get out
As I gidget along the edges of
     the perfect point of the hollow
     munched tooth of a second
Waiting
To death

The floor never picks itself
     up and walks away

On my brain are welts from
     the moving that never moves
On my brain there are welts
     from the endless stillness

I don't want to intone
     "See how she suffers"
     "See how she suffers"
(The sting of eyes reminds)
That's not really, or only what
     I mean—among other things I am not
      permitted to feel that much
      tick tock

But that the truth I guess of
(Even were I to KNOW it)
Is EVERYONE'S
And what is not this, is a
      rag flapping
      sometimes on the window in the wall
      across the shaft
Just more waiting, with bells on,
And that Truth, is it only the FACT
      of WAITING, the flash at the end
      of cosmic striptease?

I wants a little something for itself
 unique, a single word
               treasure
               act
               perfection
If only to give away
      Only to "He scatters
            his blood on the street."
Love? Is this where, what, why
      love, loving—all this time?

(No,—but there's something in it . . .
      to be continued)

■ ■ ■

THE LADY . . .
The Lady is a humble thing
Made of death and water
The fashion is to dress it plain
And use the mind for border

■ ■ ■

This is believed to be the last poem that Elise Cowen ever wrote:

No love
No compassion
No intelligence
No beauty
No humility
Twenty-seven years is enough

Mother—too late—years of meanness—I'm sorry
Daddy—What happened?
Allen—I'm sorry
Peter—Holy Rose Youth
Betty—Such womanly bravery
Keith—Thank you
Joyce—So girl beautiful
Howard—Baby take care
Leo—Open the windows and Shalom
Carol—Let it happen

Let me out now please—
—Please let me in

Joyce Johnson
A True Good Heart
(1935–   )

"Joyce was a city girl, bookish, the closely watched only child of more ambitious Upper West Side parents . . . . But she was writing—a novel, already under contract—and that was her good fortune, I thought. We shared what was most important to us: common assumptions about our uncommon lives. We lived outside, as if. As if we were men? As if we were new, freer versions of ourselves? There have always been women like us."

—Hettie Jones

Joyce Johnson's ironically titled *Minor Characters* was the first book to focus specifically upon Beat women. Joyce was Jack Kerouac's lover during 1957 and 1958, the two crucial years that brought the Beat Generation into public awareness. In her 1983 memoir, which received a National Book Critics Circle award, she recreates her time in the Beat inner circle during that period, writing not only about herself but about two other women in their early twenties who became her close friends: the doomed Elise Cowen and the stalwart Hettie Jones. Johnson gives an eyewitness account of Kerouac's catastrophic encounter with fame when *On the Road* became a cause célèbre in 1957 and inspired many young people around the world to identify themselves as Beatniks. We see how the members of the Beat Generation, such as Allen Ginsberg and LeRoi Jones, managed to thrive while others like Kerouac and Cowen were unable to survive the seismic shift in sensibility.

But *Minor Characters* is first and foremost Joyce's own story, showing us what it was like to be a young woman coming of age on the tumultuous and transitional fifties, as the youth of postwar America chafed against the constraints of a buttoned-up, conservative society. Joyce, Elise Cowen and most of their contemporaries were

Facing page: Joyce Johnson (Glassman) at the Staempfli Gallery in New York City, May 1960.

expected to marry a wage-earning male as soon as possible and settle down to raise a family. Parental pressure to conform to this ideal was high as Hettie Jones also testifies in *How I Became Hettie Jones.*

Strangely enough, Johnson grew up on West 116th street on Manhattan just around the corner from the apartment salon of William and Joan Vollmer Adams Burroughs where Ginsberg and Kerouac were frequent visitors during the late forties; her parents, Daniel and Rosalind Glassman had moved there from Queens when she was eight years old. The Glassmans, a quiet, hardworking Jewish couple, placed their hopes on Joyce, their precocious only child, and her potential as a librettist and composer of musical comedies; they certainly did not expect her to hook up with a hard-drinking, vagabond writer like Jack Kerouac. At the age of thirteen Joyce began rebelling against their attempts to control her life and started making illicit trips to Washington Square. Overwhelmed by a love affair with an instructor during her last year at Barnard College, she fell short of getting her B.A., and she abandoned music, refusing to be the surrogate for her mother's frustrated ambitions. There was a rift with her family, when she left home following her non-graduation.

In 1955 at the age of twenty, she began her first novel *Come and Join the Dance*, and supported herself by working for literary agents. One of her employers, Phyllis Jackson, turned out to be the agent who had rejected three manuscripts of Jack Kerouac's, including *On the Road* (Kerouac's staunch advocate Allen Ginsberg had once made a memorable trip to the agency to retrieve Jack's work).

Joyce found her way to the heart of the Beat scene through her Barnard classmate Elise Cowen, who had begun a relationship with Allen Ginsberg on 1952, two years before Ginsberg fell in love with Peter Orlovsky. In January, 1957, Ginsberg arranged a blind date for Joyce with Jack Kerouac; the 21-year-old Johnson and the 34-year-old road-weary Kerouac met at a Howard Johnson's in the Village.

As photos of the period attest, the two were a study in contrasts: Joyce all wistful, delicate features and demure blond freshness; Kerouac darkly handsome with striking blue eyes and a rugged, wild air. Joyce was with him the day he went from unknown writer to Beat icon. On September 5, 1957, *On the Road*, the novel he had typed on a long scroll of drawing paper during two feverish weeks in 1949, received an overwhelmingly laudatory review in the *New York Times*. The prescient critic Gilbert Millstein, cited its publication as "a historic occasion…the testament…of the Beat Generation." After that the phone in Johnson's apartment, where Kerouac was living never stopped ringing. Kerouac had become famous overnight.

To read about Joyce's two-year love affair with Kerouac in *Minor Characters* is to hope against hope that somehow Joyce will be able to save Jack from crushing, unwanted notoriety, from his crippling emotional dependence upon his mother, Mémère, and from alcohol. It was not meant to be.

It was not an easy time for either of them; but for Kerouac it proved disastrous. Joyce writes:

As of 1982, there is the Jack Kerouac Society for Disembodied Poetics, founded in Boulder, Colorado, in 1976. There is *Jack's Book,* as well as *Desolation Angel: Jack Kerouac, the Beat Generation and America* and *Jack Kerouac: A Biography* and—the one I like best—*Kerouac: A Chicken Essay,* by a French-Canadian surrealist poet; as well as proliferating pamphlets, theses, articles, chapters in books. A journal published annually celebrates the Beats and the "Unspeakable Visions of the Individual." It's hagiography in the making. Jack, now delivered into the Void, would be amazed to know there's even a literary fan magazine devoted entirely to him, called *Moody Street Irregulars* (after the street in Lowell where he lived as a child). For a back issue, a graduate student somewhere put together a rather randomly chosen chronology of Jack Kerouac's life. In a column labeled 1957, there's a cryptic entry: *Meets Joyce Glassman.*

"Hello. I'm Jack. Allen tells me you're very nice. Would you like to come down to Howard Johnson's on Eighth Street? I'll be sitting at the counter. I have black hair and I'll be wearing a red and black checked shirt."

I'm standing in Elise's kitchen, holding the phone Allen has just handed me. It's a Saturday night shortly after New Year's.

"Sure," I say. I put on a lot of eye shadow and my coat and take the subway down to Astor Place and begin walking westward, cross-town, passing under the bridge between the two buildings of Wanamaker's Department Store and the eye of the giant illuminated clock. It's a dark, bitter January night with ice all over the pavements, so you have to be careful, but I'm flying along, it's an adventure as opposed to a misadventure—under which category so far I've had to put most of the risky occurrences in my life.

The windows of Howard Johnson's are running with steam so you can't see in. I push open the heavy glass door, and there is, sure enough, a black-haired man at the counter in a flannel lumberjack shirt slightly the worse for wear. He looks up and stares at me hard with blue eyes, amazingly blue. And the skin of his face is so brown. He's the only person in Howard Johnson's in color. I feel a little scared as I walk up to him. "Jack?" I say.

There's an empty stool next to his. I sit down on it and he asks me whether I want anything. "Just coffee." He's awfully quiet. We both lack conversation, but then we don't know each other, so what can we say? He asks after Allen, Lafcadio, that kind of thing. I'd like to tell him I've read his book, if that wouldn't sound gauche, obvious and uncool.

When the coffee arrives, Jack looks glum. He can't pay for it. He has no money, none at all. That morning he'd handed his last ten dollars to a cashier on a grocery store and received change for five. He's waiting for a check from a publisher, he says angrily.

I say, "Look, that's all right. I have money. Do you want me to buy you something to eat?"

"Yeah," he says. "Frankfurters. I'll pay you back. I always pay people back, you know."

I've never bought a man dinner before. It makes me feel very competent and womanly.

He has frankfurters, home fries, and baked beans with Heinz ketchup on them. I keep stealing looks at him because he's beautiful. You're not supposed to say a man is beautiful, but he is. He catches me at it and grins, then mugs it up, putting on one goofy face after another; a whole succession of old-time ridiculous movie-comedian faces flashes before me until I'm laughing too at the absurdity of this blind date Allen has arranged. (The notion of Allen Ginsberg arranging blind dates will crack people up years later when they ask me how on earth I met Kerouac.)

As for what he saw in me that night, I'm not sure at all. A very young woman in a red coat, round-faced and blonde. "An interesting young person," he wrote in *Desolation Angels*. "A Jewess, elegant middleclass sad and looking for something—she looked Polish as hell…" Where am I in all those funny categories?

As our paths converge on Howard Johnson's, we're looking for different things. At thirty-four, Jack's worn down, the energy that had moved him to so many different places gone. He's suddenly waited too long. The check for *The Subterraneans* will never arrive, *On the Road* will never be published. Why not let Allen rescue him? He can't go back to the two Virginias.

I see the blue, bruised eye of Kerouac and construe his melancholy as the look of a man needing love because I'm, among other things, twenty-one years old. I believe in the curative powers of love as the English believe in tea or Catholics believe in the Miracle of Lourdes.

He tells me he's spent sixty-three days on a mountaintop without anyone. He made pea soup and wrote in his journal and sang Sinatra songs to keep himself company.

Some warning to me in all this. "You really liked being alone like that?" I ask.

"I wish I was there now. I should've stayed up there."

He could somehow cancel you out and make you feel sad for him at the same time. But I'm sure any mountaintop would be preferable to where he's staying—the Marlton Hotel on Eighth Street, with the dirty shades over the windows and the winos lounging on the steps.

"And where do you live?" Jack asks. He likes it that it's up near Columbia and the West End Bar where he used to hang out. Was Johnny the bartender still there? Johnny the bartender would remember him from the days he was a football hero at Columbia but he broke his leg in his sophomore year and stayed in his room reading Céline, and Shakespeare and never went back to football again—thus losing his scholarship at Columbia, but he's always had affection for the neighborhood, "Why don't you let me stay at your place?" he says.

"If you wish," I say in *Desolation Angels,* deciding fast. And I know how I said it, too. As if it was of no great moment, as if I had no wishes of my own—in keeping with my current philosophy of nothing-to-lose, try anything.

We stood up and put on our coats, we went down into the subway.

And there on the IRT, on a signboard I'd never seen before that night, was an ad for an airline with a brand-new slogan: FLY NOW. PAY LATER.

"That's a good title for a novel," I said, and finally told Jack I was writing one, I wasn't just a secretary. He said Pay Me the Penny After would be a better title, "You should call your novel that." He asked me who my favorite writer was. I said Henry James, and he made a face, and said he figured I had all the wrong models, but maybe I could be a great writer anyway. He asked me if I rewrote a lot, and said you should never revise, never change anything, not even a word. He regretted all the rewriting he'd done on *The Town and the City*. No one could make him do that again, which was why he always got nowhere with publishers. He was going to look at my work and show me that what you wrote first was always best. I said okay, feeling guilty for all that I'd rewritten, but I still loved Henry James.

All through this literary conversation, Jack stood swaying above me on the subway. Hanging on to the strap. Just before we got off, he leaned down. Our foreheads scraped, our eyeballs loomed up on each other—a funny game where I knew you weren't supposed to blink, no matter what.

That was the start of *Meets Joyce Glassman*.

The apartment I lived in at the time was dark and cavernous, on the first floor of a brownstone halfway down the block from the Yorkshire Hotel. Two furnished rooms—the furnishings being the uselessly massive, weak-jointed kind found in the lobbies of antediluvian apartment buildings. A small refrigerator and a two-burner stove stood behind a screen in one corner of the living room, but you had to wash your dishes in the bathroom sink. The windows looked out on a rank back yard where a large tree of heaven battened on bedsprings and broken bottles. I always felt very small in that apartment. One night outside the house a huge grey tomcat with a chewed ear had rubbed against my legs. I'd hauled him inside under the impression I was rescuing him, but he spent his days on the windowsill longing for the street, trying to pry the window open with his paw, or he lurked in the closet vengefully spraying shoes. Jack was the only person I'd brought home so far who saw the beauty of this animal, whom I'd unimaginatively named Smoke. He said he was going to call it Ti Gris, after a cat he once had in Lowell. He seemed to like to rename things. On the walk from the subway I'd become Joycey, which no one had called me since I was little, and he'd put his arm around me, leaning on me playfully and letting his hand angle down over my breast—that was how men walked with their women in Mexico, he said. "Someday when you go there, you'll see that for yourself."

When we got in the door, he didn't ask to see my manuscript. He pulled me against him and kissed me before I even turned on the light. I kissed him back, and he acted surprised. He said I was even quieter than he was, he had no idea quiet girls liked kissing so much, and undid the buttons of my coat and put both his hands up my back under my sweater. " The trouble is," Jack said with his voice against my ear, "I don't ... like ... blondes."

I remember laughing and saying, "Well, in that case I'll just dye my hair"—wondering all the same if it was true.

In the morning Jack left to get his stuff out of the Marlton. He returned with a sleeping bag and a knapsack in which there were jeans and a few old shirts like the one he was already wearing and some notebooks he'd bought in Mexico City. That was all he owned. Not even a typewriter—he'd been borrowing other people's typewriters, he said. I'd never seen such foreign-looking notebooks, long and narrow with shiny black covers and thin, bluish paper on which Jack's slanted penciled printing sped across page after page, interrupted here and there by little sketches. One notebook was just for dreams. He wrote in it every morning.

There was something heartbreakingly attractive in these few essentials to which Jack had reduced his needs. He reminded me of a sailor—not that I knew any sailors—something too about the way he looked coming out of the shower, gleaming and vigorous and ruddy with a white towel around his neck.

Very quickly it didn't seem strange to have him with me, we were somehow like very old friends—"buddies," Jack said, squeezing me affectionately, making me feel both proud and a little disappointed. Crazy as it was, I sometimes really wished I was dark—like this Virginia I felt jealous of for making him so wild. Or the girl named Esmeralda who lived in Mexico City and whom he'd loved tragically for a long time and written an entire novel about in one of his notebooks, calling her Tristessa. But he'd slept with her only once, She was a whore and saint, so beautiful and lost—one of his mysterious fellaheen women, primeval and of the earth.

I was inprimeval and distinctly of the city. I was everydayness, bacon and eggs in the morning or the middle of the night, which I learned to cook just the way he liked—sunny-side up in the black iron frying pan. I'd buy slab bacon in the grocery store, like he'd always had in Lowell—not the skinny kind in packages—and add canned applesauce (a refinement I'd learned from Bickford's Cafeteria), which Jack had never thought of as anything that might enhance eggs. He took extraordinary pleasure in small things like that.

As a lover he wasn't fierce but oddly brotherly and somewhat reticent. I'd listen in amazement to his stories of Berkeley parties where everyone was naked and men and women engaged in some exotic Japanese practice called yabyum (but Jack, fully clothed, had sat apart brooding over his bottle of port, something he didn't tell me). In my memories of Jack in the good times we had together, I'm lying with my head on his chest, his heart pulsing against my ear. His smooth hard powerful arms are around me and I'm burying my face into them because I like them so much, making him laugh, "What are you doing there, Joycey?" And there's always music on the radio, Symphony Sid, whom he taught me to find on the dial, who always comes on at the stroke of midnight, bringing you the sounds of Charlie Parker, Lester Young, Miles Davis, and Stan Getz, and who, according to Jack, is a subterranean himself—you can hear it in his gravel voice smoked down to rasp by innumerable weird cigarettes. "And now—after a few words about that fan-tastic Mo-gen David wine—the great Lady Day…" In the darkness of the room we drift together as Billie Holiday bewails lost love…

But then Jack leaves me. He goes into a small back bedroom where I never sleep because there's no radiator there. He pulls the window all the way up, closes the door, and lies down on the floor in his sleeping bag alone. This is the cure for the cough he brought with him from Mexico City. In the morning he'll do headstands with his feet against the wall, to reverse the flow of blood in his body. He tells me a frightening thing about himself. He's known for eight years that a blood clot could finish him off at any minute.

How can you bear living, I wonder, knowing death could be so close? Little by little I'm letting go of what I learned on the abortionist's table in the white upstairs room in Canarsie.

I'm good for him, Jack tells me. I don't mind anything he does, I don't mind about the sleeping bag, do I?

I didn't really mind, that was the strange part. Everything seemed so odd, so charmed, so transformed. At night when the cold air came with a rush into the little room where Jack was sleeping, and seeped under the edges of the closed door, I could imagine myself on a place without walls, an immense campground where, lying wrapped in blankets, I could feel in my own warmth absolute proof of my existence.

I'm a regular fool in pale houses enslaved to lust for women who hate me, they lay their bartering flesh all over the divans, it's one fleshpot—insanity all of it, I should forswear and chew em all out and go hit the clean rail—I wake up glad to find myself saved in the wilderness mountains—For that lumpy roll flesh with the juicy hole I'd sit through eternities of horror in gray rooms illuminated by a gray sun, with cops and alimoners at the door and the jail beyond?—It's a bleeding comedy—The Great Wise Stages of pathetic understanding elude me when it comes to harems—Harem-scarem, it's all in heaven now—bless their all their bleating-hearts—Some lambs are female, some angels have womanwings, it's all mothers in the end and forgive me for my sardony—excuse me for my rut.

(Hor hor hor)

Not for Joyce Glassman to read, this bleak passage later written in *Desolation Angels*, this awful metaphysical linking of sex, birth, the grave. I hate Jack's woman-hatred, hate it, mourn it, understand, and finally forgive.

Working as a publishing secretary by day, writing her first novel at night (a Random House editor had bought it after reading only 50 pages), and hanging out at the Five

Spot and the Cedar Tavern with "regulars" such as Willem DeKooning, Franz Kline and Frank O'Hara, Joycey, as Kerouac fondly dubbed her, became a full-fledged artist and bohemian herself. She would never turn back.

Come and Join the Dance was published when Johnson was twenty-six, four years after she and Kerouac parted company. Soon afterwards she married James Johnson, a young abstract expressionist painter, who was killed in a motorcycle accident a week before their first anniversary.

Johnson went on to become a respected writer and editor in the New York publishing world, with five books to her credit and numerous articles. She became married to another painter briefly and raised a son as a single mother. She is now on the faculty of the graduate writing program at Columbia University and is working on a new novel.

These excerpts from Minor Characters *show that Johnson has the rare ability to recreate a specific time and place and make it immediate. Through her words we all get an opportunity to live, for a moment, at the heart of the Beat Generation.*

Periodically the young revive the Beat Generation. 1993 was the year of a Beat revival in downtown Manhattan where a wave of cafe poetry readings made the cover of *New York* magazine. In a Gap ad for khakis, I came upon Jack Kerouac posed on a warm September night outside a bar on MacDougal Street called the Kettle of Fish. Part of the original shot had been cropped away. In it, well out of the foreground, arms folded, dressed in black of course, with a look on her face that suggests waiting, you would have found an anonymous young woman. It was strange to know everything about that woman who wasn't there, strange to be alive and to be a legend's ghost.

■ ■ ■

In the late 1950s, young women—not very many at first—once again left home rather violently. They too came from nice families, and their parents could never understand why the daughters they had raised so carefully suddenly chose precarious lives. A girl was expected to stay under her parents' roof until she married, even if she worked for a year or so as a secretary, got a little taste of the world that way, but not too much. Experience, adventure—these were not for young women. Everyone knew they would involve exposure to sex. Sex was for men. For women, it was as dangerous as Russian roulette; an unwanted pregnancy was life-threatening in more ways than one. As for art—decorative young women had their place as muses and appreciators.

Those of us who flew out the door had no usable models for what we were doing. We did not want to be our mothers or our spinster schoolteachers or the hard-boiled career women depicted on screen. And no one had taught us how to be women artists or writers. We knew a little about Virginia Woolf, but did not find her relevant. She seemed discouragingly privileged, born into literature, connections and wealth. The "room of one's own" that she wrote about presupposed that the occupant had a small family income. Our college educations enabled us to type our way to fifty dollars a week—barely enough to eat and pay the rent on a tiny apartment in Greenwich Village or North Beach, with little left over for shoes or the electric bill. We knew nothing about the novelist Jean Rhys, an earlier runaway from respectability, dangerously adrift in the Parisian Bohemia of the 1920s; we might have identified with Rhys's lack of confidence in her writing, found a warning to take to heart in the corrosive passivity of her relationships with men. Though no warning would have stopped us, so hungry were we to embrace life and all of reality. Even hardship was something to be savored.

Naturally, we fell in love with men who were rebels. We fell very quickly, believing they would take us along on their journeys and adventures. We did not expect to be rebels all by ourselves; we did not count on loneliness. Once we had found our male counterparts, we had too much blind faith to challenge the old male/female rules. We were very young and we were in over our heads. But we knew we had done something brave, practically historic. We were the ones who had dared to leave home.

■ ■ ■

[Upon the death of Elise Cowen]
All I could do was write a poem, which I did in my own adaptation of beat style:

> Elise
> got on the Greyhound Bus.
>
> Having sabotaged
> a few of the clocks
> in the city—
> she left me the rest,
> and a destiny
> of endless chop suey
> a beat-up copy of The Idiot
> She didn't own much.
>
> When the electrical doors closed
> and the air conditioning began,
> the black leather roads
> took her.
>
> Her friends
> celebrate her departure
> with beer and a fist fight.
> Her parents
> in their impenetrable living room
> have drawn the blinds.

■ ■ ■

I'm walking east in a winter twilight some twenty five years ago, about to pass Cooper Union, where I'll run into a young woman I'll someday think of as my oldest friend. For an hour already she's been standing out there, braced against the freezing wind that blows through the empty spaces around Astor Place. A very small person in an old tweed coat left over from college days, and several knitted scarves, she's handing out mimeographed leaflets—or trying to—about some poetry reading taking place that night that everyone's too cold to be interested in. Extracting one with a numbed hand while clutching the rest with the other, she holds it out to me. "Take One!" There's such laughing desperation in her voice that I have to stop (I think I recognize her anyway) and I end up staying there and helping her until snow starts falling on us—which is too much, we agree, even for poetry. So we walk to the B&H deli and thaw our fingers out against thick brown mugs of coffee as a snowstorm thuds against the window and Second Avenue's sparse neon turns to water color.

"Oh come to the reading!" she urges when I reluctantly say I really should go home. Her husband is one of the poets, and she's a woman in love. For him she would stand on innumerable freezing street corners. She writes poetry herself, but has never stood up with it at a reading of her own—makes no particular mention of it, in fact— telling herself it isn't good enough ("Some of it was good enough," she'll admit fiercely, years later).

Two months ago I'd seen and heard her husband the poet; privately I wonder if his stuff is really so great. He'd been reading in a new Bleecker Street coffee shop Jack took me to one night, a tiny place that had opened in the basement of a flophouse. Every head had turned as we walked in. "That's Kerouac," people whispered. The poet, a young black man, short and graceful with a neat professorial beard, glanced up from his page nervously; the poem was academic, with a few deliberately hip touches. He came up to us afterward and introduced himself as LeRoi Jones. "And this woman over here is Hettie," he'd said proudly. So that was where I knew her from. She'd smiled at us, but the protective passion in her eyes was for him. Despite the complications of race, they'd seemed more coupled than most people. Even their smallness somehow made them fit together.

■■■

Blind intuition guided me that night as I went through Cess' (Lucien Carr's wife) spice shelves, smelling the contents of the small glass-stoppered jars, sprinkling a little of this and a reckless amount of that on my sliced apples. "How about cloves, Cessa?" She'd laugh and say, "Why not?"

I liked her enormously. She was a tall, beautiful, capable woman; her long delicate face was slightly worn around the eyes, which somehow made her all the more lovely. She'd already bathed her little boys and put them in pajamas and made stuffing for roast chicken and picked squash from her garden. Even when she was furious with Lucien, you knew she was crazy about him. Because of her, Lucien had the most settled life of any of Jack's friends—a life that resembled that of ordinary people and was almost the real thing, despite the edge to it that you always felt, the shadows gathered in the corners.

To Jack, Cessa was a goddess of domesticity, second only to Mémère. It meant a lot to me to have her acceptance. Now that I'd launched myself into what I'd once childishly considered "real life" ordinary life was coming to seem exotic, like the trees I saw on the highway.

I've never tasted pie as good as the one I made that night. "Ecstasy pie!" Jack shouted. He put down his fork and ran out to the kitchen for the Reddi-Whip I'd forgotten. He and Lucien squeezed great swirling drifts of it over everybody's portion, which only made everything that much more ecstatic.

In one biography it was later said, "Lucien called Joyce 'Ecstasy Pie' and her affair with Jack would endure for an erratic year and a half," which aside from obliterating the historic actual pie, allows for no nuances whatsoever.

There was an early-morning walk with Jack on the Sunday of that weekend, which was also, as it happened, my twenty-second birthday. Wet September woods that smelled as if we were inside a mushroom, jack-o'-lanterns hanging on dried stalks, scarlet-berried bushes, a mistiness around us like a web. Under pines we discovered moss like a constellation of tiny milky-green stars. We came out finally into a meadow where the sun had already warmed the grass. We lay down on it together. I put my head on Jack's chest, and his heart beat into my ear like a slow clock. After a long time he said into the silence, "Well, I know we should just stay up here and get married and never go back." Feeling the saddest happiness, I said that was what I knew, too.

But my next thought had to do with being twenty-two, which, although it was older than I had ever been, was also, I suddenly realized, quite young after all; and, as if I were floating above Jack and me, looking down, I thought, I can do this now, be here with him like this. It's all right. I have all the time in the world.

We went back to the city that afternoon, and Jack's fame. Since the measurements of its ingredients were unrecorded, ecstasy pie turned out to be unduplicatable—or could only be made with apples from Lucien's orchard, on a day when they'd achieved a precise state of ripeness.

Hettie Jones
Mother Jones
(1934–   )

"The Idea . . . is to change first of our own volition and according to our own inner promptings before they impose completely arbitrary changes on us."

—Jane Bowles, in the epigraph to *How I Became Hettie Jones*

Hettie Jones describes a singularly compelling moment in her memoir, *How I Became Hettie Jones,* that, almost like a still from a movie, crystallizes in one frame the essence of who Hettie was and would become. It is a childhood memory of summer camp, lying on her back in the grass. Hettie, a young white Jewish girl from Long Island, is looking up at the clouds with her hands in the air, trying to weave the clouds.

There is a creative energy inside Hettie that is beautifully captured and held for a moment in this childhood scene. It is at once both idealistic and practical, and if there is any common thread in the life of Hettie Jones, it is that—practical idealism.

Hettie goes on to describe how startled she was when her parents came upon her unexpectedly there in the grass and, of course, never guessed she was weaving clouds. It was also at this moment that some understanding of how different she was from her parents came to her, that sense of almost being from the wrong family. It seems as if Hettie's sensibility was fully developed at a very young age and she knew she would have to leave to become herself.

Hettie Cohen made a choice to leave behind comfortable Long Island and the fifties' ideal of a cookie-cutter marriage when she went to a women's college in Virginia to study drama. There she explored the creative arts, discovered jazz, and realized there was no turning back. In 1955, Hettie graduated with honors and, with the

Facing page: Hettie Jones in her Greenwich Village Kitchen during the production of *Yugen.*
photo © James O. Mitchell

help of her parents, moved to an apartment in New York City.

Her first job was at a small film library. When that lost funding, she moved to Greenwich Village and worked part-time at *The Record Changer,* a jazz magazine. Hettie was working there when LeRoi Jones (later to rename himself Amiri Baraka), a young black poet bristling with intelligence and intensity, joined the staff as shipping manager. Falling in love with him was only a matter of time. Soon they were living together. Hettie writes:

> One windy late fall Friday just after we moved to Chelsea, Roi and I went out to hear Jack Kerouac read his poetry. Jack's life had so far led him from working-class Lowell, Massachusetts, where he'd been a football star, past Columbia University, the Merchant Marine, Mexico, both coasts, two marriages, many liaisons, and a child he wouldn't acknowledge. In the year since ON THE ROAD, he'd been celebritized, endlessly criticized, pressed for definitions of Beat. The attention hadn't helped. I didn't know him, and after our one brief meeting at Jazz on the Wagon I'd only caught glimpses of him haggard, drunk, and surrounded.
>
> The reading was at a newly opened, out-of-the-way place, the Seven Arts Coffee Gallery, a second-floor storefront on Ninth Avenue in the forties, the transient neighborhood near the bus terminal. The audience, mostly friends, numbered only about thirty. Unexpectedly, Jack was sober; all slicked down and lumberjacked up, an engineer scrubbed clean for the evening (on the West Coast he'd worked as a trainman). I decided I liked this good-looking, friendly man whom everyone loved and admired, and I certainly admired his work, so when the reading began I sat alone at a table up front to pay attention. He noticed. He kept catching my eye and reading to me, and he was marvelous: relaxed, confident, full of humor and passion—and he wanted the meaning CLEAR. At the end we all stomped and whistled and clapped and cheered.
>
> A crowd of thirty, thus inspired, needs a big enough place to party. Our new house was a straight mile downtown, just off Ninth Avenue, and we had nothing but party space to offer, so after the reading we just brought the audience home, to 402 West Twentieth Street, a once elegant six-room parlor facing the weatherbeaten brick of the Episcopal Seminary.

In the arrival melee of coats and drinks and glasses and ash trays, I caught some puzzled glances from Jack, who looked as if he couldn't place me, as if he'd read to me as an interested stranger, and only now had noticed the burgeoning rest of me. To whom was this pregnant woman attached? I saw him whisper the question to Allen, who pointed to Roi.

The connection seemed to please Jack enormously—his face lit in the strangest, gleaming little grin. The music was on and a few people were already dancing. Suddenly he ducked and wove his way through them— fast, as if in a scrimmage—to Roi, who was at the other end of the two adjoining front rooms. Then dragging bewildered Roi by the hand he maneuvered back to me and grabbed me too, and then, with amazing strength, he picked us both up at once—all 235 pounds of us, one in each arm like two embarrassed children—and held us there with an iron grip and wouldn't let go!

What pleasure to meet this funny, visionary Jack, who appeared to have such sympathy in him, a sweetness similar to Roi's that I found attractive. Word got out and soon the party grew to fifty, and all night Jack kept running to me with different people: "I didn't remember who she was," he kept saying, "but she was listening so hard at the reading, she was really listening to me—she UNDERSTOOD what I said!"

Hettie and LeRoi worked together at *The Record Changer* until the fall of 1957. Hettie left the magazine and began working at *Partisan Review,* a magazine she discovered in college. Both Hettie and LeRoi went to poetry readings at cafes and bohemian bars like Jazz on the Wagon, where they met many poets including Gregory Corso, Diane di Prima, and Frank O'Hara.

LeRoi began reading his poetry at these events and, while Hettie continued to work at *Partisan Review* by day, the duo founded *Yugen,* a magazine featuring the work of poets and writers of this new literary scene. The entire magazine, from type to layout, was put together in their Morton Street kitchen. *Yugen* was an immediate hit with the bohemian literati, and the first issues published, along with LeRoi's poetry, the writings of Philip Whalen, Allen Ginsberg, Denise Levertov, Frank O'Hara, and William Burroughs.

Hettie handled production for *Yugen;* its new ideas and the hands-on act of creating were of importance to her, and she worked hard to make it happen. Hettie was developing her formidable editing skills and, though not publishing her own work, knew she wanted to write and that editing was helping her hone her craft. "All my late-night cutting, pasting, aligning, and retyping finally taught me—what comes from reading things over and over, taking apart and putting together, the heart of the matter, the way it feels."

When Hettie discovered she was pregnant, she and LeRoi decided to marry. By 1961, they had two daughters, Kellie and Lisa. Despite the Beatnik scene, New York in the early sixties was still a difficult climate for a biracial family—a place of cold stares, rude remarks, and stereotypes. Hettie bore the brunt of much bigotry and got the opportunity to see the world through the eyes of her husband and daughters. This affected her deeply and became a recurring theme in her writing, then and now.

LeRoi became closely involved in the Black Power movement and, consequently, grew apart from his white wife. His highly political play *Dutchman* was quite a success, and he was criticized for not being with a woman his own color. Hettie and Roi divorced in the spring of 1968.

Billie Holiday

Born Eleanora Fagan, Billie Holiday was gifted with a deep lyrical voice that inspired an entire generation; Jack Kerouac once called her "the Heroine of the Hip Generation." Her emotional connection with her songs came from a life of struggle and pain punctuated by prejudice and heroin abuse. By the age of twelve, she had turned to the streets in order to survive the brutal inner city of Baltimore. In 1932, she moved to Harlem and began singing at her first professional job. She traveled with a dance band for two years before she found her niche back in Harlem.

Onstage, she was a soulful blues singer with a sweeping vocal range. Her popularity spread to black and white audiences alike, crossing all boundaries through the appeal of her emotion-filled voice. She performed with musicians as diverse as Count Basie, Lester Young, Dizzy Gillespie, and Teddy Wilson. She also performed solo at the Apollo Theater, and on television. Slowly, her ambition and lifestyle collided. She was arrested on drug charges throughout her career and the jail time, harassment by the police, and her inability to shake her heroin addiction all contributed to the downfall of Lady Day. At the end of a sour marriage, Billie entered a rehabilitation clinic but ultimately died in 1959 from complications resulting from her hard living.

Her death marked the loss of one of the few female voices to capture the emotional torrent of the times. Her soulful sound played a vital role in the jazz influence of the Beat and other poetry, and writers such as Hettie Jones, Amiri Baraka, Jack Kerouac, and Frank O'Hara all acknowledge her inspiration.

Though circumstances weren't the easiest, Hettie thrived on her own with her two daughters and made a living for them through teaching as well as her writing and editing. In 1968, she helped run a community-based project for disadvantaged children and helped design a Head Start program for greater New York. When Hettie broke her silence and began getting published, she proved to be a gifted writer: "Without a him in the house, there was more space/time for her, and I tried to redefine the way a woman might use it," she writes.

Hettie Jones' poetry and prose deals with issues she cares about and those she experienced firsthand. She has written several children's books of note, including the well-received *The Trees Stand Shining* and *Big Star Fallin' Mama: Five Women in Black Music,* as well as many short stories. Her memoir, *How I Became Hettie Jones,* received critical acclaim upon its publication in 1990, and provides a rare glimpse into the downtown New York Beat, art, and jazz scenes of the fifties and sixties.

Hettie Jones still lives on New York's Lower East Side and, in addition to her own writing, runs writing workshops for the homeless and at the New York State Correctional Facility for Women. Weaving hope out of compassion and understanding, she recently published a volume of writing by women prisoners, *More Out Than In*, and works on the committee of PEN's Prison Writing Committee. She is a very popular reader and lecturer and has taught writing at New York University, Hunter College, Parsons School of Design, and the University of Wyoming.

The beauty, power, and range of Hettie Jones' writing is evidenced here in a previously unpublished short story and several poems.

Sisters, Right?

"Sisters, right?" says the woman who owns the grocery, when the middle daughter and I step up to her counter.

At the same time she says "sisters, right," the grocery woman gives a little squeeze to my hand and makes a gesture just short of a wink to show us she's well aware that this is a mother-daughter duo.

The middle daughter and I burst out laughing. She—like her sisters—is now a grown woman, a black woman. In the past week, we have encountered two different women who could *not* see our relationship.

"How did you guess?" the middle daughter asks the grocery woman, who is laughing with us.

"Because you look exactly alike!" she shouts gaily.

My daughter and I have been together this week for another rite of passage: from minor we have progressed to major surgery. Both of us have survived the knife.

What, then, had the grocery woman seen that the others hadn't? What has appeared to augment our resemblance—pain?

And does this shared pain create the same face, differently skinned?

And who else sees it?

In the recovery room I had asked on my daughter's behalf for pain medicine. "Not yet," said the nurse of the snapping eyes.

A few moments later I asked again. "Sorry," I said, "but you know how mothers are."

"You're her *mother*?"

Courtesy falling like rain.

But who had she seen before? Who was that woman hung over the bedrail, loving someone?

Soon, another nurse—a young one, mean to the bone—has the middle daughter out of bed and in the bathroom with the water running full force.

I offer instead to whisper in her ear, the way I used to.

"What are mothers for?" I joke to the nurse, who overreacts with even more noise than the splashing water, on and on about how I couldn't possibly be, I'm too young, etc., but we know what she's covering.

"*Loud*," says the middle daughter, back in bed, thumbing the painkiller button.

Later, I muse about these two women.

Flowers on the bed table, heart balloons in the air, the middle daughter, propped up and frowning dismissively, says, "Oh, they probably just thought we were dykes."

At her house, in the beautiful spread of her life, I tell her I'm going to write this story. That I'll begin with the grocery woman, because she had good eyes.

The middle daughter jumps on this. She says. "There you go, Ma."

2

And off *she* goes, to work again. The two of us sit side by side in the small city airport.

There's always something at the airport. This time it's a young black man, with a young white woman seeing him off.

They're not lovers, that much is clear, perhaps new acquaintances. They sit facing us in the narrow lobby. The plane is delayed, and we four—he, she, the middle daughter, and I—have nothing to do but scope each other.

Suddenly, between us intrudes a noisy, excited group, led by a sexy overcontrolling mother in a black catsuit, missing her two top front teeth.

Into my ear the middle daughter whispers, "Somebody couldn't take it and popped her."

I laugh out loud.

"Ma, it's rude to laugh at people in airports," she says, laughing, and when I look up, still laughing, I catch the eye of the young black man. He's now standing, his face a mask of controlled amusement. He almost smiles. Perhaps, as he passes me, the one who catches his smile is the middle daughter.

Or perhaps not. Gently, gallant in the bumrush, he spreads a protective hand on the back of the woman he's with.

I know my daughter doesn't miss this.

I think about black and white women in competition. For what hard reasons? What's to be addressed? What will happen if we don't? If my middle daughter—my sister, right?—is black, and I am white, we have to keep thinking.

We lean against each other and talk. She says, "Three minutes more, you'll have to pay to park another hour."

She's old enough to dismiss me; still I dawdle, kiss her goodbye twice. On the way out, I'm thinking in Spanish, *m'ija, mi hija,* such a pretty way to say it.

The parking lot gate is manned by a boy, whose sweet smile recalls to me the middle daughter's high school boyfriend. I know his mother loves him. I wish I were looking at a million of him. And he doesn't charge me for another hour, although according to the clock in my car I am nearly *five* minutes late leaving.

In my gratitude I fumble a dime, which gets lost on the seat.

"Well," he says with a pleasant laugh, "at least you know where it's *at.*"

Which, I suppose, is both the problem and the start of any solution.

■ ■ ■

WELCOME TO OUR CROWD

I've slept
in every room except
the kitchen, and that
includes alone or
with others, in symphony
or cacophony.   Now
the man in his socks, the one
asleep on his own pillow,
the tender lover, curious
youth, bossy fuck
—all these clothed and naked visions—
are sharing particular angles
of light, the rushed or
lingering presence of time.
They hang off the splintering
beams.   On the uneven floor
we all lie down in layers,
a hologram of lovers, his pillow
under another one's head,
the constant drift of old perfume, a jacket
left behind on a chair, shoes
later buried with the dead.

They needed heels. The jacket is minus
a button. Torn sheets, the windows
unwashed. We breathe and
don't breathe, lie, pass
in the hall, fall
into all our arms, live again
           gone soon

■■■

SONNET

Love never held my hand
like those summertime couples
palm to palm, the perfectly
interlaced fingers
the pressures

Love never flung himself
around my shoulder, or
measured my convivial waist

Love was a grandmaster though,
and he laughed when he came on
like gangbusters, who
could refuse him, ah.

I knuckled under, no regrets
but I've always wondered

■■■

WORDS

      are keys
or stanchions
      or stones

I give you my word
You pocket it
and keep the change

Here is a word on
the tip of my tongue: love

I hold it close
though it dreams of leaving

■■■

TEDDY BEARS ON THE HIGHWAY

Saturday the stuffed bears were up again
over the Major Deegan
dancing in plastic along the bridge rail
under a sky half misty, half blue
and there were white clouds
blowing in from the west

which would have been enough
for one used to pleasure
in small doses

But then later, at sunset
driving north, along the Saw Mill
in a high wind, with clouds big and drifting
above the road like animals

proud of their pink underbellies,
in a moment of intense light
I saw an Edward Hopper house,
at once so exquisitely light and dark
that I cried, all the way up Route 22
those uncontrollable tears
"as though the body were crying"

and so young women
here's the dilemma

itself the solution:

I have always been at the same time
woman enough to be moved to tears
and man enough
to drive my car in any direction

■■■

RABBITS   RABBITS   RABBITS*   **2/1/80**
When I leave you this morning
I go to the clinic
with a volume of poems
in my pocket

But I find I can't suffer the pain
of another woman's love, or
absorb her losses
because I am so full of pleasure
(sir what is yr pleasure) I am
that full I could hardly take
the sun in my eyes on my way here

so I sit and wonder why

the woman beside me
has a face full of wrinkles
above her pregnant belly
   and if that is the same story
   as my book of poems
while around us the white nurses
flit in Chinese and Spanish
and English to the dyke doctor

*To ensure good luck for any coming month, say these words immediately upon awakening on the first day.

■ ■ ■

Hettie Jones and Joyce Johnson (Glassman) at the Artists' Club, March 10, 1960.

From "Your House Is Mine," a collaborative project on homelessness at the New Museum of Contemporary Art, New York:

HOME: Deep, to the Heart, as "The Truth Strikes **home**." Ladybug, Ladybug, fly away **home**.

Home in. **Home** is the sailor, **home** from the sea. The hunter **home** from the hills Welcome **home**. Safe **home**. **Home** port. **Home** Base. Harvest **home**. **Home** of the brave. Be it ever so humble, there's no place like **home**. Chickens come **home** to roost. Charity begins at **home**. **Home** is where the heart is. **Home** is where you hang your hat. **Home** sweet **home**. Make yourself at **home**. "You'd Be So Nice To Come **Home** To." Something to write **home** about. A man's **home** is his castle. Keep the **home** fires burning. Till the cows come **home**. Lassie Come Home. Bring **home** the bacon. For hearth and **home**. **Home** brew. Don't leave **home** without it. To market, to market, to buy a fat pig/ **home** again, **home** again, jiggity-jig. This little piggie stayed **home**. Ate us out of house and **home**. **Home** folks. **Home** grown. **Home**bound. **Home**boy. **Home**girl. **Home** team. **Home** game. **Home** run. **Home** plate. Down **home**. **H o m e** s t e a d. **H o m e** f r o n t. **H o m e** g r o u n d. **H o m e** stretch. All the way **home**. **Home** at last. **Home** free.

Homeless tempest tossed. Can't go home again.

Homesick. With no direction home.

Broken home.

Joanne Kyger with Buddha in Japan.

Joanne Kyger
Dharma Sister
(1934–)

"...We met the Dalai Lama last week right after he had been talking with the King of Sikkim, the one who is going to marry an American college girl. The Dal is 27 and lounged on a velvet couch like a gawky adolescent in red robes....And then Allen Ginsberg says to him how many hours do you meditate a day, and he says me? Why I never meditate, I don't have to."

—Joanne Kyger, in the *Japan and India Journals, 1960–1964*

At the age of five, Joanne Kyger published her first poem in the literary and news magazine of Naples Elementary School in Long Beach, California. She closed her eyes and told it to the teacher, who wrote it down. In high school in Santa Barbara, California, she wrote the school newspaper's feature page with the help of poet Leland Hickman. "He was sophisticated, worldly to me, but was also able to laugh at my pieces, like 'From Dinah Shore to Dinosaur,' about Mr. Meen, tracer of lost bones."

At the University of California at Santa Barbara, Joanne pursued her interests in poetry and philosophy. In 1957, she moved north to San Francisco, where the "Howl" obscenity trial was in full swing. She became immediately immersed in the city's blooming poetry community, meeting, among others, Gary Snyder.

Joanne moved into the East-West House, a communal living project, and began sitting with Zen master Shunryu Suzuki Roshi, who had recently come from Japan to teach at the Soto Zen Church. In 1960, she left for Japan and joined Gary Snyder. They were married at the American Consulate in Kobe three days after her arrival. Five days later, they were married again in a Zen ceremony at Daitoku-ji, a large and beautiful complex of temples in Kyoto.

I had met Gary Snyder in 1958 in North Beach when he was visiting the United States, back from his first trip to Japan. I was a part of a group of young writers clustered around the poets Robert Duncan and Jack Spicer. Gary came to our Sunday poetry group and read from *Myths and Texts* sitting cross-legged on a table with Jack Spicer sitting cross-legged under the table. "Do you like this Boy Scout poetry?" Spicer challenged me. I did indeed, very much.

Ruth Fuller Sasaki, who was Gary's sponsor in Japan and ran the First Zen Institute in Kyoto, which hired him part-time, made it clear that I could not come and "live" with Gary. We would have to marry. She wrote to him, "If you and Joanne want to marry at any time, and then live in your little house in the mountains, fine. But living together in the little house before marriage won't do. There are certain fixed social customs that the Institute expects its members to respect." I bought a wool dress with a scooped neckline, basic black, so I could wear it a lot, starting with the wedding, which happened a few days after I arrived.

Joanne lived in Kyoto for four years, writing poetry, studying flower arranging, and practicing Zen Buddhism at Daitoku-ji with Ruth Fuller Sasaki, the experience of which she has chronicled in *Japan and India Journals: 1960–1964*. To help make ends meet, she also taught conversational English and obtained English-speaking parts in low-budget Japanese films.

In 1964, she returned to San Francisco, where she started writing prodigiously, gave readings, and participated in the Berkeley Poetry Conference. In 1965, her first book of poems, *The Tapestry and the Web*, was published. Her second book, *Places to Go,* was published in 1970 by Black Sparrow Press. Alicia Ostriker wrote in the *Partisan Review,* "Risking folly, let us propose that Joanne Kyger is a genius, though a weird one. Handling her work is like handling a porcupine traveling at the speed of light. She is not 'disciplined' but is a radically original combination of symbolist and comedienne."

Gary and Joanne divorced, and in 1966 she traveled to Europe with Jack Boyce and sojourned for a time in New York. The two returned to San Francisco and, in 1968, together purchased land in Bolinas, just north of the city. "It was a time of inventive country living, dirt roads, no street lights, interesting plumbing, and an hour away over the coast range for shopping. Robert Duncan called us the 'Bolinas bucolics.'"

Seven years later, she was at the Naropa Institute in Boulder, Colorado, with Allen Ginsberg and Anne Waldman. Based on the same principles as the legendary Black Mountain College, Anne and Allen founded the Jack Kerouac School of Disembodied Poetics, which continues to this day as the forum for counterculture humanities where Buddhism meets Beat. Here Joanne met Chogyam Trungpa Rinpoche and the Sixteenth Gyalwa Karmapa, head of the Kagyu school of Tibetan Buddhism. It was while teaching at Naropa in 1978 that she met Donald Guravich, a writer and artist from New Brunswick, Canada. When she returned to Bolinas, he joined her and they have shared a household ever since. She now sits at the Ocean Wind Zendo in Bolinas.

Joanne Kyger has published many books of poetry. Recent collections of her work include *Going On: Selected Poems 1958–1980* and *Just Space: Poems 1979–1989*. In a voice that is immediate and accessible, her poems are often snapshots of the realities of daily life. The combination of these characteristics and her Buddhist beliefs meet to form precise imagery and powerful ideas.

> The "Square Zen" Alan Watts spoke of, the Zen of the established tradition, was not an accessible practice for me. But the sheer caprice of "Beat Zen" with its "digging of the universe" seemed out of hand too. Sitting with the sangha at Suzuki's San Francisco Zen Center when I returned, I was struck with the simplicity of zazen, nothing to prove, nothing to gain. But I was also grateful for the established traditional rules of the zendo, unquestioned, that allowed one's mind freedom within the form.

Buddhism was a major influence on Beat writers, a philosophy and teaching that they embraced in rejection of fifties' materialism. For a literature in celebration of the open mind and the open road, Buddhism offered a transcendental grace and deeper consciousness for Kerouac's spiritually weary "seeking" generation. Joanne Kyger's poetry is exemplary of Buddhist consciousness in Beat writing, of a sensibility for which wisdom is the greatest beauty.

Breakfast.   He assured me
orange juice, toast & coffee.
Just the way I like it.   I flang
the cawfee cup to de floor.   After
three times it split into a million
pieces.   She worried about the
small supply of dope in the other room.
                              Both
of them, Lewis and Tom, were busy
collaborating.   The record
playing.   The wind howling
The electric heater going by
her side, as an ache over
increased herself.   It was a fact
about what she thought
a moment before, which
was me, it was the love, He's
fine.   I wonder why he
doesn't exchange some of the
mescaline for dope.   Give Tom
some of the dope.
    I wouldn't go there, into their
minds.   I'm here, ain't I.   Now
thru the mirror one can she see
pine branches nodding nodding
in the blue California sun.

■ ■ ■

he makes love to her

    he talks about

afterwards

when some years

ago

he worked

    for the welfare

department

    in New York City

She starts up

  a hue

    and cry

  oh the money, the electricity

    give me

      some clothes, some jewels

      some food, some love

■ ■ ■

what I wanted to say

   was in the broad

sweeping

form of being there

     I am walking up the path

     I come home and wash my hair

     I am bereft

     I dissolve quickly

I am everybody

■■■

My vision is a large golden room
Where your ancestors dwell
And you give your heart to them
And having given your heart to them

         You're there to move out
      from that source.
   God's mountain, Sun Street.

■■■

I want a smaller thing in mind

Like a good dinner

I'm tired of these big things happening

They happen to me all the time

■ ■ ■

It is true, there is power within us.   But I am so
improperly trained.   Mostly it is
get your own 'thing' going, facing
each day's rise and set.
                         Maya, Maya,
on de foot afternoon.

I am veering closely back and forth

Oh! Half moon behind the slim holder of the lotus
Oh! she's a poet.   Joanne Kyger
Who was that woman?
Oh come over and visit.
Oh it's all passed, gone, gone, gone.

■ ■ ■

It's a great day.   Last night I visited my old
childhood town of Lake Bluff, Illinois. The
Creeley's and Philip Whalen were there.   I took
a walk to Lake Michigan with Philip to see it all
built up in the form of a great amusement center.
Lost in its intricacies I go to work.   Stepping out
a door I land in a great field and run a tractor up
and down the rows, not exactly enough, to be sure
and run back into the amusement center, donning my
waitress uniform on the way, before I get caught,
before I get caught. Oh Ladies of the Middle West,
how do your hands get rough. What is this self
I think I will loose if I leave what I know. Back
to the dark bedroom, and aimless unhappy adolescent
lives. Lacking any commitment to the actual living
ground, life becomes pointless in its urge for culture,
quote unquote, Art. There, I've said it, in all it's
simpleness—the best teacher lives outside, the best
teacher lives inside you, beating blood, breathing
air, the best teacher is alive.

Denise Levertov
Fortune's Favorite
(1923–   )

- **Remember Mallarmé's words that "Poems are not made with ideas, they are made with words."**

- **Beware of consciously searching for the original; nothing is more likely to lead to the banal. The *fresh* word is not necessarily the *odd* word.**

- **Strength of feeling, reverence for mystery, and clarity of intellect must be kept in balance with one another. Neither the passive nor the active must dominate, they must work in conjunction, as in a marriage.**

—Denise Levertov on the craft of poetry

A t the age of twelve, Denise Levertov sent several of her poems to T. S. Eliot. Far from thinking her cheeky, the great poet wrote back two pages of "excellent advice" and encouragement to continue writing based on what he deemed to be great promise.

It was an auspicious start. The young poet wrote with an even greater fervor and sent her poems to other noted writers and, at age seventeen, was published for the first time in *Poetry Quarterly*. "In no time at all," Kenneth Rexroth recalled, "Herbert Read, Tambi Mutti, Charles Wrey Gardiner, and incidentally myself, were all in excited correspondence about her. She was the baby of the new Romanticism. Her poetry had about it a wistful Schwärmerei unlike anything in English except perhaps Matthew Arnold's 'Dover Beach.' It could be compared to the earliest poems of Rilke or some of the more melancholy songs of Brahms."

From such beginnings, Denise Levertov has gone on to become one of the most beloved, critically acclaimed and highly awarded poets in the English language. The success and praise she received by such icons as Eliot and Rexroth as an adolescent

Denise Levertov at a poetry reading in 1959.

seemed to point to a destiny Denise recognized as a child.

Born October 24, 1923, in Essex, England, Denise Levertov was the daughter of an Anglican priest. Privately educated (the only formal education she received was in ballet), her earliest influences were within the confines of the suburban London parsonage in which she was surrounded by the thousands of secondhand books her father collected, often buying entire lots just to obtain a certain obscure volume. Her father, a highly productive writer in German, Hebrew, Russian, and English—his third language—was a Russian Jewish immigrant who converted to Christianity before moving to England to become a priest. Though home-schooled, Denise was exposed to the masterworks of the nineteenth century; her mother, also her teacher, often read aloud to her from the canon of beloved British poets, particularly Tennyson.

Compared by one biographer to the childhood of poet Robert Browning, Levertov's upbringing in a nurturing home immersed in writing and many different languages was an ideal beginning for a poet. Her lack of formalism was an asset from the beginning. Untethered by convention, tradition, and literary self-consciousness, the young writer thrived, decided to become a poet at the age of five, and began writing poems almost as soon as she knew how to read.

Spurning academia to train as a nurse, Denise spent three years in London rehabilitating war veterans during World War II. She wrote every night after her shift at the hospital and published her first book of poetry, *The Double Image,* in 1946. *The Double Image* was received by some as overly sentimental; its theme was the loss of life, no surprise considering she wrote after long days of nursing patients, many of whom were permanently maimed. What *The Double Image* proved though, notes Jean Gould in *Modern American Women Poets,* was that "the young poet possessed a strong social consciousness and . . . showed indications of the militant pacifist she was to become."

Two years after the debut of her first book, Denise married American writer Mitchell Goodman, and the young couple moved to the United States. With the change of location and lifestyle, her writing changed and began the shift toward a stark, muscular elegance. She published a second book of poetry, *Here and Now,* displaying her new, more American voice.

Kenneth Rexroth, her mentor at the time, noted of her work, "the Schwärmerei and lassitude are gone. Their place has been taken by a kind of animal grace of the word, a pulse like the footfalls of a cat or the wingbeats of a gull. It is the intense aliveness of an alert domestic love—the wedding of form and content." Rexroth was struck by the new sinew in her poetry and felt her to be emerging as a force to be reckoned with, declaring, "What more do you want of poetry? You can't ask for much more." Her next book, *With Eyes at the Back of Our Heads,* established Levertov as a great American poet, her British origins nearly forgotten by the reading public.

As the shape of American poetry was being forever changed by the arrival of Denise Levertov on the literary landscape, so was she being influenced by a different force: the Black Mountain poets. This trio included Robert Duncan, Charles Olson, and Robert Creeley, who founded in 1933 the revolutionary albeit short-lived liberal arts school in North Carolina whose impact upon art and literature was monumental. Levertov's former style was now further stripped to a core of spare, yet not raw, beauty and power. Denise was excited by this courageous new approach and embraced what she saw as a "projectivist poetry" wherein the writer projects herself via the poem through a free, natural flow of words instead of a formalist standard form of strict verse and meter.

In the fifties, Robert Creeley began to publish Denise's work in the *Black Mountain Review* and in *Origin,* published by Cid Corman. Her affiliation with this group of writers also led to her becoming one of the stable of authors published by New Directions in New York. Though she is considered by many to be a member of the Black Mountain school of poets, she herself believes a "'school' is any group of poets who talk and write letters to each other." Indeed, Denise's development and poetry stands alone and is difficult to categorize in its widely divergent styles, themes, and influences.

In 1957, the year that Allen Ginsberg's "Howl" set the world on fire, Denise Levertov felt compelled to check out the bohemian poets of the "left coast." Robert Duncan, the bastion of the San Francisco Renaissance, arranged a poetry reading in honor of her visit. He hoped to usher Denise into the San Francisco scene with an opportunity to meet the local poets and showcase her talent. The event was nothing short of a disaster. Jack Spicer chose this moment to read his infamous "Admonitions" and test the mettle of this potential interloper with some insidiously misogynist doggerel, setting off a poetic debate that turned the Beat and Renaissance communities on their ear for a time. It reads, in part:

> People who don't know the smell of faggot vomit
> will never understand why men don't like women
> Won't see why those never to be forgotten thighs
> of Helen (say) will move us into screams of laughter.

At this point, Spicer's poem moves into a more vicious attack on women, culminating in insults to the female body. Denise's rebuttal was to strike back from a place of female power, fully taking on male condescension and the "hypocrite women who whorishly accept any lesser position from men":

> And if at Mill Valley perched in the tree
> the sweet rain drifting through Western air
> a white swearing bull of a poet told us
> our cunts are ugly—why didn't we
> admit we have thought so too? (And
> what shame: they are not for the eye!)
> No, they are dark and wrinkled and hairy
> cover of the moon

She made quite a splash that day, forever gaining the respect and standing with the Beats and besting Jack Spicer on his own ground.

In the sixties, Denise's social consciousness drove her to found the Writers and Artists Protest against the war in Vietnam with like-minded writers. While teaching at the University of California, she took part in several antiwar protests in Berkeley, once landing her in jail. She also supplied staunch support for students and young poets who opposed the Vietnam War, including a young nun, Sister Mary Norbert Körte, for whom she felt a special kinship.

To this day, Denise has remained vocal in her protests against nuclear arms and the United States' role in El Salvador. Her poetry reflects these concerns, most notably in *The Sorrow Dance, To Stay Alive,* and *Candles in Babylon.*

Yet, the very people who formerly praised her now vilified her political poetry, demanding a separation in her work. She refused, saying that poetry cannot be "divided from the rest of life necessary to IT. Both life and poetry fade, wilt, shrink, when they are divorced."

The confidence she showed as a child writing to Eliot did not abandon her when her poetry and politics became suddenly unpopular. Her memories of London during the war would allow for no compromise of her ideals just to keep a few critics at bay. Her husband, Mitchell Goodman, shared many of her antiwar sympathies and supported her choice to go to Hanoi during the war; he was, himself, codefendant in the draft resistance trial of Dr. Benjamin Spock.

In addition to being a prolific poet, Denise Levertov has had a flourishing career as a teacher. Beloved by her students for her sensitivity and sense of how best to help a budding writer tune his or her poetic voice, she takes her role as teacher very seriously. She is in great demand and has taught at a number of institutions, including Drew University, CCNY, Vassar, UC California, Stanford, and Tufts University. Levertov has also translated dozens of poems from other languages and has published articles in many literary journals, as well as a volume of her translations of Eugene Guillevic's poetry.

In 1972, Denise and Mitchell divorced after a quarter century of marriage. This resulted in a more confessional style of poetry:

> A kind of sober euphoria makes her believe
> in her future as an old woman, a wanderer
> seamed and brown
> an old winedrinking woman, who knows
> the old roads, grass-grown, and laughs to herself . . .

Time has served Denise Levertov well. She has fulfilled the promise that T. S. Eliot and Kenneth Rexroth saw in her and has become one of the greatest poets alive today. Her poems are part of many poetry curricula in America, and her advice to writers illuminates the creative process as hard work, urging writers in the "focusing of attention upon *what is given*, and not in the 'struggle for expression.'"

Although enormously gifted, Denise Levertov reminds us that the muse cannot be made to appear on demand. The following poems span her career from her earliest American writings to more-recent work.

THE GYPSY'S WINDOW

It seems a stage
backed by imaginations of velvet,
cotton, satin, loops and stripes—

A lovely unconcern
scattered the trivial plates, the rosaries
and centered
a narrownecked dark vase,
unopened yellow and pink
paper roses, a luxury of open red
paper roses—

Watching the trucks go by, from stiff chairs
behind the window show, an old
bandanna'd brutal dignified
woman, a young beautiful woman
her mouth a huge contemptuous rose—

The courage
of natural rhetoric tosses to dusty
Hudson St. the chance of poetry, a chance
poetry gives passion to the roses,

the roses in the gypsy's window in a blue
vase, look real, as unreal
as real roses.

■ ■ ■

ANOTHER JOURNEY

From a world composed, closed to us,
back to nowhere, the north.
                              We need

a cold primrose sting
of east wind; we need
a harsh design of magic lights at night over
drab streets, tears
salting our mouths, whether the east wind
brought them or the jabbing
of memories and perceptions, who knows.
            Not history, but our own histories,
a brutal dream drenched with our lives,
intemperate, open, illusory,

    to which we wake, sweating to make
substance of it, grip it, turn
its face to us, unwilling, and see the
snowflakes glitter there, and melt.

■ ■ ■

THE DEAD

Earnestly I looked
into their abandoned faces
at the moment of death and while
I bandaged their slack jaws and
straightened waxy unresistant limbs and plugged
the orifices with cotton
but like everyone else I learned
each time nothing new, only that
as it were, a music, however harsh, that held us
however loosely, had stopped, and left
a heavy thick silence in its place.

Joanna McClure
West Coast Villager
(1930–   )

"Through all those years from the mid-1950s to the publication of her first book, *Wolf Eyes,* in 1974, [Joanna] McClure wrote quietly, unheralded, and often in the middle of the night in ecstasy, or pain, or drunkenness, or a state of joy. There is probably no more honest, intense, or personal portrait of a period than is made through her poetry—for she is a very sensuous and sensual as well as musical poet."

—Michael McClure

nlike so many other Beat writers who have an urban background, poet Joanna McClure née Kinnison was raised in the desert in the foothills of the Cataline Mountain Ridge near the small town of Oracle, Arizona, and these beginnings inform her poetry with a sensitivity to nature absent from much of the Beat writing. She was born to a family of ranchers—Henry Almyr Kinnison and Ramona Jane Hoffman Kinnison—who owned an eighty-acre spread called the U Circle.

The sparse beauty of this desert ranch touched the young Joanna deeply and filled her early memories with the sounds of unforgiving winds and the sight of fierce cacti, canyon cottonwoods, hardy scrub oak, and manzanita struggling to survive the harshness of the lonely mesa. Joanna developed the quick, loving eye of a naturalist combined with a poet's soul that shaped her life to come:

> I come from dusty desert mountains
> Where people only killed other people, bad
> > people,
> And rattlesnakes, and deer to eat
> And valued their horses and families.

Michael, Joanna, and Jane McClure sailing with Larry Keenan, San Francisco Bay, 1966.

During the Depression, Joanna's family lost their ranch. This was shortly followed by Joanna's father's diagnosis of Parkinson's disease, from which he suffered terribly. They moved to Tucson, still more of a town than the city it was to become, where Joanna felt out of place. "Growing up in the desert was mostly a time of waiting," she recalled. "Soaking in the beauty of the place—but waiting and not even knowing what I was waiting for."

Noting Joanna's gift for language, her mother encouraged her to learn Spanish in her early teens, which helped the family earn their keep when they moved to a horse ranch outside Guatemala City, Guatemala. Joanna translated for the ranch owner, an American. She remembers there were plenty of horses for her to ride and that they watched with fascination from their rural vantage point the Guatemalan revolution of 1944.

Later, Joanna returned to the United States to attend the University of Arizona, majoring in literature and history. After graduation, she married a chemist, Albert Hall, the son of a local judge. The marriage was brief and not quite over when Joanna met someone who excited her with his brilliance and curiosity. Michael McClure had arrived in Tucson to study at the University of Arizona and went on to become one of the key figures in Beat poetry.

> Michael was startlingly different. He had exciting ideas, and I was immediately drawn to him. He was a look at another universe. He brought me Bartok, James Stephens, Yeats, and Pound. After I met Michael, my life was very exciting and interesting, but I was married to someone else. When that marriage collapsed, I came to San Francisco. It was 1954. When I got here I was fascinated. I was working at Paul Elder's Bookstore and living in Pacific Heights. I was enchanted to be living by myself for the first time. I wore Guatemalan skirts and rope-soled shoes. My landlady tried to talk me into dressing well. I went over to North Beach for the first time and thought, this is amazing, there's sunshine, and children's voices, people out playing their radios and washing their cars. I thought, life is passing me by in Pacific Heights. I've got to move to North Beach. Even then it was hard to get apartments there, but a friend from the bookstore, Allen McCabe, moved and passed on his small two-room apartment to me. It rented for $45 a month.

Suddenly at the heart of the Beat scene in North Beach, Joanna blossomed creatively—and so did her relationship with Michael. He moved into her flat and together they explored the revolution in art and poetry that was taking place all around them. Joanna, whose visual sense had been sharpened by the desert landscape she grew up in, was deeply influenced by the art she was seeing. She mentions in particular Jay DeFeo's "existential expressionist" paintings show at the North Beach hangout of choice—the Place—along with Richard Diebenkorn's art and a memorable Place exhibit of Robert La Vigne's paintings hung beside Allen Ginsberg's poems.

Joanna's relationship with Black Mountain expatriate Robert Duncan and his lover, Jess Collins, was enormously influential upon her poetic sensibility. At the two men's art-filled flat, choked with bric-a-brac, Robert and Joanna spent hours discussing art, poetry, philosophy, and all imaginable arcana, which resulted in her receiving a finer graduate education than most. Robert's vast personal library was also available to her, and she eagerly read volume after volume of both classics and obscura.

A similar household-salon Joanna frequented was that of Wally and Shirley Berman, where she met other young, burgeoning Beats including the artist Jay DeFeo she so admired. The Bermans propounded a quasi-mystical philosophy of life *as* art, which the younger generation eagerly adopted as Beat credo.

At the same time, Joanna's husband, Michael, was carving out a unique role for himself as a poet with a strong and singular new voice and as a protégé of the great poet and Beat mentor, Kenneth Rexroth. On October 7, 1955, Rexroth helped Allen Ginsberg unleash his "Howl" upon the world, when he introduced the young New York poet to the eager crowd at the Six Gallery in San Francisco. Yet another literary lion, William Carlos Williams wrote a preface for the City Lights pocket edition of the poem. The publication of "Howl" resulted in the book's infamous obscenity ban and a police raid of Lawrence Ferlinghetti's City Lights bookstore in North Beach. Joanna attended the historical reading, heavily pregnant and very excited by this new, raw energy let loose by the readings by Allen Ginsberg, Michael McClure, Gary Snyder, Philip Lamantia, and Philip Whalen.

Joanna and Michael's circle of friends expanded to include Miriam and Kenneth Patchen and Allen Ginsberg, whom Michael met at a party for W. H. Auden. Two days after the historic reading of "Howl" where Ginsberg changed the face of poetry forever, Allen stopped by Joanna and Michael's place with his friend Jack Kerouac, who impressed Joanna as "handsome and nervous." Michael spent a great deal of time with Kenneth Rexroth and the younger writers, engaged in literary discussions that would prove seminal to the full blossoming of the Beat sensibility.

Soon after the post-"Howl" poetic awakening, Joanna and Michael moved out of the now tourist-ridden North Beach to the Western Addition district of San Francisco, filling their apartment with the possessions of Robert Duncan and Jess, who had relocated to Mallorca, Spain. Joanna gave birth to a daughter, Jane, and the couple began a press in their basement—*Ark II/Moby I,* a revival of the forties' anarchist review *Ark.* Their huge Fillmore flat was, in fact, a small commune, a favorite stop for Beats and other San Francisco anarchists, poets, and painters. Joanna recalls when Neal Cassady stopped by to try to sell a brand-new Nash for two hundred bucks. She also fondly remembers Philip Lamantia and Philip Whalen, who provided impromptu storytelling and poetry salons and often baby-sat Jane.

The McClures also started exploring other parts of California, traveling down the coast to Big Sur, where they met literary legends Henry Miller and Robinson Jeffers, who both welcomed the young couple and their friends to their idyllic hideaways. Joanna was struck by the stunning landscape with its rugged cliffs and endless ocean beaches and found her naturalist urges stirred to poetry. Later episodes traveling down the California coast were forever immortalized by their friend Jack Kerouac in his book *Big Sur.*

In 1958, Joanna wrote "Dear lover," the first poem she shared with others, excerpted here:

> I have only lately learned to wear pointed
> shoes with delicate straps
> And realize the value of a pearl choker with
> High delicate necklines & short black gloves
> Topped by wild cropped blonde hair.
> And I am glad and would wear them through
> a war
> If I had to.
>
> I have no heart for wars I can't fight
> Or bombs that destroy.

Like a dam bursting, Joanna wrote prolifically thereafter, filling dozens of notebooks with her quietly powerful verse. She and Jack Kerouac preferred the same kind of artist's notebook for their writing, and she was one of the few of their contemporaries who produced as much writing as Kerouac did, though she kept much of hers private. Gradually, with the encouragement of her husband and Robert Duncan, she began to publish her poems.

In 1959, the McClures moved briefly to New York, where they quickly fell in with the New York Beats, including LeRoi and Hettie Jones, Diane di Prima, and New York School poet Frank O'Hara, as well as other literati and artists of the East Coast scene. Upon their return to the West Coast, due partially to lack of finances but mostly to the difficulty of raising Jane in New York City, Joanna read A.S. Neil's *Summerhill.* This began a study of education and developmental psychology that led her to a career in early childhood development and parent education.

> I was reading Erickson and Bettelheim as well. I experienced the same feeling of being home, the feeling of place, as I had earlier at the first poetry reading I went to, when I met the group of co-op teachers under Frances Miller, the group I have continued to work with in early child-hood development and parent education for seventeen years.

Joanna still lives in San Francisco on a hill above the Haight. Though she and Michael are now divorced, they remain linked by poetry. Her poetic voice has grown through the years, her desert naturalist eye sharper. Currently, she publishes her poems in limited-edition chapbooks.

Joanna McClure's book Wolf Eyes *is a spiritual autobiography. Selections from it are in-cluded here, along with some of her newest poetry.*

excerpt from WOLF EYES

A woman was
Destroyed by
Wolf love

I give thanks
For my
narrow escape.

■ ■ ■

HARD EDGE

The crow watches.
I wait upon anger
Now gone,

Wait upon it for
The edge only it
Gives,

For the clarity of
A cold eye,
After

Leaning
Too far
Out!

■ ■ ■

JUNE 18, 1984

Bills,bills,bills
Thrills, thrills, thrills
Skills, skills, skills

   metacognition
   memory
     &
   metamorphosis

    . . .

   cocoon me out
    right now!

■ ■ ■

COLLAGE

Quiet the tension
Pauses of interwoven silence
Smells, textures, buds
Tastes, textures, touches
Braid in with surprises

. . .

Each new discovery as
Slow and quiet as a
Possum's front feet.

■■■

NIGHT

Wandering from room to room
Smiling.
How can life be so full at 52?

■■■

SAPPHO

The spirit matters
Most of the words gone

The simplicity
And ardor

Reach out and
Catch a resonance

That time and fragments
Only enhance.

■■■

PEARLS FOR KATHIE

My pearls
Sit in the cupboard

And I feel sad
Seeing the opalescent

Colored contoured
Nacreous gloss—

Reflecting your
Cosmic eye

Which suffers
Sans hope

While I sit
Comforted

    by oak arms.

Janine Pommy Vega
Lyric Adventurer
(1942–   )

"At the dock, Elise peering over her eyeglasses, Janine whitefaced blond in black jacket waving scarf, & Lafcadio with half smile, fluttering a straw hat ambiguously—Peter above deck cupping his hand to heart in a Russian cap—and when I called their names I saw them, drifting away with their skulls."

—Allen Ginsberg, "Dream Record," March 23, 1961

Janine Pommy Vega has always been a seeker. She sought out the Beats in her teens and now she travels "in search of the Mother Goddess, in search of shamanic teachings, sometimes setting out without knowing exactly what I was searching for, but that it was something." Her poetry, which she has been creating and performing steadily for the past thirty years, reflects the power that travel can have in one's search for self. She also uses her work to reflect on the past and look toward the future.

Janine grew up in a working-class neighborhood in Union City, New Jersey. Her early years were spent happily; she particularly remembers occasionally helping her milkman father with his deliveries. These experiences gave Janine her first feel of travel. While in high school, her wanderlust took her to the Beat scene in Manhattan, attracted by the mobility that *On the Road* represented. There she became lovers with Peter Orlovsky and friends with Herbert Huncke and Elise Cowen.

When she was twenty years old, she met and fell in love with a painter named Fernando. She traveled and lived extensively in Europe with him until his sudden death of a heart attack at the age of thirty-three. Janine then used travel to try to escape the pain of her loss and finally ended up back in New York. Realizing that she would end up dead from drugs or a broken heart if she stayed there, she moved west to California.

Her first book of poetry, *Poems to Fernando,* was published in 1967, and she became active in the poetry scene in San Francisco until the seventies, when wanderlust overtook her again. Never in one place too long, Janine has been performing her work, with and without music, in English and Spanish, to enthusiastic audiences throughout North and South America and Europe. She is the author of five major collections of poetry and five chapbooks. Her most recent publications are *Threading the Maze*, a prose work on the Mother worship spots in Europe, and *Drunk on a Glacier, Talking to Flies,* a collection of poetry. She has edited numerous anthologies, has been translated into six languages, and her autobiography is being published by Lawrence Ferlinghetti's City Lights.

Presently living in the Catskill Mountains north of New York City, she continues to travel extensively, exploring new parts of herself and her personal mythos. As she says:

> My desire to slip away from the stories, and the choices we make to secure our identity in everyday life has borne fruit again and again. To go on a pilgrimage, I discovered, you do not need to know what you are looking for, only that you are looking for something, and need urgently to find it. It is the urgency that does the work, a readiness to receive that finds the answers.

The following is an excerpt from Janine's memoir of her time with the Beats, in which she shares her initiation into Beat life. Several of her poems round out the selection.

Seeds of Travel

In high school, I found a friend, Barbara, who was different from the other kids. She looked like a showgirl; it was what she wanted to be. She wore eye makeup, and had a sophisticated air. She was willing to take a risk. We took dance classes together on 32nd Street in Union City. I had been reading Jack Kerouac's *On The Road*. All the characters seemed to move with an intensity that was missing in my life. A magazine article about the Beats mentioned the Cedar Bar in New York City. Barbara agreed to go with me and check it out.

Outside the bar on University Place, we were nervous. We were both sixteen; would we get in? We tried to look as nonchalant as possible as we cut through the crowd of people and sat in the back. From our table we watched the bar through the cigarette haze: the drinkers were mostly men—big men, it seemed to me—with large hands jabbing the air as they shouted at each other and laughed.

We ordered beer. Opposite us sat a dark haired man, drinking wine at a table full of crumbs. He had just eaten a meal of pasta and French bread. He introduced himself as Gregory Corso, and talked with us, but especially with Barbara, whom he seemed to like.

He began to speak about *Allen,* and *Peter,* and *Jack*—meaning Ginsberg, Orlovsky, and Kerouac. He was calling them by their first names. I was thrilled. I told him I'd seen his name in a Time Magazine article. He invited us to come with him to the Lower East Side and meet his friends.

At the apartment he brought us to, on Second Street between B and C, a handsome man answered the door. Gregory introduced us to Peter Orlovsky. He looked like one of the men in the photo accompanying the article I'd read. Peter led the way into the main room, where there was a double bed and an easy chair, and invited me to sit down. Gregory and Barbara stayed in the kitchen talking.

Elsie John

One of the carnies who introduced Herbert Huncke to the concept of Beat was carnival freak Elsie John. Elsie was a denizen of the road, a weary, drug-hazed, jazzy fringe world where real Beat was born long before John Clellon Holmes quoted Jack Kerouac in the *New York Times.* Elsie was a hermaphrodite whom Huncke met when he was sixteen, working as a shill for her popular act on the carnival midway. Herbert also procured marijuana for Elsie at the going rate of seven joints of "high quality" for a quarter, as well as the heroin she loved. Elsie was a very large person; her feminine side was prettily shaved, powdered and made up with Veronica Lake–hennaed hair, while her masculine side was very hairy and muscular.

Elsie fascinated the young writer with her glittering eyes and endless stories of the road. Exhibiting her maternal side, she tried to keep Herbert out of trouble and wouldn't allow him to deal heroin. Elsie was the subject of his first short story, which was so well received he was spurred on to continue writing. It is rumored that Elsie's participation, at Herbert's urging, in the first Kinsey Report skewed the famous sex survey's data. No doubt, Elsie John knew firsthand about "exalted exhaustion."

Janine Pommy Vega and Herbert Huncke having fun in New York City.

Peter was wearing a gray and white bathrobe. He had straight brown hair and candid hazel eyes. He read me a poem he had written, called "First Poem," and we chatted a while. Barbara and I had discussed at length our desire to jump into life and experience it fully, as adults; our virginity seemed to stand in the way. That's what I thought about as I watched Peter. He said he'd like to keep talking, but had to go out and meet Allen. We made a date for Barbara and me to return on Sunday, and meet him and Gregory again.

On Sunday morning, we were back. Gregory answered the door, and took Barbara to a side room, and closed the door. I sat in the kitchen. It was so quiet. Allen and Peter were, I guessed, still sleeping. I was a little nervous; I had no way of knowing what would happen. The room was warm, but my hands and feet were cold. I began leafing through the Sunday papers piled on a chair.

A dark haired man came out, and washed his glasses in the sink. Then he put them on, and looked at me.

"Hi," he said, "I'm Allen Ginsberg."

"I'm Janine." I hoped I looked cool. I didn't know what else to say.

"Peter will be right out."

It looked like they had just woken up. Peter looked very handsome with his hair disheveled. Barbara screamed from the side room, and I didn't know what to do. Allen left shortly afterwards. Peter took my hand, and led me through the big room, where we'd sat before, to a little room with a single bed.

My main feeling was fear. Was it going to hurt? Would there be blood? Maybe it wasn't a good idea, after all. But Peter was sweet, and quiet, and tender. He took my clothes off, then his own. Every move he made was gentle. He took his time. He insisted I keep my eyes open. There was no blood. His face was very beautiful.

Back in high school, word circulated that we'd gone to New York City. Barbara and I ignored the questions. We returned to the City as often as we could, though not to Second Street. Peter and Allen had left for the west coast. Barbara was seeing Gregory, and meeting his friends. I got a waitress job on weekends in the Bizarre Coffee Shop, and started hanging out with people from the village. John Rapanick and Arnie Levin, co-owners of the Seven Arts Coffee Gallery in Hell's Kitchen, asked me to work for them. As long as I was working my mother accepted, albeit reluctantly, my irregular schedule and lengthening absences.

When summer ended, I had to go back to finish my last term in high school. Barbara quit, and went to live with Dave Simon, a goodlooking actor she had met and fallen in love with. During that fall, at the Seven Arts, I met Herbert Huncke. Arnie Levin told me he was an old friend of William Burroughs, and had just come out of prison.

Huncke was sitting along at a table, wearing an olive green sweater. His hair was straight and almost black; his eyes were hazel. He looked to be in his mid-forties. We started talking. He told me about having lived around Times Square in the 1940's and '50's; he had been one of the people interviewed in the Kinsey Sex Report. Huncke had the voice and captivating gestures of a natural story teller. I liked him immensely.

One night at a reading, Peter and Allen came in. They had just returned from the coast. I realized Peter did not recognize me. I felt I'd obviously changed a lot from the naive girl he had met the year before. After the reading, I asked if I could go back to the Lower East Side with them. I wanted to visit Huncke, who had become my friend and mentor. He lived two floors above them, in the same building. 270 East Second street was home as well to Elise Cowen, a close friend of Allen's, and poets Bob Kaufman and Jack Micheline.

On the train, Peter asked my name. When I told him, he cocked his head to the side, and looked at me.

"Janine? Did I, I mean did we…. Oh my dear, I'm so sorry."

I was glad he hadn't identified me with the nervous girl I'd been in his kitchen.

"That was a long time ago. I've changed a lot."

That Christmas I wanted to surprise Huncke with a little Christmas tree, and set it up while he was out at work. I bought the tree, and some lights, but I couldn't get it to stand up in the corner. I went down to Peter's and asked for help. Between us, we got the tree positioned between bricks, then put on the colored lights. I wanted to leave before Huncke came back. Peter looked very handsome in the light from the tree.

In January, I graduated from high school. Though I had done virtually no work in the last semester, I was named Valedictorian. Both my English teachers counseled me to apply for college scholarships, but I had no interest in returning to school. My mother, with whom I'd been battling constantly over my freedom, wanted to throw a party to celebrate the honors I'd received. She was very proud.

I made a deal with her: I would go to the party, and stay until the last person left; then I would leave myself, and she would never again ask where I was going. I was still underage, as she was fond of reminding me; the party was my only bargaining chip. I loved her and my father very much. She was selfless in her love for me, but I had to be about my business. She agreed to the deal. That night I took my suitcase onto the last bus from New Jersey to the city, and went straight to Huncke's.

I got a job in an office near Bryant Park. Peter and I became lovers again. From Huncke's, I moved one block down into a new apartment with Elise Cowen, a strik-

photo by Ira Cohen, courtesy of Janine Pommy Vega

Janine Pommy Vega with Jack Micheline in San Francisco, 1981.

ingly intelligent poet and copy editor, and old friend of Allen's from college. Though most of her affairs were with women, secretly she was in love with Allen.

All that winter, and into the spring, I read. Emily Dickinson, Christopher Smart, Catullus, D.H. Lawrence, Gertrude Stein, Charles Dickens, William Blake, John Weiners, Arthur Koestler, Albert Camus: anything anyone else was reading. After work, I would hang out or read. This was my education.

I was shy about showing anyone my writing. Sometimes I showed a poem to Elise, who had constructive comments; mostly I kept my work to myself. Peter gave me *Moby Dick* to read; I finished it in a weekend, and decided on the spot that I needed a passport. I began, one night a week, to visit the Public Library on 42nd Street, and read, in the quiet of the long tables, the journeys of Marco Polo.

Allen left for South America, and I found myself spending more and more time with Peter and his younger brother, Lafcadio. Laf was kind of a hermit: he seemed unable to work or deal with the world, and had no friends of his own, which was why Peter took care of him. When I came back from work, we would eat cheap dinners, which Peter cooked, and go to the movies, or stay home and read.

I was learning with Peter not just how to make love, but how to open up and take his intimacy in my life as a constant. He would read me some of the letters that arrived from Allen. Wrapped up in Peter's robe, I tried to imagine the jungle Allen described in Colombia where he was taking *yage,* and the scary snakes he'd seen, glowing in the dark.

When I brought Peter home to Weehawken, where my family had moved, my mother looked askance at his beard. Hearing *Orlovsky,* she spoke to him in Polish, which he didn't understand. She steered me to her bedroom and confided in a whisper that I might be hanging out with Bolsheviks.

One night, Peter took a bath, and put on the gray and white bathrobe he had been letting me wear. He looked exactly like he had the first night I'd met him. Someone knocked on the door. It was Allen, with a huge duffel bag on his shoulder. I left them together, and went back to my room at Elise's. In the ensuing weeks, we juggled who slept with whom. With their single bed and double bed, somebody usually slept alone, and it wasn't Peter.

Some months later, Allen announced that he and Peter were leaving the country en route to India. I had my passport but no money, so I stayed at my job; Peter helped me find a bigger apartment, where I would live with Huncke, and the two of us would take care of Lafcadio. I read all the works of Herman Hesse and Dostoyevsky, and *Mount Analogue* by Rene Daumal. I began to walk the streets at night, and imagine magical existences behind the lit-up windows.

Peter's letters came to me from the warm sun on the rooftops of Morocco, where he described the smells coming up from the alleys, and the dreams he'd had of us making love above the city. I missed him. He'd been my first real lover. But I was angry that they hadn't invited me to travel with them. Is that how it was in the world of the poets? I thought I'd rather meet painters and musicians.

■ ■ ■

[Ah certainty of love in the hand]

Ah certainty of love in the hand
a bright new corner, spasms of clarity

/ day throatwinded walking I am
filled with unmotion, singing
A turned around tree dances
sparrows in her hat/ a
canopy of canaries

    Spring!
& I not with you?

                        paris, spring '65

■ ■ ■

[Here before the sunrise blue &   in this solitude]

Here before this sunrise blue &   in this solitude
to you: come home. The moon is full over morning
buildings, the shade of solitude is upon my hand:
Come home. In this empty loft of high windows
the shades are lifting, and people are arrived;
To you: in the early silence between us that IS,
folded deep into night & the black well of Sources
in-here is gone forth to meet in-there, &
we ARE bound below a sound or gesture;
beneath distance, before time, at the foot of the
silent forest, meet me here, I love you.
A fire is crackling, I have risen early
before the dawn—love and how long I have
need of you all I feel; don't know
where you are or what's happening, yet

surely the morning stars will shed their light
in desolate places, and this just from me
first thing in the morning, love.

paris, 1/18/65

■ ■ ■

M42

M42
M42
the 42nd interruption
in Charles Messier's quest for comets
the 42nd suspect on the list
the 42nd blotch and *poseur*
is not a shooting star
is not a star
What is it?

M42 in Orion's sword
is a scintillating branch
the fish mouth of the Great Nebula
the next spiral arm out from us in the galaxy
the seamless coat of Christ
a stellar swan
The pulsating blue Trapezium
in a *cuna,* a cradle giving birth
to star after star after star

From the Chinese enamel lamp
a gorgeous goose flew off
through a hole in the beaded curtain
to the recesses of stellar space
she was laughing to herself, she was shaking

with mirth, her flight described an arc
of maybe twenty-five light years
across, from wing to wing

Her laughter flew
uncontrolled from the throats
of the ancient queens
as they swigged another ale down
broke another neckbone
and threw it to the dogs

She laughed in the midnight graveyards
with adept yoginis, who sang to each other
in secret
surrounded by bones jutting through
the earth and the grinning skulls
they reeled in ecstasy

O dazzling fecund nebula
in her blue and white robe!

If you want to be present at creation
see the Goddess in Her radiant dress
the Shakti
the Shekkinah
Get a telescope
buy binoculars
point it at the cloud in Orion's sword,
galactic pulse of the universe,
Look at this!

Fall on your knees in the snow and weep
in gratitude
Look at this!

The bird flying off into starry space
Look at this!

Willow, New York, November 11, 1994.

■■■

FEBRUARY THAW
The birds are coming back
and with them, the old longing
for wet seeds, sleek skin, the moist earth
reaching up with bare arms,
and mine among them

the birds
congregated in the hemlocks
are not just chattering
but the first mighty chorus
of return

the body hums and trills
with each wisp of cloud, each
feathered wing and starry catkin
dropped on the snow, in the advent
of my own year also

I clear away the entrance in the tree
to the animal cave
clean the entrance of raggedy wet leaves
crystal snow
clear the entrance for easy access

and I ask myself,
what hole is this?

The ear, the drum,
the tunnel to the psyche,
the vagina?

A sun harvest
creaks and knocks on the wood
above me. I am the surface
and underground cave
I am the thaw and the cold snap
and the thaw again

With their peeping and piping
the tiniest birds
have returned with their indomitable
song, with their small happy
voices, to the light

the wind combs the hillside
for dead branches, bodies at rest
and winter returns
implacable wind, dead leaves scoot
over the snow like frightened animals

but the green shoot thrusting through the ice
is strongest
the wind the snow the cold
can slow her, put her down,
but they cannot stop her

From the dream church where I knelt
and knew
I could never be separate
from what I love, these tears
in the snow

celebrate return
not the mind or the will
or the heart
but something
singing with the crowd in the hemlocks

flowing with water under the ice
in globules, like amoebas
migrating over rocks to the pools below
and no matter how long I have left
on the earth, I have loved it here.

February 5, 1993. Flanks of Mount Tremper, Willow, NY.

■■■

A young Janine Pommy Vega enjoying a smoke and a cup of coffee.

THE DRUM SONG

Red and white candy striped
Exit sign:
enter a hole in the wall
to a hidden world of juju beads
and maps the size of Atlantis
and little boys stalking the deer
of imagination

Red and white
Peruvian flag, the Polish flag,
and other breastplates
and gee-gaws of domination
since there ever was a war
since there was the idea
of conquering your neighbor

Red and white
the woman in her childbearing
years, and then herself, soft haired
watching the fire, taking to her
the grandchildren who want her stories
red and white, the passionate
female, the passionate male

Orgasm and abstinence
hosannas coming up from the belly
to the top of the head
red/white
the blood and bone, the skeleton
in its scarlet flag

the two-step zigzag dance
across the tightrope, the red and white

agenda, wavering like a flock
of geese, like a ribbon
across the sky.

February 1994, New York City.

■ ■ ■

GREETING THE YEAR 2000, WITH RESPECT

Glancing back at the millennium we are leaving,
I see a cannon roll out into the dust
of a tiny war in the patch of sun
in a store window
on the Lower East Side
Noise, blood, suffering, even the animals
take part; no one is winning

Great theaters of carnage
bright science yoked to bleak
military arsenals, kids are killing kids
people are torn between nationalism
and compassion, and the entire human species
is hurling itself headlong off the edge.

And he laid hold on the dragon, the old serpent,
and bound her for a thousand years
and cast her into the abyss
and shut it and sealed it over her
that she should deceive the nations no more
until the thousand years be finished;
after this she must be loosed a little while. *

She must be loosed a little while?
How little a while?

238

Lording it over the beasts in the field,
the trees in the forest, the air, the water,
with the rapt egocentric stance that nature
is the devil, we have been supremely free
to disrespect whomever we choose.

I think of the lovely Lilith,
tossing her hair as she leaves the abyss
the unbound fire in every atom
She steps out into a vacant lot
in the Southeast Bronx, where to *dis*
somebody is to face down a handgun

A serpent curls among the streets
of the world, a naked energy
climbs our spine and gazes from our eyes
Don't cut the trees, don't blaze more trails
across the mountains, leave a little
wildness for the next inheritors,
with respect.

Monte Alban for a thousand years
was a sacred city and civilization
of peace. With plentiful fields of corn,
the people were free to serve and adorn
their temple. In synchronicity
with the earth
they derived their names from what they did.

Let us go out and greet the new
century, said Seraphita, Balzac's angel,
and the icy fjords cracked and melted
the bells rang wildly
With great respect, with great love

she said, and the energy
crackled across the sky like lightning.

Look at the serpent
curling through the green woods
spiraling up the hills from the flat land,
and greet the new millennium with complicity
for the unchained nature in the earth,
the air, the water,
the snake undulating up our spines
and the dragon in the stars.

*Revelations 20; *2–4*.

Willow, NY, January 1, 1994.

ruth weiss
The Survivor
(1928–   )

"A fine funkiness: Beat Generation goddess ruth weiss (she launched the jazz-poetry readings at The Cellar) and trumpeter Cowboy Noyd will have their first reunion since what John Ross calls 'the bad old days'..."

—February 15, 1993 item in Herb Caen's column in the *San Francisco Chronicle*

Austria, 1938. Amid political strife and religious genocide, some Jewish families managed to escape the horror of the Nazi regime. One was ten-year-old ruth weiss, born in Berlin in 1928, who in 1933 escaped with her parents to Vienna, where she began her schooling and wrote her first poem at the age of five. In 1939, on the last train allowed to cross the Austrian border, they fled to Holland to board ship for the United States. Though her immediate family survived, most of ruth's relatives perished in the Nazi concentration camps.

The family's first years in New York were far from their comfortable life in Berlin. ruth's parents, struggling with a new language and long hours with low wages, placed her in a children's home to prevent her from wandering the city streets alone. Even though ruth was eleven at the time, she was so small that she passed for eight, the maximum age for the housing facility. Her parents visited on weekends.

Eventually ruth's family settled in Chicago, where she graduated eighth grade from a Catholic boarding school. During high school, ruth felt alienated from her classmates; she kept to herself and studied hard, graduating in the top 1 percent of her class with high grades in every subject—including all *A*'s in Latin, solid geometry, and English. In 1946, she and her family left their upper-middle-class Jewish neighborhood to return to Germany, where her parents worked as American citizens with the Army of Occupation. She then spent two years in Switzerland at the College of

Neuchatel, hitchhiking and bicycling through the countryside, learning French, learning to drink, and, as she recalls, "learning little else." ruth wrote several short stories during this period and kept a journal, which she later destroyed. This was to be the only time she ever destroyed her writing.

ruth returned to Chicago with her parents in 1948. This time, she moved into the Art Circle, a rooming house for artists on the Near North Side, where she gave her first reading to jazz in 1949. Shortly thereafter, ruth began her Bohemian wandering, which led to New York's Greenwich Village and the French Quarter in New Orleans. In 1952, she hitchhiked again, this time from Chicago to San Francisco's North Beach, moving into 1010 Montgomery, later occupied by Allen Ginsberg and his last girlfriend, Sheila. ruth wrote poetry in the Black Cat, a bar two blocks away, and she entered the all-night jazz world across town in the Fillmore at Bop City and Jackson's Nook.

Haiku has long been a favorite form of ruth's, and there have been many exhibits of her watercolor haiku. In the early 1950s, when she was living at the Wentley Hotel, Jack Kerouac would stop by. "You write better haiku than I do," he'd say. After a night of writing, talking, and sharing haiku, Neal Cassady would show up, insisting they join him in a drive to Portrero Hill to see the sunrise. ruth fondly recalls the wild ride down "that one lane two-way zig-zag street."

Through a piano player she knew from New Orleans, ruth met many jazz musicians in San Francisco and jammed in their sessions with her poetry. When three of these musicians, Sonny Nelson, Jack Minger, and Wil Carlson, opened The Cellar in North Beach in 1956, ruth joined them onstage, performing her poetry to jazz accompaniment, creating an innovative style whose impact would reverberate throughout the San Francisco art scene.

During this time, ruth published in the majority of the early issues of *Beatitude,* one of the first magazines to give voice to the Beat Generation. Wally Berman also included her in the Mexican issue of *Semina,* a Beat art-and-poetry magazine.

In 1959, ruth returned from traveling the length of Mexico with her first husband, having completed her journal *COMPASS,* which includes an excerpt of her memorable meeting with two close San Francisco friends in Mexico City—poet and photographer Anne McKeever and poet Philip Lamantia. After talking all night in a

© C.R. Snyder

ruth weiss reading at the Grant Street Fair.

Aya Tarlow

Aya was born Idell Rose Tarlow on August 14, 1932 in Los Angeles, California to the son of Polish/English/Jewish immigrants and the daughter of Romanian Jewish immigrants. She grew up in Los Angeles surrounded by a large, loving family. As a child she studied piano and dancing and inherited her love of photography and writing from her father, who was a pharmacist.

She began writing at 13 and started compiling collections of observations, poems and drawings. After high school, she attended L.A. City College, but dropped out after the first year to get married. She continued attending poetry and writing classes and slowly began to have work published in small magazines. At 23, she met her second husband Lee Romero in a poetry class and created a scandal by getting a divorce to marry him. They moved to a farmhouse in Riverside, California, and from there on to San Francisco. They arrived unwittingly just when all the signs of the Beat movement were emerging and it swept them away. They frequented the coffee houses and became part of the scene, and it brought a freedom of spirit neither one had known before. She fell in love with the new Bohemian life, and wrote constantly about the romance of the senses, the music, the ongoing spiritual highs of that time.

In the early sixties, collections of her poems were published, including *Poems for Selected People* and *Marks of Asha*. A play *The Edge*, was produced in Open Theater in Berkeley in 1966 when she returned to San Francisco for another period. While there she was drawn to a Zen Buddhist Temple and soon began practicing Zen with the famous master Suzuki Roshi. She then returned to L.A., and her play *Honeylove* was produced by East L.A. Jr. College in 1967. *Zen Love Poems* also came out.

In 1969, after surviving a near-fatal miscarriage, she met her third husband, astrologer/artist/filmmaker William Royere, and adopted his young son. For the next twenty years until his death, they formed the nucleus of a large magical family of like-minded comrades. During their intensely dramatic ride together, they produced several experimental movies with such playmates as Beatle Ringo Starr, Mellow Yellow minstrel Donovan, and their extended families.

In 1971 another play, *Dialogue with Feathers* was produced by the L.A. Feminist Theater. She also began publishing *Matrix: For She of the New Aeon,* a seminal three-volume literary journal in university libraries worldwide.

In the mid-1970s she and Royere co-founded Araya Foundation, a healing arts corporation and school were they taught astrology. The Foundation also produced a benefit concert at the Shrine Auditorium in L.A. Later she, Royere, and a friend formed Jade Productions and produced a 90-minute documentary, *A Religion in Retreat*, about the Buddhist persecution in Southeast Asia. Aya became active in the L.A. Vietnamese/American Buddhist community and later took her vows as a Buddhist layperson. During that time she also appeared in a film *The Beats: An Existential Comedy* by Philomene Long, and gave readings with poets Cameron, George Herms, ruth weiss, and Frankie Rios.

Aya and Paul-O and their two cats live in a cabin under an extinct volcano, tucked in the mountains at the west end of Sedona, surrounded by pine trees and lush national forest. They continue their astrological work for clients nationwide and Aya, as ever, continues writing, and has just completed *The Crone Poems*. She also surfs the Net, coordinates a Wise Woman Lodge, stays active in several other groups, and waits for the next Assignment, still considering herself a Messenger-in-Waiting.

cafe, they decided to climb the Pyramid of the Sun in the Mayan ruins outside Mexico City and catch the sunrise. Neither guides nor other tourists were there in the pre-dawn chill. The climb to the top of the pyramid was easy, but ruth, paralyzed by a fear of heights, had to be carried all the way down.

That same year, ruth published a book, *GALLERY OF WOMEN,* poem-portraits that included poets Aya (born Idell) Tarlow, Laura Ulewicz, and Anne McKeever, written out of "my respect and admiration for these women with whom I felt a kind of sisterhood."

ruth's first marriage was to artist Mel Weitsman, who studied with artist Clyfford Still. They met in 1953, lived together for a year, split up for a while, and then married in 1957. In 1963, their lives moved in separate directions and they parted as

ruth weiss performing in "Kubuki, U.S.A." with Howard Hart (L) and Dion Vigné at Fugazi Hall, San Francisco, 1957.

friends. Weitsman went on to become a Zen priest, and ruth kept on with poetry as the central focus of her life. ruth's second marriage, to sculptor Roy Isbell in 1966, lasted less than a year; Roy, imprisoned on a drug charge, was later murdered in prison by guards.

North Beach has always been "home turf" for ruth. Here, in 1967, she met her life partner—artist Paul Blake—at the Capri, a classic North Beach watering hole. During the Vietnam War, Paul was a conscientious objector, and he and ruth went to Los Angeles while he worked his alternative service for two years as an attendant in the psychiatric ward at Los Angeles Country General Hospital. During this time, ruth expanded her artistry beyond the written form and worked with San Francisco artist and filmmaker Steven Arnold, playing major roles in all of his films. Their collaboration received international attention when Arnold's film *Messages Messages* premiered at the Cannes Film Festival in 1969. In the early sixties, ruth, excited by the new wave of films coming out of France, Italy, Sweden, and Japan, began a series of filmpoems and plays, including *FIGS, NO DANCING ALOUD,* and *THE 13TH WITCH.*

Throughout the decades, to support her poetry career, ruth worked at part-time jobs that included waitress, chorus girl, gas station attendant (even though ruth doesn't know how to drive), postal employee, museum cashier, and accountant. Mostly, she worked as a model, sitting for artists and students. In the early 1970s, she tended bar at the Wild Side West, a lesbian bar in San Francisco's Bernal Heights where she did Sunday afternoon poetry readings with her long-time friend, Madeline Gleason. ruth also ran various poetry series in San Francisco, including Minnie's Can-Do Club, Intersection, and a poetry theater, *Surprise Voyage,* at the Old Spaghetti Factory, connecting with many of the younger poets.

In 1981, ruth and Paul moved to Inverness, fifty miles north of San Francisco. A year later, after a flood threatened their lives and their life's work, they moved further north to the small town of Albion in the coastal redwoods. The peaceful surroundings have been good for ruth, and these later years have been some of her most productive. In 1990, ruth won the Bay Area "Poetry Slam" and released *Poetry & Allthatjazz,* volumes 1 and 2, on audio and videocasette, collected from her live performances.

ruth weiss is finally getting the attention she has long deserved. In 1996, *The Brink,* the 1961 film that ruth wrote, directed and narrated with jazz, was screened at The Whitney Museum of American Art during their exhibit *Beat Culture and the New America, 1950–1965,* by the Bancroft Library at the University of California Berkeley's Pacific Film Archive, and at the Venice Biennale Film Festival. The San Francisco Main Public Library held a three-month exhibition of ruth's and Paul's individual work and collaborations over the past twenty-five years; her work is also in over fifty special collections at universities and libraries across the United States.

And ruth continues to perform. Since their heyday in the fifties, ruth is one of the few Beat poets to have continued reading poetry live in North Beach, proving how she has honed her craft to become one of our finest living poets. She and her jazz collaborators are at The Gathering Caffé on Grant Avenue on the last Monday of every month. For anybody who missed out on the Beat scene the first time around, this is a rare and wonderful opportunity to experience one of the original Beat poets firsthand. To hear ruth weiss read her poetry in a dimly lit coffeehouse in San Francisco's North Beach is to understand why our fascination with the Beat Generation will never die.

As poet Jack Hirschman said, "No American poet has remained so faithful to jazz in the construction of poetry as has ruth weiss. Her poems are scores to be sounded with all her riffy ellipses and open-formed phrasing swarming the senses. Verbal motion becoming harmonious with a universe of rhythm is what her work essentializes. Others read *to* jazz or write *from* jazz. ruth weiss *writes* jazz in words."

Included here are pieces from SINGLE OUT, *a prose-poem recalling her Nazi refugee past, and recent work.* I ALWAYS THOUGHT YOU BLACK *is the title story for a series of autobiographical "synchronistic reminiscences" chronicling her relationship with black people in her life.* MY NAME IS WOMAN *comprises her prose-poem sketches of women friends.*

FOR BOBBY KAUFMAN

crossed your bridge
with your big word
and your huge silence

■ ■ ■

POST-CARD 1995

> JOHN HOFFMAN died in MEXICO
> RON RICE died in MEXICO
> ANNE McKEEVER vanished in MEXICO
> ALEX wife & child died in MEXICO
> and what about SHEILA
>
> BOB KAUFMAN wanted to die in MEXICO
> and so did JACK KEROUAC
> and what about NEAL CASSADY
>
> SUTTER MARIN swam in PLAYA ANGEL
> made a pact with the angels
>
> all mad to be reborn
>
> i die every time i go to MEXICO
> and return reborn

JOHN HOFFMAN your poetry lives with PHILIP LAMANTIA
RON RICE your films are flower-thieves of the night
ANNE McKEEVER your poems, your voice, your toreador's baby
where are they
ALEX left his name ERNEST ALEXANDER & paintings in CHICAGO

and SHEILA of the blues voice
once married to A. GINSBOIG

said she took a dope-rap for him
died in a south-of-market hotel dreaming of MEXICO

BOB KAUFMAN is equal to anything
especially in FRANCE
and JACK KEROUAC is everywhere
daughter JAN KEROUAC carries his face
and what he faced
and what he didn't
and what about NEAL CASSADY swinging his lantern
to the night-train

SUTTER MARIN did it all to his own beat in SAN FRANCISCO
before the beat & after

      this night
      in a room
      of reflections —

      like what put us here
      like changes in reflex
      like changes in pace

      this night
      in a room
      of reflections

      the patterns of self on the wall

      at the shore of the sea
      sparks from the red tide
      a movement of self
      fire-works on the water
      the eye a reflection of stars
      what put us here

the self of course

the course is not always clear
the water is not always clear
the sky is not always clear

it is still —
a time for reflection

■ ■ ■

FOR MADELINE GLEASON

"do your poems haunt you?"
oh Maddie
is not the poem of our life
a haunt
drawing us
releasing & drawing us?
A stronger line each time
drawing us the artist
drawn & quartered
into seasons, elements...

■ ■ ■

excerpts from SINGLE OUT

II — INCIDENT

october 1938 we had to flee vienna.
my grandmother hungarian boarding house
was wanted by a nazi official.
hungary was still out of nazi clutch & my grandmother hungarian.
we were austrian citizens—
my father, his mother's only son.

we left quickly in the night for the swiss border.
the border had closed one night before our arrival.
rain—
dizzy alp trails—
we climbed to slide muddy back to the border village.
another try—
now a desperate 20 (mostly young men)
with hired guide across the flooded rhine.
one woman slips in the mud…
shotssinging above our heads
not really meant to hit us (the swiss sharpshooters)—
the warning realenough—
go back we can't take any more.
we couldn't either.
the three of us penniless in the innsbruck trainstation—
obvious unaryan.

what now?

any moment the question—
the only answer!

a young woman brushed by—
a whisper the follow-me.
what could we lose?

wet night
narrow streets—
we kept a block behind
until she vanished into a doorway.
a slit of light—
we entered.

are you hungry? she said.
i'll show you your bed.

all night the venetian blinds caught light.
once there was a knock.

the sun rayed through the blinds
when she called us for breakfast.
a young man with unslept eyes was sipping coffee.
where are you headed?
vienna.

the man nodded, kissed the woman, left.
her hands put money & tickets into ours.
she directed us to the station—
first checking the street.

at the station an official gleaming a huge swastika neared us.

what now?

then we saw his face.
it was the young man who hadn't slept.
there had only been one bed in the flat.

in vienna our visa from new york awaited us.
there was still time to leave.
december 31st, 1938—
midnight—
the last possible moment.

we boarded a train for holland.

in switzerland we would have spent the war
in an internment camp.

        * * *

the party was in full swing—
chicago 1950

i had just come back from new orleans & making circles.

old faces
new faces
lifetalk
deathtalk
any talk to keep the thread & nervous.
are you here?
is he?
is she?
she is.
he is.
he is who?

you have an accent; yes viennese.
a young face—
coal
old as coal.
smooth.
i'm an expert.
besides I have a friend from vienna.

the circles stopped.
we were hanging over the back of an overstuffed couch—
four feet dangling over the heads who filled it.

my feet stopped dangling.
is it a she?
is she black but light?
is she tall?
very.
does she dance?
yes he said & she comes from vienna.

oh how we talked that night!

in her tiny attic-room that night.
up stair after stair
i'm sure it's her.
it's she, he said.

she made coffee, scrambled eggs.
circus.
the war.
i'm an acrobat when I have to be.
the war & after a GI from detroit.
no more—
but always the dance.
and now
always the dance!

IV - DANCE

naked
lined up for the gas chamber
shame & blame & guiltless guilt
take a shower
wash clean the sin
the lie
hypnotic shuffle in
SOAP & SILVER CLEAN LIKE RAIN

he follows order
he follows orders
he wanted a joke
SS commanding officer
YOU THERE!

the nameless numbered girl numb

you're a dancer

DANCE!

and the word struck lightning
and she danced as it struck
CLEAN   LIKE   LIGHT
and took the gun from his dumb hand
and struck him down
like thunder
and thunder again

from where the shocked guard stood
she went down
CLEAN   LIKE   LIGHT

■■■

excerpts from I ALWAYS THOUGHT YOU BLACK

oh there is literature at the ART CIRCLE. living literature. WILLARD MOTLEY
comes to visit. *KNOCK ON ANY DOOR.* GWENDOLYN BROOKS comes to visit.
A STREET IN BRONZEVILLE. A fine tooth-comb.
WILLARD'S lover is lovely BILL. BILL in
my class at sullivan high. BILL dies young. "i want to die young & have a beautiful
corpse."

* * *

ERNEST ALEXANDER long & brown listens to my poem. in my black blue-bulb
room. pulls me upstairs. sez now read to these folks. they gotta hear this.

my first own home. my first turntable. my first modeling nude. my first poetry aloud.
someone blows a horn. someone brushes a drum. i'm reading to a jazz man.

* * *

i'm 22.

don't think i'll make it to 30. don't think. write.
words are my friends. words are wings. protect.

255

i have a room of my own. i shall always have a room of my own.
that i will. this cancer girl gotta have a room of her own.

* * *

one by one the ones who must play—enter.
the search for that note—that only one. it's a jam for the
heartbeat. no feet tapping. no hands clapping.

i walk slow through daybreak-blue. back to north beach.
my lids fold around my whole being.

■■■

from MY NAME IS WOMAN
ANNA MARIE

barefoot in winter. in the city. in the mid-west winter of the USA. i am seven years
old. my toes are cold. too cold to tell me the stories that keep me going in the summer. the blood in my toes tells me all the old stories. the stories that tell me i am a
gypsy.

momma sez this is not true. how did you ever get such an idea. gypsies steal & make
up lies about the future. how did you ever get such an idea. that you are a gypsy.

it is winter. my toes are cold all the way to my fingertips. and i tell my toes. don't
worry. i am a gypsy. i will find you shoes to make you warm. so you can keep telling
me the stories

in a building where many people live i look at galoshes outside the doors. one black
pair after another they don't belong to me i keep on walking down the halls. a red pair
shouts. try me. they fit. almost. but i like my sandals better. the ones that i buy in a
store. many many years later.

i am looking at my toes. in my sandals. where i sit by an ancient redwood tree. to keep
the chainsaw from cutting it down. and my toes tell me the story of the redwood. and
about surviving.

Mary Norbert Körte
Redwood Mama Activist
(1934–   )

"A series of women poets emerged in San Francisco who identified with the established Beat Poets even as they challenged them on their grounds [including] Joanne Kyger and Mary Norbert Körte... Of these, the career of Mary Norbert Körte most sharply defines the historic tension between the women of service and the women of passion. The strongest woman poet to emerge in the West.... She became a student of Lew Welch, cracking convention within the bastion of the religious order."

—Brother Antoninus (William Everson)

Mary Norbert Körte grew up along the eastern skyline of the San Francisco Bay Area in the Oakland-Berkeley hills. She was born into a long line of devout Catholic teachers and lawyers reigned over by her grandmother, a Bavarian dowager who wore severe formal gowns at all times and enforced strict propriety in her offspring. One of Mary's earliest memories is of her grandfather's funeral, where her grandmother marched her up to the open casket, made her take hold of his cold, stiff hand, and solemnly promise, "In front of God, to remain ever faithful to Grandfather's memory." The adult Mary is quick to add with a laugh, "And I have. No man has ever measured up, including Jesus."

Mary was encouraged by her deeply religious family to join the convent right after high school; dutifully, in 1952, she entered the St. Rose Convent on Pine Street in San Francisco at the age of eighteen. Here she exchanged the bustle of a busy family for the solitude of a strict order. She earned a master's degree in the specialized field of Silver Latin, the more obscure Virgilian period of the language that followed the great Golden Age of Latin. All in all at this point in time, Mary Körte, now Sister Mary

Norbert, was an ideal young bride of Christ.

Then two events took place that drew her attention outside the walls of the St. Rose convent. The first was Martin Luther King Jr.'s speech for the march on Washington; she watched it on television and felt her "consciousness open." Then she attended the Berkeley Poetry Conference in 1965 and heard readings by Robert Creeley, Jack Spicer, Charles Olson, Robert Duncan, Gary Snyder, and Allen Ginsberg, among many other poets and writers who moved her enormously. She remembers being the only nun in attendance and was treated as rather an exotic, but very warmly welcomed.

Sister Mary Norbert Körte's life changed completely on that day. She found her true calling—poetry—as she experienced an ecstasy in the auditorium she had never experienced in any cathedral. She recorded the impact on her life and her religious community in the lighthearted poem, "Eddie Mae the Cook Dreamed Sister Mary Ran Off with Allen Ginsburg," but remarks in all seriousness, "and that's exactly what happened!"

It didn't happen overnight, however, and Sister Mary Norbert tried hard to make her previously chosen vocation work, no doubt with the memory of her grandfather's cold hand and her childhood promise in mind. To the abject horror of the sisters at St. Rose, Sister Mary's idea of good works was to sneak food out of the pantry to give to poet activists like Diane di Prima and Lenore Kandel. She had met the two in the Haight at the headquarters of the Diggers. "The Diggers were a community of people in the Haight Ashbury modeled after the fourteenth-century English group devoted to the simple life and helping the poor," recalls Mary. "I got involved when I hustled food from the convent to feed starving poets, some of whom were Diggers."

Sister Mary also began writing a new, freer kind of poetry that really excited her and was met with praise from her sisters at St. Rose and her new bohemian buddies. She also made two important friendships at this time. She met the young Beat poet David Meltzer and felt an immediate affinity with him. David recognized that Mary had a rare gift for poetry and urged her to act on it. He introduced her to Robert Hawley, who took one look at her writing and offered to publish her in *Oyez*. Later, Hawley published Mary's first book of poetry, a beautifully lyric volume entitled *Hymn to the Gentle Sun*.

By 1968, it became clear to Sister Mary Norbert that her divine inspiration might be more pagan than befitting a nun of the Catholic Church. She realized that she lived in an extremely conservative community, one that didn't share her interests in poetry, liberalism, and the outside world. Knowing that the concerns of the Church were no longer her primary values, she decided it would be hypocritical to stay. She left the convent and the Church and became Mary Körte.

She moved to Berkeley and began to explore life beyond the walls of her order, thrilled at her newfound freedom to write and do as she pleased. At her new job as a secretary in the psychology department at the University of California, she made another important friend, who gave her great encouragement in both her writing and her activism—Denise Levertov.

At the time Mary moved out of the convent, the riots in Berkeley were starting to really heat up, and, as luck would have it, she rented an apartment one block away from what was to become People's Park. She remembers how Denise Levertov would sometimes call on a particularly riotous night to make sure the young ex-nun was safe. Denise also touched Mary when she wrote to Thomas Merton on Mary's behalf, explaining how much trouble the ex-nun was in for her activism. Merton wrote back immediately, offering to "help in any way I can."

Denise nominated Mary Körte for a National Endowment award in the Fall of 1972. Mary remembers it as one of the greatest moments of her life. She greatly enjoyed being in the same

courtesy of Mary Norbert Körte

Sister Mary Norbert Körte with a younger member of the congregation.

anthology as Senator Eugene McCarthy and William Saroyan, Jr. and used the $500 to buy some food, a winter coat, and the shorter *Oxford English Dictionary.*

In 1972, Mary Körte answered a classified ad seeking a caretaker for some land in northern California, north of Mendocino. She moved to the property in a remote valley and has lived there ever since, learning carpentry in order to add to the crude one-room cabin. A few years after moving, she bought the property from the absentee landlords and has since added a library and an altar, where the Virgin Mary and Frida Kahlo stand side-by-side. Except for a seven-year period in which she lived with a man—another poet—Mary has lived alone in the ever-changing woods she has come to love.

The move to the redwoods affected Mary Körte deeply, and she found another calling: environmentalism. Throwing herself into the Save the Redwoods movement, she has participated in every way short of "lock-down," the most extreme protest which takes the form of chaining oneself to a tree, although "it may come to that," she comments. Like many other environmentalists, she sees the old-growth forests of the Pacific Northwest and the Amazon rain forests as the "lungs of the planet" and has written and handed out dozens of poems on this increasingly important issue. "Those woods are *allowing* me to stay there."

Mary Körte supports herself through teaching writing in the Poetry in the Schools project and by teaching at the college on the Native American reservation near her home. She truly enjoys "teaching kids about poetry and sharing your process with them and getting them to write. It's a lot of fun." She has had four fifteen- and sixteen-year-old students publish their own books after her classes.

She also derives great satisfaction from her job at the reservation school, which is part of a recovery program after the government policy of forced assimilation, known as termination, that began in California in 1934 in which, for a small sum, Native Americans gave up their tribal status and their languages. At this school, Native American students are learning their own languages for the first time in sixty years, many of which were on the verge of extinction. Notes Mary, "Sinead O'Connor said it best: If you want to really oppress a people, take away their names, their language, their traditions, their dance, their religion."

Mary Körte reads a lot in the quiet of her beautiful woods, including certain writers whom she reads over and over, such as Gertrude Stein, Gerard Manley Hopkins, and Gabriel García Márquez. She writes every day and publishes beautiful broadsides of her special-occasion poems on holidays, Earth Day, or for events such as the opening of the Mendocino Book Festival, where she received a standing ovation for the reading of her wondrous epic, *Throwing Firecrackers Out the Window While the Ex-Husband Drives By*. Like other poets who developed their craft during the Beat Generation, Mary Körte believes it is very important to "be there and read to the audience, to connect with the people you're writing for."

The writings included here represent the range and movement of Mary Körte's writing, showing her development from nun-poet to "redwood mama" activist.

EDDIE MAE THE COOK DREAMED SISTER MARY RAN OFF WITH ALLEN GINSBURG

The halls dark long hard
enough to have survived
the '06 Quake where survival
was measured by the sound of
Mother Superior's Rosary Beads
                        she dreamed
the cook dreamed the other nuns
dreamed impossible dreams of silver
visions pelagic noises in the
                        groaning night
Dreaming was a mission she could not
renounce night as a place to see
all freedoms looming ahead
like a sweet dragon like
a cross with its circling tail

She ran away in everybody's dreams
calling out like a booming flame
running running into the lines
of bards & lions lovers & birds
running with her arms out wide
into the bright   flapping   dark

(A true story about a dream really dreamed by the cook at the St. Rose Convent after
Sister Mary Norbert Körte attended the Berkeley Poetry Conference.)

■ ■ ■

excerpt from THROWING FIRECRACKERS OUT THE WINDOW
WHILE THE EX-HUSBAND DRIVES BY

It is 50 years figuring out how to
make it down to the end of the road
to make it up & out on the ridges
the mountains along the Eel
brought from her Grandmother
            Sister   Mother
            Mother Courage women
she went to school with lived with
prayed with settled all the great
affairs around midnight cramped for—
bidden tables 50 years
brought to a time
of sunset noises and the time
of 2 women walking in autumn apples
talking of how quiet
            how quiet it is
            in a Redwood Forest
how sometimes quiet is frozen river
held fast in rocks and reeds

the furtive burrowing of birds
singing in a frail winter sun
quiet singing quiet

■ ■ ■

TURNING 40 IN WILLITS
you could see the path the wild oats
disturbed with her dying   she slid relaxed
in to the sun her ears moving through the wind

Mary Norbert Körte after leaving the order.

courtesy of Mary Norbert Körte

(we thought)   it was a long path she slid
down the hillside   some body hit her
with a .22 and she ran away to die
you run away to the city   to get a boat
why did you leave the Midwest   too many
friends (he said) he came to California
and the man who has too many friends
in California runs to sea or the city
it's all mixed up in who dies running
and who dies down a long slope
of peach grass with the fledgling hawk
wheeling and complaining with the wind
twining wild oats around your still still ears.

■ ■ ■

This year will be the winter spring the summer
of our discontent the fall
having shown its colors
poisoned overfed bloated
    with names:
oriented strand board
late seral stage heartwood
5000 year old redwood rhizomes
ground down to disposable diapers
managed forest clear
cut to infinity well
infinity is her dig it

New Year 1995

■ ■ ■

REMEMBERING BILL EVERSON, POET

They brought him back home to be buried among his Brothers. To be buried with all the bowing mystery of a Dominican Funeral is to get a grand good-bye indeed, and Brother Antoninus—Bill Everson's Vespers and Mass took their place in a long tradition of those "Birthdays into Heaven" read about in the daily martyrology.

The last years of Bill's life were, indeed, a martyrdom. That a man of such passionate intensity, one of the great bears of my life should be trapped within a body cruelly assaulted by Parkinson's Disease was a blow to the heart. That he slipped away in his sleep was a blessing.

And over his body, his poems were read: "A Frost Lay White on California" the poem born in the very St. Albert's Chapel where his friends bade him Godspeed. "The Poet is Dead" for Robinson Jeffers. My God! How he had such raging patience. That was the one he showed me in Draft #68, pencilled neatly in the top (left-hand) corner. He shared this with my great heroes: the Catholic poets of the century—Hopkins, Frances Thompson, T.S. Eliot, Merton, C.S. Lewis—they brooded with a howlingly intense stamina and glorious image. And they had reason: a Church structure that didn't understand, a horribly repressed era that looked upon books with pleasure, but was appalled by the cranky persons who wrote them.

Bill and I entered the Dominican Order at the same time—the early '50s; he, to the Priory at St. Albert's College, I, to the Convent at Dominican College. We left the Order at the same time, too—the late '60s. He found his place at Kingfisher Flat, miles down the

Coast from my bench of land on the Noyo.
But we each lived with the Redwoods and the salmon
streams that somehow—I don't know—the Order had
made us ready to find. We talked about that the last time
I visited with him. About people flying in the
Face of God. Well, he did. And he's resting there
now. Well done, Bill. O, well done.

■■■

THERE'S NO SUCH THING AS AN EX-CATHOLIC

(The Spotted Owl & Chain Saw Scapular for Erni Pardini)

Scapulars worn next the heart contain
relics of Martyrs
Martyrs are those who have lived and
died with Heroic Virtue
Heroic Virtue is a condition to which we
are increasingly called by the abuse of
Technology
Technology must be put in its proper
place only one life form among all those
others who share this Planet
This Planet will survive only if All
recognize a Common Mission

The Common Mission is Mutual Respect

■■■

THE ROOM WITHIN

this room within my self wants light
a flowing-in with flowers that I take of you
shot prisms and candles pierced through walls
built of my fear-kept hands that now you
bear to earth rich and quick at my door
thrusting aside the vines long grown hanging
about my careful house wherefrom that reasoned place
we would sing the pattern dance dancing
through the ritual hieroglyphs of passion
when we would go moving as people do with
purpose would take apart this room stone
by stone and set ourselves outdoors
to mate with the sun

courtesy of Janine Pommy Vega

Janine Pommy Vega and Brenda Frazer at Allen Ginsberg's farm in Cherry Valley, New York.

Brenda Frazer
Transformed Genius
(1939–   )

"The women I knew best were imports like me and they may have been free spirits but it didn't show at first. Diane di Prima was the only one making her own statements that I knew. Others like Hettie Jones were competent but family and husband oriented as I was. Some of Ray's jail friends used to pick up women that had jobs and allowances and made their lives comfortable with such 'Angels.' Like my mother, my generation still wanted women to accept roles instead of create them."

—Brenda Frazer

The shy, slim, brunette Brenda Frazer loved Ray Bremser passionately. A hipster poet-author, Ray introduced the nineteen-year-old Sweetbriar College student to the world of marijuana, psychedelic mushrooms, and heroin. Born July 23, 1939, in middle-class Washington D.C., Brenda attended Princeton High School. Her parents, especially her mother, were unhappy in their marriage, which cast an uncomfortable sadness over the household. Brenda remembers struggling with disorientation and a feeling of not fitting in anywhere during her teen years.

The intensity of her connection with Ray Bremser made her feel that she had finally found a place where she could fit in. They married just after her high-school graduation in 1959. Six months later, Ray was jailed on a narcotics charge and was paroled soon after. Meanwhile their daughter, Rachel, had been born prematurely. Shortly after Rachel was released from the hospital, the trio skipped town and moved to Mexico. Changing her name to Bonnie Bremser was the first of many transformations Brenda Frazer would undergo in her lifetime.

"I married Ray Bremser, poet seer, when I was nineteen," recalls Brenda. "He wore an olive drab fatigue jacket and a red hooded sweatshirt to the ceremony. I adored him, even his eccentricities, and justified my existence by typing his poems. I identified with Fidel Castro. His patriotism, presented in lawyer truth, moved me. His actions inspired me to quit school and give thought to the shameful corrupting influence of capitalism. The Beat movement provided me with a husband and a rationale. Ray Bremser's penal/political history began to involve me also."

Life was hard in Mexico. To support their daughter and their drug habit as well as feed themselves, they relied upon various means of financial support, from Bonnie's prostitution (pimped by Ray) to panhandling. Soon her robust, brunette beauty gave way to bleached hair and a drug-wracked, emaciated physique. Five years later, Bonnie escaped Mexico and Ray, leaving Rachel at the border. In 1969, she chronicled her life in Mexico in her autobiography, *Troia: Mexican Memoirs*.

In New York City, Bonnie met Allen Ginsberg and moved to his farm in upstate New York, where she regained her health and vigor. Inspired and rejuvenated by rural life, she saw in it a lifestyle in harmony with the earth that was capable of revolutionizing the culture by getting it back to its roots. She embraced the agricultural sciences, transforming the place into a model farm far in advance of its time. She tried hard to make a go of Allen's farm—and very nearly pulled it off.

Her friend Janine Pommy Vega spent some time with her at the farm and remembers Brenda as an absolute genius. Brenda worked, studied, and experimented diligently, earning several master's degrees, including one in biochemistry, and she devised a method by which compost and manure were used to manufacture methane, upon which the farm was powered. All through the seventies and eighties, Brenda stayed in upstate New York, continuing her agricultural education and commitment to environmentally conscious farming.

Eventually, Brenda moved to Michigan, where she now works as a consultant for the U.S. Department of Agriculture. She writes and publishes a lot of technical articles under a different name and only occasionally writes poetry, having left her Beat life far behind.

Brenda Frazer's writing tells the story of a woman transformed. She notes: "I defined myself when I sat down to write. It was a rebellion against my most immediate authority figure, my husband, who was once again in jail. Writing was a therapy I could afford. It was exciting then and still is to give myself that freedom. Alone I evolved my personal story. There is no mentor or male muse to be a live-in example for me. I have more faith in my creativity now. Creativity is in the middle, at the turning point of gender, either, neither, nor."

Soft Birdwing Hat (1943)

A child of four with violent emotion "It is not enough! One night together only, mother and I. But I put that from my mind for she has told me she is going and I have only this time to enjoy her presence. The moments tick away too fast and I cannot control their passing. A world I took for granted is ending. I must be more careful of my feelings from now on. I must arrange my life to somehow satisfy my needs. I wonder if my father can understand and help me through our future alone together. This painful pact of leaving between mother and me. It dims my sight, a loss like death and I'm afraid. The shock is too great to face and to diffuse it between half-closed eyes as I watch her pack."

High

"up on the top shelf, the closet in the furnished room, is her traveling hat. My mother is a bird flying away. When she puts her hat on, the birdwing swoops curving up over her right eye. She has a forties hairdo and I know how she fixes it because I love to watch. She uses rattail cushions from the store, their netting fibrous in a mass of rounded shape. She brushes the hair up over her beautiful brow forming a soft roll over the rattail. I wish that I had rattail nets to catch and make her stay. But she gently brushes her hair getting ready for the necessary flight. I hold the birdwing hat of dead dreams against my cheek and then put it back in its tissued hatbox nest."

"I wonder if I'll be a mother and have girls to lose. I'll go away and come back to find my daughters gone from the nest, eaten up by unknown dangers. The pact of soul closeness broken. The pain I carry dead upon my brow beautiful in the eyes of lost children."

Postnote: My daughter Rachel Bremser (1960) was given up for adoption in Fort Worth, TX at a year old. I haven't seen or heard of her, nor know her name since then. I want to.

excerpt from *Troia: Mexican Memoirs*

First off I want to tell a few really important things about me. I know that continuity is necessary, and I do my best up to a point, but I believe in distortion—I believe that if you get to a place where something is taking shape and want badly to comprehend the thing that you have created, supposedly for yourself (Since everything is personal anyway), then any old thing to fill the gap will do and that is the point where you come in… in looking back, what's important is not the technique or lack of it, but those few minutes when you overcome the frustration, bridge the gap, and hold something incredibly beautiful to you; the point where you don't see yourself anymore but you are there, and OBOY, that's the way you really are… Here is the way I really am: I HAVE GOT PLENTY OF NOTHING, if you will excuse my banality. My heart belonged to Ray since the day I met him in Washington, that is the basis of my life, and all life before that can only be explained this way: that my heart knew that Ray was on his way to me. My heart has a mind of its own—and speaking of minds, this is where I want to explain me: I have a dirty mind.

My mind is on my needs. I walk down the street and feel the thigh within my raincoat warmed by the sun. I like to think of other people helping me. It occurs to me that everything will be OK, because there will always be someone to help me get the things that I want. I like the people who help me, as a rule, because their existence adds to the thought that everything is going to be OK.

When I have no money I am able to desire vividly the things that money can buy. I look at them and am pleased at their availability; even looking at money pleases me. With a dime I walk into a restaurant and take a long time over a cup of coffee and am pleased to see people buying things that I don't have the money to buy, and a green bill passing hands is especially beautiful to me. A person sitting next to me complains of the food and the proprietor calmly throws it in the garbage and when the man leaves he pays for it, though he is not asked to, and leaves a tip for which the proprietor thanks him. I find them both admirable.

Walking by a wholesale jewelry store I am called into a dream by the fairy tale beauty of diamond bracelets, and moreover, I think of the people I could have buy me those things; nothing more than that, the moment passes but leaves its impression of a completed sensual experience. I decide that I will go without money more often to enjoy this feeling: the anticipation of confidence, the lilting dream which grows upon itself is a reality I had not expected to encounter.

I am pleased at my lack of clothing. My nakedness is anticipated much more in dreams than my eyes can ever plan for it in covering, and the means to the dream is a whole other dimension I hesitate to describe. The ideal covering for my body is sunlight, and in sunlight I will be admired (foremost by myself)—the afternoon sun I wile away thus with my dirty mind....

[She and Ray head to Mexico]

Once across, we were quickly tired of Matamoros and purchased tickets to Mexico City. Transportes Del Norte, maroon buses, nothing to complain of in these first class accommodations, we had enough money to get safely to Mexico City from where we were somehow to get safely to Veracruz, where we were to find our refuge...had I already exchanged one fear for another? Had the cold damp night of Matamoros put another chill into my heart? Was my fear at this time all composed of not being able to handle external circumstances, afraid I would not be able to keep Rachel healthy, or at least not crying (and that was a feat I didn't often succeed in), and not to be able to satisfy Ray—what was happening in his head, something similar? And it all was so extremely personal, this service of responsibility, that the failure of it and maybe the success I have not had much chance to experience up to this point was a very lonely thing; we were not really helping each other too much now. Each of us was just clinging as well as possible to what shreds of strength were left in the confidential self. The bus ride to Mexico City, full of this, I am constantly with the baby on my lap, broken hearted at every spell of crying, the frustration of not being a very good mother really—trying to groove, trying to groove under the circumstances—and in spite of it I have impressions of dark shrouded nights of passage through the hills, of an oasis of light in a restaurant stop. 2 A.M. with everyone sitting around the narrow lighted room—with a sense of it being the only lighted room for fifty miles around—eating eggs Mexican style for the first time. Ray got his *huevos rancheros* and me eggs scrambled with fried beans and this was a sort of prelude to our Mexican trip. This meal in itself would come to be one of the great Mexican treats; eggs, how many places have we had those eggs I came to remember with great pleasure, but then, at that time, it was fear and anxiety not even to know how to ask for an egg in Spanish an though I probably exaggerate now the lostness of not being able to make myself understood, I can now see that it was not just the language that caused the fear. Somehow the fear was cumulative, the desire growing as the inability increased.

The trip—maroon bus awaits us beside the low immigration building, near the broken-down bridge—beer cans clatter in the dusty road afternoon no sunlight but the approaching lowering clouds of a thunderstorm spreading out over the sky into gray vastness of a depressing standstill underneath any tree; lonely your reality here in Matamoros, the streets which carry through the center of town growing in importance to the four central parallels which cut out the square of the plaza, where afternoon *bistek* eaters and shoe-shine boys eye each other from across the unpaved streets; these same streets spread outward into the still mathematically correct city layout but sidewalks disappear and houses rise in midst of a block shacked upwards from a broken down fence entryway by eroded paths; a house may take any shape or position within a block and weeds of menacing aspect care little for the store on the corner so drawn into its cache of paper candies and orange soda signs it has shrunk to the stature of a poverty-struck doll house—the incredible ironies of Mexico—the wild-flung filth of Matamoros. Leaving town on the bus, mud hole crossroads fifty yards wide of rutting and industry—some International Harvester or reaping machine showroom with its economic splendor surveying the city; it will grow on, and the sky disapproves. Pass Sta. Teresa, a cafe faces east on the flat land. Look across to the Gulf, and nothing looks back, save the mesquite bushes, a mangy dog chases a couple of not promising cows across a landscape you would not expect to carry even that much vision of life. Seen from the air, Transportes Del Norte carries on, a vision of good service, sixty people burning up the dust on the first stretch of the roads which do indeed all lead to Mexico City—San Fernando, Tres Palos, Encinal. The sun shines briefly as I change the baby's diaper and we have a cup of coffee and head back to the bus. Santandar Jimeniz, we do not know yet that from here dots one of those "almost" roads perpendicular to the route of travelling civilization. A road which grows out of the solid surety of modern highway dotting in weak secrecy into the plain to Abasolo where another almost not to be seen road, goes nowhere, but goes—we want to see where all the roads go, since then, but this first trip just get us there and quick, get us there where we are going, and we don't know yet that nothing waits but the bottom waiting to be scraped in our own whimsical and full-of-love fashion—got to get there and quick—damn the crying and wet diapers and laps full of Gerbers on the bus, of leg cramps and not much to view—Padilla, Guemez, Ciudad Victoria, chicken salad sandwiches and the unknown feeling of a waterfall. In all of these places we stop, passing through, rushing downward, seeking our level, slowly dying, get it over, let's get there. Ciudad Monte, non-stop Valles, passing in the night the bus driver picks up on lack of sleep, answers on the wheeling whispering pavement. We take our first curves into the hills, the roads start to swing—Tamazunchale, lights seen across a valley, Jacala, pencil marks on maps of future excitement. We turn East in the night approaching Ixmiquilipan, herald Indian feathers, the driver mutters incoherent names over the sleeping passageway, the bus careens as we shoot through Actopan, come another and final turning point at Pachuca. The driver announces the last lap and everyone stirs and gets excited at the news, not realizing it is more than 3 hours of approach to Mexico City. I look out and God drops from his hand the myriad stars and constellations I have never seen before, plumb to the horizon flat landed out beneath the giant horoscopic screen of Mexican heaven.

Why do I hold back and hide, when I am sure at least of one person as understanding as I of my own faults and maybe as proud of our achievements. Oh yes, let's don't get personal about it at this late hour—had we done so earlier, tempestuous natures would have wracked to the lowest hill what now begins to seem almost a peaceful Arcadia we retire to, even in exile, now....

Two o'clock *en la mañana,* we arrive in Mexico City and the bus leaves us off at ADO and not at the Transportes Del Norte bus terminal. In a swelter of homeless appearing people whom we don't recognize there are many who are waiting for the morning bus perhaps, and though they look disreputable something will eventually be brought out of their packs to make them proud—like us, our records, our chevrons at that point I guess, on our way to make the scene at P's and it couldn't be too soon for me. I was cold, tired and ready for the new day to dawn with everything O.K. as usual. Taxi drivers, *caldo* eaters of the night, our soon-to-be compadres of doubtful reckonings on Mexico City taxi meters. When the meter registers two pesos, the passenger somehow must pay four and even more surprisingly we find out this is not just tourist graft and that the taxi in Mexico is one of the cheapest rides anywhere with privacy like a king; cheapest except for the bus ride, if you are game, but that is more rollercoaster thrills.

P was not at home. We walked looking for a place to have coffee and get warm, for though we travel light we have the burdens of 300 miles in our heads. I remember now the opposite trip for me later when I flew from Mexico City to Washington in five hours and was dizzy for days afterward, unbelieving—and now I make the trip in my head, slowly, in pieces, this morning with the sun I climb the overhanging hills of Acapulco, alone, lonely, alone full of the meaning of death, and life, either end of it, Mexico, Mexico, your sun crashes me in the head obliterating all bodily care, all shame, shameless Mexico, I am your child, and you have my child as the token.

Like the man who taps you on your waiting-for-hours shoulder, P finally comes to the window, ahh, relief, I give the baby a little jiggle for joy, ooyboy, baby, this is it, we enter. Five flights up, an imposing building, strange this is for us, even in a strange country. In Hoboken we live in houses of the renovated artist type, to put it politely. We live in ramshackle houses where we can and love it—modern apartment buildings for us, whafor? But I am tolerant for once, maybe even glad, I want to flake, a couple of hours of peace, unmoving. But there is no peace for our bodies, more food for the soul on top of all the rest, and maybe it is better, the truth, soul full of food in Mexico....We turn on, do indeed at this point display our chevrons and for once they are appreciated, but we were used to that, Change of the Century, Ray Charles. We all were there at that first meeting, P, L, his blond stage-managing wife, in bed asleep, no doubt working the next day, in spite of our cataclysmic arrival, but P knows and believes, as all groovy poets who dig us, no one otherwise could. We had met P in our marriage year, arriving in San Francisco on foot, having just aired our souls on the Mojave Desert. He took us to his room in the B Hotel and, handing us one enormous reefer, proceeded to read stuff that will knock you out, poetry that cannot fail to hit you in your own personal cause of it all, and therefore we love him, that is P still, I believe. N was there, as I say, the whole Mexico crew, jive N, the first of the absconders, who had I believe invited us to Mexico, in lieu of staying to testify at Ray's trial, whereby we would have had double strength of truth on our side, but what does that matter, all visions of trial and parole past, have we not achieved our escape, have we not disembarked from it all and many mornings together in the waste of a life will prove it's no mistake. Salvage what you can, when there is no hope, run for your life, this is what I felt all along, the closing, around the ears like a bad drug taking hold which has been administered involuntarily.

Melchior Ocampo in the morning light is not half so scary and we all retire to the nearby hip food stand and eat hamburgers and apple pie with ice cream and coffee. It is one of those great pot feasts that are always for all time remembered like some memorial along the road of our beautiful experiences. God praise marijuana, yes, my baby, I will never put you down. A few things stay close to our hearts, definitive, a happy to have habit thing with no pain, no remorse, no sickness—although we did contact some people in Mexico who were profound expostulants of LOCOS who had smoked too much, (this was more a way of bragging that the pot you buy for an arms length thick amount costing less than a dollar is likely to shack you up until you decide to buy again), we have never had more than one or two disagreements with them, and that purely external, say for instance once or twice not having the mini-mum of survival and therefore having to do without, and only then, and then it was a frenzy to get straight and quick, and nothing wrong with that I guess. Sweet mari-juana—lotus blossom I am entitled to call you now, being thoroughly a member of the club.

Ray was perhaps responding to the illusion of everything being beautiful. He always was ahead of me in that respect, and I do respect, although it in fact leaves me behind. He decided to stay in Mexico City for twenty-four hours more while it is decided for me that I will travel to Veracruz by bus with N and the baby. Ah bitter, I was not about to accept with grace my maidenly burdened-by-baby responsibility at this particular time. I should have put my foot down instead of being shuffled because see what it did in rebellion (sure! almost sure! suspecting something really wrong since Matamoros—that Ray had already set his eye on something that didn't include me—what could it be—my perceptions were not sharp) and my survival reflexes were working overtime, I guess. But I go—midway between holding the baby on the eight hour bus trip, the night quickly sets in and I decide to try my seductive powers on N, and the mistaken blue jeans, not to survive this episode, did indeed entice his hand where it should have by any standards stayed away from, the baby on my lap, we arrive in Mexico, me zipping up alone, my lonely pleasure, had I known I could have got in any restroom by my own mechanics—damn N.

If I could only do more than grab at a passing branch over my head, but the trouble with that is everything up until now has taken place fast on the go, the screeching terror of speed of everything falling out from underneath you—the recurring dream of bridges falling and falling away from beneath your very feet into rushing water, the resulting social shock, but more than that, knowing what it is to fall for the last time forever.

I set down in Veracruz, not I alone, me and the little me, Rachel, we arrive there escorted into taxi cab jive and Veracruz barely registers our arrival. The America Consul is not informed, the DA knows not what is about to hit him, the FBI thinks that we are maybe laid up with a cold in Hoboken. And yet we are already doing the dance; the Paso Doble of passionate worth dissembles all other meaning of life and we dance, we all dance, Veracruzano's Negroes, the woman on the corner shakes her wet clothes into a floating heap on some not so precious patch of grass, gelatinas yelled through the streets, the palms again, all dancing dancing, the sun rises, Veracruz rises, some altar on this Easternmost coast, the morning of Mexico, Veracruz rises beyond the sugar fields. Oh Cordoba, the plaza dances, the streetcar certainly dances, this is the dance of the sun I have fallen into and knowing my own heart also at least dance, abide the sacrifice, it is unimportant, but dance....

Lenore Kandel
Word Alchemist
(1932–   )

"I will always remember being met at the airport by the most downtrodden pickup truck I had ever seen, driven by Lenore Kandel, whilst a Digger moppet, age about two, stood beside her in the cab, naked from the waist down and chewing on a hot dog (horrific to my macrobiotic mind). Miscellaneous mutts—mostly canine—shared the back of the truck with us, as we drove into town. My infant refused to stop screaming."

—Diane di Prima

Bold and beautiful, Lenore Kandel's poetry attempts to bridge the chasm between the sacred and the sexual, between religion and the eroticism of the body. Replete with Tantric symbolism, her works reflect her Buddhist influence as well as a celebration of the corporeal.

Born in New York City in 1932, Lenore moved with her family that same year to Los Angeles, when her father, the novelist Aben Kandel, got a movie deal for his novel, *City in Conquest.* A minor classic, the film starred Jimmy Cagney.

By the age of twelve, Lenore had decided to become a Buddhist and started writing. She spent the next fifteen years going to school and reading voraciously, "everything I could get my hands on, particularly about world religions." In 1959, she began sitting zazen in New York and had three short collections of her poetry published. In 1960, she moved to San Francisco and met Beat poet Lew Welch at East-West House, a co-op started by Gary Snyder and other Zen students.

Lew Welch was on the scene in the early part of the San Francisco Renaissance, the collection of poetry schools in the Bay Area pulled together by Robert Duncan in his efforts to create community after the fall of Black Mountain College in North

Carolina. Lew was intertwined in the mesh of the Beat and Black Mountain College scene, but refused to align with any one school of poetry. He was friends with Jack Kerouac, Lawrence Ferlinghetti, and fellow Buddhist scholar Gary Snyder.

Lenore recalls how she ended up in San Francisco. "I'd been meaning to come to San Francisco, and I decided to come here for a weekend and I stayed. I met Lew and all the people in that whole trip and when Jack came into town, we all went to Big Sur." During these forays, she met other women of the Beat such as Carolyn Cassady and Joanne Kyger, but her closest friendship was with Diane di Prima, whom she met when they both joined the political group, the Diggers. "I knew the Beat men a lot better, was better friends with them. They took my poetry seriously." She lived at the East-West House and studied with Shunryu Suzuki Roshi.

An "omnivorous reader," Lenore was very familiar with Jack Kerouac's work and

© 1978 by Ed Buryn

Lenore Kandel at the Tribal Stomp, October 1, 1978, in Berkeley, California.

was especially fond of *On the Road*. His poetic style piqued her interest, and she found him to be inspiring to her own work. He too, was impressed by her intensity and intellect as well as her physical stature. It would be in his *Big Sur* that he would immortalize Lenore as "a big Rumanian monster beauty of some kind I mean with big purple eyes and very tall and big (but Mae West big), ... but also intelligent, well read, writes poetry, is a Zen student, knows everything..." She *was* tall, indeed taller and larger than Lew, yet she carried a distinctly female aura, described by Carolyn Cassady in *Off the Road* as a "Fertility Goddess."

Like many of the other Beats, her work provoked controversy. *The Love Book,* her most notorious collection of what she calls holy erotica, sent shock waves throughout the Bay Area when it was published in 1965. After police raids on the Psychedelic Shop and City Lights bookstore in San Francisco, the chapbook was deemed pornographic and obscene. When challenged in court, Lenore defended it as a "twenty-three-year search for an appropriate way to worship" and an attempt to "express her belief that sexual acts between loving persons are religious acts."

Although Lenore has been incapacitated since 1970 from a motorcycle accident with her then-husband, Hells Angel William Fritsch, she still reads voraciously on all subjects, including religion, and writes daily. "It's important to be a speaker of truth, especially if you put your words out there, they gotta be true."

Kenneth Rexroth once praised the fluidity and striking austerity of her words, which he saw as delineating the sharp paradoxes of the body and soul. Disregarding convention, she delves into the essence of being, writing provocative poems that intend to stir the heart as well as the mind. Her strong Buddhist influences mold emotions into stanzas, giving shape to the ineffable.

As evidenced by the following selections of her beautiful and controversial poetry, both old and new, Lenore Kandel is a true word alchemist.

ENLIGHTENMENT POEM

we have all been brothers, hermaphroditic as oysters
bestowing our pearls carelessly

no one yet had invented ownership
nor guilt   nor time

we watched the seasons pass, we were as crystalline as snow
and melted gently into newer forms
as stars spun round our heads

we had not learned betrayal

our selves were pearls
irritants transmuted into luster
and offered   carelessly

our pearls became more precious and our sexes static
mutability grew a shell, we devised different languages
new words for new concepts, we invented alarm clocks
Fences   loyalty
still…even now…making a feint at communion
         infinite perceptions
I remember
we have all been brothers
and offer   carelessly

■■■

SMALL PRAYER FOR FALLING ANGELS

too many of my friends are junkies
too many of my psychic kin tattoo invisible revelations on
    themselves
signing their manifestoes to etheric consciousness with little

hoofprint scars stretching from fingertip to fingertip
a gory religiosity akin to Kali's sacred necklace of fifty human heads

Kali-Ma, Kali-Mother; Kali-Ma, Kali-Mother
too many of my friends are running out of blood, their veins
are collapsing, it takes them half an hour to get a hit
their blood whispers through their bodies, singing its own
    death chant
in a voice of fire, in a voice of glaciers, in a voice of sand that
    blows
forever
over emptiness

Kali-Ma, remember the giving of life as well as the giving of
    death
      Kali-Ma...
Kali-Ma, remember the desire is for enlightenment and not
    oblivion
      Kali-Ma...
Kali-Ma, their bones are growing light; help them to fly
Kali-Ma, their eyes burn with the pain of fire; help them that
    they see
with clear sight

Kali-Ma, their blood sings death to them; remind them of life
that they be born once more
that they slide bloody through the gates of yes, that
they relax their hands nor try to stop the movement of the
    flowing now

too many of my friends have fallen into the white heat of the
    only flame
may they fly higher; may there be no end to flight

■ ■ ■

GOD/LOVE POEM

there are no ways of love but/beautiful/
    I love you all of them
I love you / your cock in my hand
    stirs like a bird
in my fingers
as you swell and grow hard in my hand
forcing my fingers open
with your rigid strength
you are beautiful / you are beautiful
you are a hundred times beautiful
I stroke you with my loving hands
    pink-nailed long fingers
I caress you
I adore you
my finger-tips...   my palms...
your cock rises and throbs in my hands
a revelation / as Aphrodite knew it

        there was a time when gods were purer
        / I can recall nights among the honeysuckle
        our juices sweeter than honey
        /we were the temple and the god entire/

I am naked against you
and I put my mouth on you   slowly
I have longing to kiss you
and my tongue makes worship on you
you are beautiful

your body moves to me
flesh to flesh
skin sliding over golden skin

as mine to yours
   my mouth   my tongue   my hands
my belly and my legs
against your mouth your love
sliding…   sliding…
our bodies move and join
unbearably

your face above me
  is the face of all the gods
    and beautiful demons
your eyes….

        love touches love
        the temple and the god
        are one

courtesy of Anne Waldman

Anne Waldman

Anne Waldman
Fast Speaking Woman
(1945–   )

"Anne Waldman is a poet orator, her body is an instrument for vocalization, her voice a trembling flame rising out of a strong body, her texts the accurate energetic fine notations of words with spoken music latent in mindful arrangement on the page."

—Allen Ginsberg

Born in 1945, Anne Waldman is a relative latecomer to the Beat scene, but her influence on the poetry world has been significant. A prolific writer, powerful reader of her own work, an editor of numerous magazines and anthologies over the years, and director of both the Seminal Poetry Project in New York and the Jack Kerouac School of Disembodied Poetics at the Naropa Institute in Boulder, she has been instrumental in creating renewed interest in poetry.

Anne Waldman's youth was anything but conventional. The family lived in Greenwich Village, the heart of the New York alternative artistic scene. Her father, a soldier during the Second World War, was, in Anne's own words, a "sensitive, literate, former bohemian piano player and a frustrated novelist." Her mother, formerly married to the son of the Greek poet Anghelos Sikelianos (whom she translated), had lived in Greece where she knew Isadora Duncan, among other "exile" artists. Both her parents and the bohemian/artistic setting in which Anne was raised were profound influences on her development as a woman and a poet. Close to the end of her life, Anne's mother was playing the role of the Spirit of Heroin in an off-off-Broadway production of William Burroughs' *Naked Lunch*.

At age six, Anne joined the Greenwich Village Children's Theatre, performing regularly until she was fourteen. As an adolescent in the fifties roaming the Village's bohemian-charged streets, she recalls seeing Gregory Corso, who then seemed to epito-mize the *poet maudit,* a romantic figure of her early imagination. At sixteen, while working with the American Shakespeare Festival, she met composer and jazz musi-cian David Amram, and a year later was introduced to Diane di Prima, who was studying Buddhism and occult religions while writing poems and plays and raising her first child.

Thus began a steady stream of friendships—with Allen Ginsberg (she lived on his farm in Cherry Valley for a time in the seventies), Joanne Kyger, Lew Welch, Philip Whalen, Michael McClure, Brenda Frazer, and later, Robert Duncan. She also was very involved with the so-called New York School of Poets and met Frank O'Hara before his death. In 1967, she met Gary Snyder and in 1968, William Burroughs. She became part of what she terms "a unique creative generation, a second generation Beat."

Beyond her own early writing, which was developing along "expansive chant-like structures" influenced by jazz, Anne's serious interest in Buddhism and subsequent travels in Asia also established a solid link to her Beat elders. (At age eighteen she had met the Mongolian lama Geshe Wangyal and later was to spend time in Nepal with Tibetan lama Chatral Sangye Dorje Rinpoche.) She identified strongly with "the ex-pansive visionary thrust of Ginsberg as poet-ambassador" and started to see herself clearly defined as "key player/persona in a hybrid outrider tradition influenced by the so-called New York School, the San Francisco Renaissance, Black Mountain," and ethnopoetics—lineages "that combined to foster a generation that would continue many of the experiments and thinking of its forebears ... a continuation of those mag-nificent epiphanies."

Anne credits the "freedoms espoused by the Beat Movement" as important spring-boards for the women's movement, noting, "I certainly felt empowered by the early shifts of consciousness that were taking place in the '60s as a result of the freedoms and explorations espoused by the Beats and others."

As a student at Bennington College, Waldman also came under the influence of Howard Nemerov, Stanley Edgar Hyman, Bernard Malamud, and Barbara Hernstein Smith. It was during this period that she first traveled abroad, to Greece and Egypt, a vivid journey that "ignited a life-long fascination with studying and traveling within other cultures." After attending the Berkeley Poetry Festival in 1965, where she heard the works of Charles Olson, Ed Dorn, Ted Berrigan, Lenore Kandel, and others, she returned to New York, where she produced poetry and plays for Riverside Radio, saw herself published in *City Magazine,* co-founded *Angel Hair* magazine (and, later, *The World)* and went to work for The Poetry Project at St. Marks Church-in-the-Bowery, becoming its director in 1968.

Her own books soon started to appear, including *Giant Night, Baby Breakdown,* and *No Hassles.* In 1974, she was invited along with Allen Ginsberg to help found what became the Jack Kerouac School of Disembodied Poetics at the experimental, Buddhist-inspired Naropa Institute in Boulder, Colorado. That same year Lawrence Ferlinghetti published *Fast Speaking Woman,* subsequent books have incuded *Makeup on Empty Space, Skin Meat Bones, Kill or Cure,* and the ongoing epic *Iovis Books I* and *II,* her "all encompassing exploratory collage/argument with male energy."

On being a woman writer she has this to say:

> I pushed myself hard and fought for having a life and career as a writer in a field that was blatantly (at first) dominated by men. You make sacrifices. Relationships suffer because men were/are not used to strong women with purpose and discipline. There's a subtle psychological discrimination that goes on. It is an added pressure for women because they are often not taken seriously and have to push against a certain bias. I think I became an over-achiever for this reason.
>
> [However,] I came later into the beat nexus (1970s) and did not experience the same frustrations as some of the maverick women did. . . . The '50s were a conservative time and it was difficult for artistic 'bohemian' women to live outside the norm. Often they were incarcerated by their families, or were driven to suicide. Many talented women perished. But male writers of this literary generation were not entirely to blame, it was the ignorance of a whole culture.

Anne, who has consistently sought "a hermaphroditic literature, a transvestite literature, and finally a poetics of transformation beyond gender," has always found encouragement, support, and inspiration from her male mentors and contemporaries:

> I was treated extremely well by male literary "elders." I have studied and absorbed and benefited by the wisdom of their own writing and activity in the world. This friendship and support has been a real blessing. I hung out with them, worked with them, travelled with them with equal billing as a poet, and have never felt an ounce of condescension.

Anne Waldman teaching at the Jack Kerouac School of Disembodied Poetics at the Naropa Institute, 1975.

excerpt from FAST SPEAKING WOMAN

I'm the woman never made a fool of
woman who hides her heart
woman hidden in long sleeves
   sleeves of green & gold
I'm the woman shelved one night
   while he beds down with the deer
I'm the woman wandering the forest
   tilt moon
   full moon lights up a honey eye
   half moon he returns
I'm the woman waiting
The woman counting moments
A moment never existed & he walks in
I'm the woman who scribes this text
   long after the animals lie down
Chopping wood outside the retreat hut
Stoking the fire with my little stick
A candle lit to light a teacher's face
I learn by books
I learn by singing
I recite the chant of one hundred syllables
I write down my messages to the world
The wind carries them invisibly,
   staccato impulses to the world

I'm the woman stirring the soup pot
The woman who makes circles
   with her arm
stirring, singing this song about the
   Woman-Who-Does-Things
many actions complete themselves
& repeat

she does this
I'm the woman who does these things
many actions carry words
I say them, woman-who-signifies
I light the fire
I sit like a Buddha
I feed the animals outside the door
I blow out the lamp

I'm the woman travelling inside her head
I'm the woman on the straw mat
I bewitch the stars to my heart
   points of light, arrows to my heart
Pierce me as I sleep

I'm the night woman
I'm the terrible-night woman
I travel to steal your lover
   to steal your food, to take your words

I'm the day woman
I'm the doll woman
I'm the dew woman

Day woman mends & organizes
Doll woman sits & stares
Dew woman is moist to the touch

I'm the Amogasiddhi woman
I'm activity demon
I wait for him
I walk away
Busy woman to light up the day!
Don't touch me I'm hurrying hurrying

fierce light of day he doesn't exist
mayhem on the next block a proletarian urge
& old tones deep from his gut I shut ears to
hold back, hold back
I'm the woman shouting "Hold"
I'm running down the street now
shout: "Hold, hold"

& old tones hold back ears sharp lobes hold
tainted I'll strap pathos back
that love comes to this ecto-morgue
& ties on craving & passion
but face I loved—
die! die! I'm the woman who loved
A woman who lost

turn it around
I'm the woman in charge
the woman who never succumbed
woman off the couch
woman up and about
I'm the organizing woman
I'll put this place under my spell

photo by Louis R. Cartwright, courtesy of Anne Waldman

Anne Waldman at CBGB's in New York City, 1978.

I'm the woman who drives
the woman who drove to Siliguri
I'm the woman who walked to Nepal
I took a train to rest my weary limbs
I'm the one who took a sponge bath
the water was cold
another woman soaped my back
I'm the woman slept upright in a cave a hundred years
I'm the woman over the next peak
I learned to drive on the Peak to Peak Highway

all my signals intact
I provided fresh fuel to the hikers
Fed children from my milky breasts
I rode the crest of my own wave
I thirsted for books, books
I took a plane to not calm my nerves
I rode a boat for expediency's sake

I'm the chopping wood woman
the woman with the axe
I'm the trailblazer
I clear the woods
I take out my own mind

■■■

TWO HEARTS

after Sir Philip Sidney

She's got my heart and I've got hers
It was fair, we fell in love
I hold hers precious and mine she would miss
There never was anything like this
Her heart in my brain keeps us one
My heart in her guides thoughts and feelings
She loves my heart for once it was hers
I love hers because it lived in me
I once wounded her, it was misunderstanding
And then my heart hurt for her heart
For as from me on her her hurt did sit
So I felt still in me her hurt hurt, it
Both of us hurt simultaneously and then we saw how
We're stuck with each other's hearts now.

■■■

A PHONECALL FROM FRANK O'HARA
"That all these dyings may be life in death"

I was living in San Francisco
My heart was in Manhattan
It made no sense, no reference point
Hearing the sad horns at night,
fragile evocations of female stuff
The 3 tones (the last most resonant)
were like warnings, haiku—muezzins at dawn
The call came in the afternoon
"Frank, is that really you?"

I'd awake chilled at dawn
in the wooden house like an old ship
Stay bundled through the day
sitting on the stoop to catch the sun
I lived near the park whose deep green
over my shoulder made life cooler
Was my spirit faltering, grown duller?
I want to be free of poetry's ornaments,
its duty, free of constant irritation,
me in it, what was grander reason
for being? Do it, why? (Why, Frank?)
To make the energies dance etc.

My coat a cape of horrors
I'd walk through town
or impending earthquake. Was that it?
Ominous days. Street shiny with
hallucinatory light on sad dogs,
too many religious people, or a woman
startled me by her look of indecision
near the empty stadium

I walked back spooked by
my own darkness
Then Frank called to say
"What? Not done complaining yet?
Can't you smell the eucalyptus,
have you never neared the Pacific?
'While frank and free /call for
musick while your veins swell'"
he sang, quoting a metaphysician
"Don't you know the secret, how to

photo by Bill Yoscary, courtesy of Anne Waldman

Gary Snyder and Anne Waldman at a poetry reading.

wake up and see you don't exist, but
that does, don't you see phenomena
is so much more important than *this?*
I always love *that.*"
"Always?" I cried, wanting to believe him
"Yes.""But say more! How can you if
it's sad & dead?" "But that's just it!
If! It isn't. It doesn't want to be
Do you want to be?" He was warning to his song
"Of course I don't have to put up with as
much as you do these days. These *years.*
But I do miss the color, the architecture,
the talk. You know, it *was* the life!
And dying is such an insult. After all
I was in love with breath and I loved
embracing those others, the lovers,
with my *body.*" He sighed & laughed
He wasn't quite as I'd remembered him
Not less generous, but more abstract
Did he even have a voice now, I wondered
or did I think it up in the middle
of this long day, phone in hand now
dialing Manhattan

■■■

XVIII

"I AM THE GUARD!"

Some years ago she founded a poetics school on the spine of the Rocky Moun-
tain continent with a close poet friend. The school carries the name of Jack
Kerouac. They both agree that the angelic writer had realized the First Noble
Truth of Suffering & composed his mind elegantly & spontaneously on the
tongue to the page. He also entered the American culture, not always sympa-
thetically. She often heard his sounds in her head, whole lines even, & many
years later is invited to participate in a reading honoring his work at the local
university. "October in the railroad earth." She writes these words, to be read
aloud, which caress his. The challenge of the elder poet-men is their emotional
pitch she wants to set her own higher than. Are these not masters? Her
presumption is boundless. Her poem sees no end in sight if she continues to
honor & measure her life & work against theirs. She visits her father, who
speaks darkly from the corner of his room. The political climate is depressing.
She likes to travel back in time.

> *"Stop the murder and the suicide!*
>   *All's well!*
>   *I am the Guard"*
>   —Jack Kerouac

You are fun
you are god
you are
"far-out-like-a-light"

Raiders, a game
   Something about skull & bones, black white logo writ 'gainst astro turf.
Everyone looks into a bowl. And then the players start ejaculating into the air
Just like the beer commercials.

Could be London, shopping for just the right male dolls, a black one, yes, a white one too. One Christian doll, perhaps a Pope. The other one is one of the 3 kings from Orient R.

They will coexist on my little shelf. And another comes in gold, Jambhala for wealth

the razor in-cut of void meat Buddha

Dear Jack Kerouac
who'd rather die than be famous
who ran away from college in 1941
into Memorial cello time
& spilt his gut
50 pesos
Aztec blues
A vast cavern, eh?
I caught (he did) a cold from the sun
upside-down language
ulatbamsi Bre-hack! Brop?
Of the cloud-mopped afternoon

and turn this lady upside down

dyuar aham, prthivi tvam

May Vishnu prepare the womb;
May Tvastr fashion the forms;
May Prajapati cause the seed to flow,
May Dhatr place the seed within thee

Let the marriage begin
Let the fucking begin
to people our numbers
what it's about, the fucking,
what it's

about to
become, a form,
to worry about fucking
& we are dying in it,
of it, inside the form
which is happy illusion's
mind bog anyhoop

but you can go (go now! go now! in spite of yr blakity blakity brain)

But keep me,
whatever-your-name-is-deity
a terrible form
A "krodha-murti"
Keep me terrible
for I curse the day
I wed the poets

for I have sinned
I have slept in the arms of
another "husband"
I have advocated revolution
in the marketplace
I have looked
in the face of
Fidel Castro

("only the laboring man adds anything to society")

& wept
but see how
he is lost in
his "grey beard & fuzzy thought"
Fidel now

I am old now
(the father is speaking now
& of Kerouac
his indulgent-boy word run,
sometimes hard to keep company with. . .
slowly, fully clothed,
lying on his bed of thorns, my father
Room shuttered,
she goes to pull the light in)

I have nothing to live for
No direction
No direction to go

Came here to die
I am waiting to die
I'd rather die than be famous
I never thought I would live it this long

Cry for the leaves to cover me come come over me

who has accomplished
his children
Don't break
your tenderness

When the wind blows
you feel it
Same for the country…
you feel it

I felt once for the oppressed of the world
& studied Marx, Hegel, Kant, Lenin
& the Communist Party meetings I went to
had no connection to reality

You see how it changes?

Creatures of light!
That's what we are & leaves
It's all happening in snow
But I shudder
what's been buried in the grave?
Dust.

Depression drives me down
Ninety devils jokin' with me
I'm not quite clinical

But we are similar in our thinking
he, me & you too

although you are super
o logistic!woman

Vishnu pervades you all through the night
& day comes
& he is still your maker & destroyer
What are the marks of existence where they
Empty of themselves?

Put away habit, come live with me

Take this love from your father
it comes through a wizened boy body

I understand how beings in their time
endure unbearable suffering

*why listen to me
an old man*

call it to action

Where were you when the last Ancient Forests were being destroyed,
along with the 6,000 species which called them home?

Old-growth forest
dies with me,
an obsolete man
Hundreds of trees
falling every day

We throw away our last ancient forest for Happy Meal boxes. . .

You could say
we live in
a life vest mentality
swim for life
Lay it all that, be bobby
be buddy

How optative?
go Sutter's home (his gold)

going my way a marriage
had a life in the war
age or ache in breast
war was a life it woke me up
a long time was always
a long time
in war

dear Jack:
not-of-war reflected in that mirror

& when you returned life was sweet

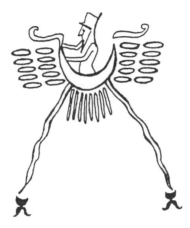

heart of breast would
swell up, proud
to die
proud to enter her womb
with renewed optimism

& thinking of all the ways to die

to die at war

to die fighting

the way he looks at home,
away at war
& how in marriage
Father, I call him,
captain Kerouac
or husband
needing him most
by his words

(forget the deeds here)

Operation a Just Cause
to weep
a cutting of deals is
1,000 Panamanians dead
is a cutter of deals
billion & $^1/_2$ property damage
is a cutting of deals
& 23 servicemen dead of the US of A
a "federal posse" intervenes
of a necessary day December 20, 1989,
a cutting day of deals

read it, get it? O cutter of deals
money lauder drive all the blame
or drug traffic doubles
& lights go out for Miami's bulletin
in a cutting of deals

narco kleptocracy
a kind of joy
Medellin cartel
a risk you run to cut a deal
kill what "we" we bounce back on you
& kill what "we" we needed once
& serve a darker purpose
Plap play play plap plap plapity gap

not to wax sentiment, a groove
but pertains to any deal
the speedboat was a vessel
quick trip outta here
(the way the sun goes down in idyllic valley)

(he said in a TV movie about
a deal, episode of a mother implicated)

It, the vessel,
carried goods
crossed a border
was fast
crossed the harmless headline
& criminality when "smoking gun"
is your
position
& headline for

growing
narco-biz
a kind of showcase
or stop
joking with men

I love you Jack
I love you Neal

you take on macho landscape with
the freeingest sensibility, men
what ban
what sex do you play
arms sales
back up to plead guilty
& make the words sigh true
political
what care they back for then
what bitch to plead
immediate action toward Syntex
toward Sabotage or reduction flight
toward Capitol Cities front for CIA
just bought by ABC
forget another *petite histoire*
I love you for what I hate
crossing the country in my way
it was fast, I kept the notebook
I said poof bang boom

I said shut a yap me mon
what cooks mon and he was his sleepy dreamy
you just gotta look at me as I crawl outta here eyes
slumps at table, wake now and me with me big sentimentally hot heart setimentalitopality

me see em
& they are all the poets in my book
a big heart church
& later down on Market Street I saw all kinda colorful street people

Dear A:

    With millions of others I spent last weekend transfixed by the Senate
Judiciary Committee hearing. Can you believe that men like Orrin Hatch are in
political power? There are others on the committee that make me nauseous, but
Hatch seems to be the embodiment of evil. It was hard to get to sleep after
watching for 9 or 10 hours this panel of middle-aged white men and listening to
their inanities. The hearing to me was not a question of Thomas vs Hill, but
instead a question of the sad state of our country.
    I'm woefully depressed here these days, thankful for your love. I can tell you
forcefully that I support you in any decisions you may make.
    Much much love,

      Daddy

        from this concentrated spark of raw energy what they call
        quantum chromodynamics predicts that a vast swarm
        of fundamental "quark" particles called "gluons"
        will spontaneously spring into existence

I, your *Clocharde Celeste,* spoke to you TiJean in a dream:
So I write about Heaven.

Jan Kerouac
The Next Generation
(1952–1996)

"I know I have my own style of writing, which is very different from Jack's.... People may read my stuff and think, This is Jack Kerouac's daughter, let's see if she's as good as he is. But it's not necessary to make a comparison like that, because I wasn't trying to emulate his type of writing."

—Jan Kerouac

an Kerouac, only child of Jack Kerouac, was a writer with her own strong voice, who seemed to touch upon many of the same subjects as her father: adventures down the open road, alienation from the mainstream, and the wild times that result from the combination of the two. Jan saw her father only twice, but his effect upon her seemed to be palpable in the wanderlust lifestyle that she led.

In her teens, before Jack Kerouac's death, he and Jan spent time on the telephone. He urged her to write and he told her about her royal ancestry, saying, "You're not a Canuck, you're a Bretonne." Two of her autobiographical novels, *Baby Driver* and *Trainsong*, are similar to the narrative style that her father employed, but Jan Kerouac seems to be able to detach herself from her circumstances more than her father was able to and writes in a less confessional way. "He was very emotional," said Jan, "and everything he saw was directly related to his soul." This detachment, coupled with her great narrative ability, makes her writing sleek and fast. Jan herself said that her writing was partially of her own design and partially an experiential search for her father. There is no denying, however, that she has an individual voice that lends itself easily to a story.

Facing Page: The Kerouac Legacy: Jan and her father Jack (inset).

Photo courtesy of Jan Kerouac; inset photo courtesy of Carolyn Cassady.

Jan Kerouac was born to Joan Haverty in Albany, New York, and the circumstances leading up to her birth are relevant to her subsequent relationship with her father. In the fall of 1950, Joan was dating a friend of Jack's and Allen Ginsberg's named Bill Cannastra. Bill was, by all accounts, a brilliant yet flawed man who fueled his self-destructive tendencies with heavy drinking. On October 12, of that year, a drunken Cannastra was decapitated when he stuck his head out of the window of a moving subway car. Jack moved into his vacant loft soon after and met Joan Haverty.

Although he had just met her, Jack fell in love with the twenty-year-old beauty, and the two were married a month later. Although the romance quickly drained from this whirlwind courtship, the two tried their best to adapt to marriage-on-the-fly. Joan finally threw Jack out when he suggested she terminate her pregnancy.

Janet Michelle Kerouac was born on February 16, 1952. Despite a remarkable resemblance between father and daughter, Jack would publicly deny that the child was his. Because of this, Jan met her father only twice: once at a blood test to determine paternity when she was nine, and once when she went to visit him when she was fifteen.

Jan moved with her mother to the Lower East Side of Manhattan and developed a rather accelerated lifestyle for a schoolgirl. Preferring the excitement of dropping acid rather than attending junior high school, she was in and out of juvenile detention centers in her teens. She began her own life on the road earlier than her father— she was only fifteen—and bounced around the states with a reckless abandon that Neal Cassady would have been hard pressed to keep pace with. She worked a variety of odd jobs to support herself and began to write accounts of her life.

Jan Kerouac's memories of childhood were of Joan, Lower East Side tenements, Puerto Rican playgrounds, stories about Jack, and juvie hall. Jan and Joan moved a lot, and thus being on the move became characteristic of Jan's life. Escaping New York in 1967, Jan went to Mexico—the first of many such trips abroad.

Marriage in 1968 did little to impede the momentum of the road. Jan and her husband, John, traveled and lived throughout the West and the Northwest. It was while living in a commune in Little River, California, that Jan learned of her father's death.

After divorce, remarriage, and divorce again, Jan experienced many moves, many relationships, and many vocations. It was during this period that she wrote *Baby Driver* and *Trainsong*. It was also during this time that she first met the cast of characters from her father's generation—Carolyn Cassady, Allen Ginsberg, William Burroughs, Peter Orlovsky, Lawrence Ferlinghetti, and Gregory Corso. Life was interesting.

In 1981, *Baby Driver* was published to critical acclaim. In it, Jan described the meetings with her father, her first experiences with drugs and sex, and the exploits of a life lived at full throttle. *Trainsong,* published in 1988, picked up where *Baby Driver* left off.

The eighties were rich with memories of travels "from Camden to Casablanca," on freighters and freight trains, through Bavaria to Berlin, with trips deviating from any direct route. Life was not easy, but then she did not make it so. Work was sporadic—a baker, a groom, a fisherman, a maid, writing the liner notes for *The Kerouac Collection,* a Grammy nominee. Indeed her father's daughter.

Joan's daughter, too. After living in New York, Maine, and Maui, and visiting her half-sister in Turkey, in 1989 Jan returned to her mother's home in Oregon. It was difficult for Jan when her indefatigable, beautiful mother died of breast cancer in 1990. Jan left her half-brother and half-sister in Eugene and moved to Puerto Rico with the intention of living on the beach and writing a third book—the wildly freewheeling and loosely autobiographical *Parrot Fever,* which has yet to be published. Her momentum was interrupted, however, when she suffered kidney failure and had to return to the States for dialysis.

Natalie Jackson

Natalie was an engaging and resourceful redhead whom Neal Cassady hung out with in San Francisco in 1955, spending their days together at the racetrack, blowing much of Neal's settlement money from a railroad accident. Natalie was a sensitive girl who became easily agitated when Neal was not around. One day, Neal became worried about Natalie when she tried to slash her wrists and he asked Jack Kerouac to watch her while he was at work. Jack tried to soothe her wounded soul with Buddhist serenades and wine until Neal got home. Once Neal was home and had fallen asleep, Natalie went up to the roof and tried to slash herself with glass from the skylight. A neighbor saw her and called the police. A rescue was attempted, but Natalie escaped and fell six stories to her death.

Jan died suddenly in Albuquerque, New Mexico, after continuing health problems. She had been fighting to gain control of her father's estate, which is currently controlled by the family of Stella Sampas, Jack Kerouac's third wife. Jan was hoping to keep her father's estate intact, not see it sold off bit by bit.

At forty-four, Jan truly embodied the notion of taking oneself where one needed to go—sometimes willfully, sometimes because that's where the road led. She was inspired by a blood legacy. Tragically, her death came too early for one with so much renewed vibrancy and commitment.

Gerald Nicosia was Jan Kerouac's best friend and advocate until her death. Here, he offers his uniquely close perspective on Jan's life and work.

I knew Jan Kerouac as a writer before I ever met her as a person. Early on in my research for my biography of her father, *Memory Babe,* I read a chapter from an "autobiographical work" by her, tentatively called Everthreads; it was published in the *City Lights Journal,* No. 4, in 1978. Her writing was unbelievably lively, sensitive, humorous, and thoughtful for a young woman of 26.

When I met Jan a few months later, I was—like most other men on the planet - captivated by her stunning good looks and scintillating intelligence. She seemed to have something interesting to say about almost everything, and—what was immediately apparent—she loved language. Putting words together for her was making something permanent, something of beauty that would last, unlike the fragile earthly beauties of home and family that kept fading beyond her grasp.

I was only two years older than Jan, but I had a couple of degrees in literature, and Jan looked to me to tell her whether what she was writing was any good. I was able to help with a little grammatical editing; but as far as I was concerned, Jan's work was basically untouchable. It already bore the mark of a unique vision and a unique voice. She was not writing because she was a famous man's daughter. She was writing because she had already lived far more broadly and intensely than most people, and because it was important to her to preserve as much of her life as possible in language.

And for someone with almost no formal schooling, she picked up new words, and even the basics of several foreign languages, with an amazingly sure grasp. She was a living argument for the fact that language ability is indeed in the genes.

After the publication of *Baby Driver* in 1981, several years went by before I saw Jan again. She was making the most of celebrity, traveling everywhere, lecturing and reading her work, going through men, drink, drugs, and every sort of experience at a frighteningly fast pace. In 1985, just back from Baja California, she stopped in San Francisco to see me, to have lunch, show off the new paperback edition of *Baby Driver* with a picture of her leaning against a big car, and to tell me about her next novel. She was calling it *Loverbs,* a title which meant to convey that action was some-how her way of searching for love. The more I got to know Jan, in fact, the more I came to realize that where everyone saw this fantastically gorgeous, sexy, daring young woman (for whom taking off her clothes at parties was no big deal), there was really

Jan Kerouac at twenty-six years old.

© 1996 by Fred W. McDarrah

inside Jan a lonely, rejected little girl dying to be truly loved. That she never found that big, true love was perhaps the greatest tragedy of her life.

Loverbs was finally published as *Trainsong,* a title which came from the area of Eugene, Oregon, near the railroad tracks where her mother lived. By and large, the book got better reviews than *Baby Driver,* and with good reason. Carolyn See in the *Los Angeles Times* picked out the tremendous sadness that underlay much of Jan's adventure writing, and it was that exquisite chord of sadness—like a Beethoven sonata—that touched me most when I read the book. My favorite passage in it will always be the scene at Allen Ginsberg's house in Boulder, on October 21, when she looks into the blue flame of the furnace grate and says "Daddy," wondering how she can ever find her father again after so much lost time.

When Jan died, she was struggling to finish her third novel, *Parrot Fever,* which would have completed the trilogy of what it meant to be the daughter of the Beat Generation's greatest icon. That book marks a great deal of growth in her as a writer. She was writing in the third person, to obtain greater objectivity, and she had split herself into two half sisters, both of them scarred by a missing father. One has gone into the depths of life, into drugs, stripping, and petty crime; the other has become a rootless wanderer and a writer. Somehow she wanted to make sense of her schizophrenic life by bringing both those characters together at the death of their mother— which was to be the death of Jan's own mother, Joan, on Mother's Day, 1990. The theme of the book was to have been loss and rebirth, something Jan knew in her soul since she was old enough to notice that "Daddy" wasn't there.

Because she was working on tape at the end of her life, it is unclear how much of *Parrot Fever* was completed. Ideally it will be published with the other two novels someday as part of the trilogy she intended—a movement from joy and exuberance through pain, sorrow, and loss, to final understanding and redemption. No other child of a Beat hero has attempted such an ambitious chronicle. Even in its incompletion, Jan Kerouac's work is a literary milestone that will surely gain in recognition and admiration as time passes and her accomplishment can stand free of the adversity and controversy that were, besides his name, a famous father's only legacy to her.

Here is an excerpt from Jan Kerouac's Trainsong, *telling the surreal story of the time she was cast as an extra in the feature film* Heartbeat, *depicting the triangle between Carolyn Cassady, Neal Cassady, and Jack Kerouac. It is at once tragic and hilarious.*

CHAPTER 22

In September I was offered a job as an extra in *Heartbeat*, a movie about my father's ménage a trois with the Cassadys. One smog-laden morn, John drove me down to the shoot on Fourth Street. The Acropolis Café was just the place for a beat generation coffeehouse scene: a Greek restaurant in downtown L.A., unchanged since the thirties, its bare green walls easily took on the ambience of San Francisco in 1956.

In the wardrobe trailer, I sat right next to Nick Nolte, who was having his face expertly plastered at the same time I was having my hair firmly yanked up into a tortuous pompadour. I had a half-pint carton of milk in my lap, and when he squeezed behind me to get out, I pulled the flimsy director's chair up closer to the dresser to give him more room and spilled the milk on my lap. Luckily I was still wearing my own jeans. That was just the beginning. Later, outside, I met John Heard, who was to play my father, and Sissy Spacek, who was cast as Carolyn Cassady. We all had plenty of time to gab in the sun, like children dressed up for Sunday School—metamorphosed into stiff anachronistic manikins. I helped John practice his Jack lip, showing him one of the few things I knew about my father, which was the way he stuck out his lower lip, easy for me because I had inherited it. And Sissy and I struck up a conversation, trading childhood stories: hers about Texas, in a husky drawl which I found to be hypnotic, and mine about New York. Meanwhile hoards of L.A. weirdos were pestering Sissy about her role as Carrie and asking her for autographs, and some energetic photographer was snapping rolls of photos of the two of us sitting on a packing crate.

Finally, we were allowed to enter the Acropolis Café. Yards of thick black cyclopsian equipment were dragged and wheeled into the cool, high-ceilinged place, where everyone again waited and waited-this time sitting at tables. Then the holy trinity took their places next to the biggest cyclops. The rest of us were supposed to comprise the background, blurred anonymous figures. My job was to sit at a table where two guys were playing a game of chess: to follow their moves like a cat, then to look mildly bored and giggle occasionally in my slinky beige crepe dress with pearl embroidery and massive shoulder pads, three-tone high heels, and heavily sprayed hairdo. We were all told to puff like mad on our Camel straights to produce a thick, smoke-filled atmosphere, and females were instructed to kiss a red blotch of lipstick onto the ends of their cigs.

Nick Nolte startled us all with a bout of spasmodic stamping and shuffling of feet, and drumming on the table, a curiously dynamic way of clearing his head—or, perhaps, essence of Neal Cassady popping through? Then he'd shout, "Okay, ready!" and the time machines would roll.

Either I was slowly asphyxiating from the Camel smoke, or toxic chemicals in the makeup were infiltrating my bloodstream, but gazing up at the lazily revolving black fans in the pressed waffle tin ceiling—I forgot *everything*. All I knew was, there I was. Camels burning in the ashtray, surrounded by outdated housewives in curlers and scarves, in some strangely contrived bubble of time when I wasn't even *born* yet. I experienced a disturbing notion: could I be my own mother? And who is that dark-haired man over there pouting in baggy blue pants, talking about poetry to the blond couple? My father? My absentee husband? Where is this? California? Colorado? New York? What is this? Who am I?

"—I'm drunk, in the middle of the afternoon—" The husky golden Texas twang of the blond woman brought me reeling back to reality, the dubious reality, of a movie set, spotlights softened with smoke spirals...*Oh, that's right, I'm just an extra. Extra, extra, read all about it!*

That afternoon I wandered home up Hollywood Boulevard in milk-stiff pants, with spray-stiff hair, feeling like some kind of a doll that had been starched and pressed flat, two dimensional, and escaped from a toy-store window. But I also felt fulfilled in a funny way, as though the Neptunian illusions of Tinseltown had wrapped my father in Technicolor celluloid and brought him back to me special delivery, straight into my arms.

■■■

CHAPTER 47

So now after all this, the true flavor comes through...You thought it would be bitter but it's only nutty after all. The cup at your teeth chatters in triumph. Like a knave caught with his pants down in a stable, *men* are finally clarified for you: little boys grown up. Innocents and psychos alike take on a new softness. A pane of glass between you and the world has been sprayed clean, though you know it will soon collect another film of dustlets. The black man in a suit, carrying a shotgun, his own little boy buried far within, sinks down into straw, preparing for a long journey. A chorus of women's voices grates from the radio—"Freeeeeeeee"—like several different kinds of vinegar.

Outside later, while trudging past dried-up adobes, a burnt smell will come to your nostrils, all the way from New York City and your childhood, a smell which was no doubt created by some men burning trash or perhaps pretzels. Men are all about—manly men, glorious men, running the world as they have indeed always done. But no man is in your bed—at the moment. What is the meaning of this masculine vacuum? Is God conducting an experiment? Men are out there being adventurous, filling the stories you've heard: wondrous tales of storms at sea, restaurant heists, smoky sixties scenes from Mitten's Playhouse in Harlem. These are the myths of your girlhood, these realms of intensely dangerous glamour, glorified crime, far-off lands, inaccessible even to most men.

So is it really any wonder that you choose the paths seldom taken? It was all in the cards, the house of cards, the condemned tenements of cards in which you grew up. And now, now that all has fluttered down to the ground, upset by the swinging pendulum of a wrecking ball which may be only the brass counterweight of a grandfather clock, now that all the bricks and lathe and plaster and cards have fallen and burned along with the trash and pretzels, now that the ash has blown away, you can finally see. The smoke has cleared and there is room now for other dreams. Ashes to ashes, dusk to dusk.

And the perennial "I love you"—so taboo that we feel compelled to try it out anyway, as a sort of exorcism to prove it doesn't matter even though it does. The eyes—*watch the eyes*. To stare unwaveringly into the eyes of the other...there's the rub.

Blue eyes looking at green eyes beholding azure eyes staring into hazel eyes piercing gray eyes bathing emerald eyes streaming through sapphire eyes adoring onyx eyes…and something magic takes place. The whole face begins to shimmer with life force, sheer animal power…a feeling of fusion—twin fetuses in cellular bondage. Sweat, heat, tears….oh so old, so well known, yet the mystery never ends, forever reborn. Flesh and blood tipping the scales of a giant golden carp.

I'm stuck fast, a South Carolina tar-baby in this ancient Chinese tapestry. With a golden needle quivering in my left ankle and a silver one in my right wrist, I lie in the realm of water dragons, utterly calm, watching blue smoke spiral up from my feet as the warm horseshoe of a meridian comes to life.

Don't fondle the doctor. Br'er Terrapin has fallen on his back an' can't get up. Lord, Lord, Lord, you don't know what trouble is till you fall on your back an' can't get up. By 'n by Br'er Rabbit come an' help you outta dat hole. But what if de doctor wear shorts, an' your hand jes' touch his balls? Br'er Fox can't *help* but fondle de doctor *den*. So shame on the shaman. Daddy don't live in dat New York City no more…Daddy don't don't live nowhere, no more.

And so time passes, passes by, passes over, passes away and through and pass the butter, please. Sometimes time passes by so fast…you can't even see those seconds make their little streaks of re-entry into your heart.

© Marie-Andrée Cossette

On top of the world:
Jan Kerouac in Los Angeles, 1978.

318

6

THE ARTISTS

The Rose, by Jay DeFeo, 1958–1966. Oil on canvas with wood, beads, pearls and mica.

Reverse: The Six Gallery, site of the "Howl" happening, circa 1957.

Jay DeFeo
The Rose
(1929–1989)

"The process of creation that unites America's many artists like the painter Jay DeFeo…is ultimately, a mystery. What is known is that it involves intellect and emotion and sheer physical power, sifted and poured and exploded through the artist's personality. It is work, and then again, it is play….But it is sublime as well, in the moment of communication: one human being to one human being. Then it is a joy to both."

—John Fitzgerald Kennedy, 1962

Jay DeFeo's paintings still shock and provoke audiences with a raw and retina-searing passion. Her multi-medium abstracts were massive—and mythic in more than proportion. Her work was an attempt to create art that "would have a center."

Born Joan DeFeo on March 31, 1929, Jay discovered her vocation early on, graduating from a San Jose High School and attending the University of California at Berkeley. Her early artistic endeavors were so impressive that she became the first woman to receive the Sigmund Martin Heller Traveling Scholarship from U.C. Berkeley. She jumped at the chance to utilize her scholarship to travel through Europe, studying masterpieces in Florence and Paris and experimenting with her own painting.

Upon her return to San Francisco, her work caught the eye of Walter Hopps, the owner of a small Bay Area gallery, and was included in his shows in 1955. By 1957, she had been featured at the Ferus Gallery's introductory exhibition. Her exposure soon moved her to the forefront of contemporary art in the Bay Area as the scene began to change dramatically from an emphasis on formalism to collage, multimedia, and abstraction.

At the same time, Jay's personal life began to thrive as well. She met another young San Francisco artist, Wally Hedrick, and they began exchanging artistic critiques. Wally, the son of a used-car dealer in Pasadena, was a Korean War veteran who attended California College of Arts and Crafts in Oakland. An iconoclastic painter, from 1957 to 1973 he challenged the Vietnam War through *The Vietnam Series,* monochromatic black paintings in various shapes and sizes. Sharing an obsession for painting and nonconformity, their friendship turned romantic.

The relationship began, according to Jay, one day when Wally scavenged for food in her kitchen. He claims, however, that her refrigerator was more useful as a hamper for dirty clothes than for food storage. Upon seeing the laundry piled inside, he said, "the scales fell from my eyes like St. Paul." Her utter disregard for convention convinced Wally of her artistry, and they were married shortly thereafter.

Their reputation soon spread to New York, and in 1959 they were featured in one of the most important East and West Coast collaborative exhibits of modern art, *16 Americans.* Shown at the Museum of Modern Art, it provided an opportunity to survey exciting new artists. Neither of them realized the impact of such an exhibit, the type of a breakthrough most of their contemporaries were dying for; they didn't even attend the show. Jay recalled: "Wally and I didn't realize the prestige of being included in such a show.... The whole show was kind of a coming out party, I discovered later."

For the next ten years, Jay and Wally were the typical bohemian couple. Though poor, they were regulars at the lavish San Francisco party scene. Musically as well as artistically inclined, Wally was adept at playing the banjo. After joining the Studio 13 Jass Band, he was introduced, along with Jay, to saxophonist Paul Beattie, who brought them to his apartment building at 2322 Fillmore Street. They moved into a $65-per-month flat in his building and turned it into an artist's dream: most of the space was occupied by their unfinished art, painting supplies, and a cache of poets and painters.

Fillmore Street was more than just a home for their paintings. Between Jay's monstrous and somber paintings and Wally's boisterous and mixed-media artwork, the friendships that formed in the flat were just as disparate. The apartment became a haven for other struggling artists and Beat poets, as well as the site of many parties. Long nights of cheap red wine and spontaneous poetry provided an atmosphere conducive to art and poetry alike. Friends such as Joan Brown, Bruce Conner, Michael

McClure, Joanna McClure, Jack Spicer, and Ed Moses could often be found hanging out in the cluttered apartment, swapping stories and drinking wine straight from the bottle.

October 13, 1955, marked the San Francisco melding of the avant garde art and Beat poetry scene. The Six Gallery, located at 3119 Fillmore Street, had begun modestly in 1954. The owners, six local artists, catered primarily to other small, locally known visual artists. Through the prodding of Wally Hedrick and poet Michael McClure, a reading was organized there for October 13. Jay's paintings lined the walls as Allen Ginsberg introduced the world to his newest poem, "Howl." Allen read while Neal Cassady listened in fascination and Jack Kerouac sat on the floor in front, exhorting Allen with shouts of "Go" while rhythmically tapping his wine jug. It was the place to be, and the Six Gallery's reading of "Howl" made literary history. The gallery's notoriety was short-lived, however; it closed thirty-six months after its grand opening.

Jay was on to other things. Along with fellow artist Bruce Conner, she and Wally Hedrick constituted the center of the hip and experimental San Francisco artists of the fifties and sixties, changing the meaning of funk art through their media as well as their intent. As art critic Harold Paris noted, previously "Funky art said that material was worthless, that only ideas were important and that the value of the art was in its making. The meaning of the art was not in any way related to the intrinsic worth of the materials." In contrast, Jay DeFeo and her peers placed great value on the materials they worked with, whether they be plaster, paint, or driftwood. The creative process alone did not define their artistry. Art was a compromise between material and mastery.

photo by Gui

Jay DeFeo and Lynn Brown abroad in Paris, Chartres Cathedral, 1951.

Not confined solely to painting, Jay experimented with other art forms and made a series of huge plaster sculptures in her studio, "done with just a lot of wood and wrapping around with rags and slapping plaster." The pieces proved to be immovable and were not exhibited, but they did influence well-known sculptor Manuel Neri, who made plaster the predominant medium of his sculptures from the fifties onward. Wallace Berman was intrigued by Jay's photocollages, and Bruce Conner credits her way of wrapping Christmas gifts and hanging them from the ceiling as a strong influence on his own assemblages. Declared one well-respected art scholar of the fifties, "She just had a flow, a creative flow, coming from her that was fantastic to observe."

Jay DeFeo's personal idiosyncrasies were artistic as well. She refused to throw out old Christmas trees. By the midsixties, she had quite a collection of bare trees in the corner of the room in which she painted. Even eating lunch was theatrical. She would prepare "a hundred little bits of things; it was like a Chinese lunch. It was by far the most arty." She was passionate about her art and was closely tied to it, even though her work has not been considered autobiographical.

Despite her experimentation, Jay DeFeo was, at heart, an abstract-expressionist painter who tempered her spontaneous inspiration with fervent labor. She worked in landscapes of color, often keying in on texture and brush strokes. Her fixation with mandalas led to a compulsion toward cyclical annihilation and reinvention. In her work, landscapes of color and textures blend together to create masterpieces that combine obsession with structure and maverick accumulations of paint. The best example of this is perhaps her most famous work, *The Rose.*

The Rose began in 1959 as an obsession with radiation. She began two paintings at the time: *The Rose* and *The Jewel.* After six months, *The Jewel* was set aside. She intended to finish it at a later date, but after a few months decided it was indeed complete.

The Rose became her fixation. Adding paints and embedding beads, jewelry, and wire to *The Rose* was her daily ritual. Although both paintings were composed of brush strokes radiating outward from the center of the canvas, the sheer mass of *The Rose* was awesome. In 1965, seven years after its inception, it was eight inches thick and weighed 2,300 pounds. This masterpiece was so large it occupied an entire bay window in her flat. When she and Wally were forced to move out of their Fillmore home in 1967 due to a hefty increase in rent, she was left with no choice but to concede to its completion.

Its removal was appropriately theatrical. A crane was required to lift it out through the window it had occupied for so many years. It took a number of moving men, dressed in white overalls, to direct the crane into the moving truck. Bruce Conner recorded the removal of the canvas on 16mm black-and-white film. He later called the film *The White Rose,* but had originally entitled it *Jay DeFeo's Painting Removed by Angelic Hosts.*

The Rose was moved to the Pasadena Museum of Art, which was then run by Walter Hopps, the San Francisco gallery owner who had given Jay her first show. When the piece started to crumble, it was removed to the San Francisco College of Art, where it was put into storage for twenty-five years. In 1995 it was displayed at the Whitney Museum in New York City.

After *The Rose,* Jay removed herself from the public eye. While other artists found new breakthroughs in their art, she kept to herself. After such a long commitment to *The Rose,* she found it difficult to become inspired again. Not only had she been forcefully separated from her life's work, but she and Wally had split up. The void created by the absence of both her central artistic endeavor and her lover brought on a severe melancholia. Jay recovered and began, in 1980, to teach painting at Mills College in Oakland, only to find that when her career began to flourish again, her body began to deteriorate.

Ironically, it would be *The Rose* that would kill her. While creating the behemoth, instead of dipping her brush into water, she used her tongue to moisten the brush tip. The white paint she used had an extremely high lead content and she unwittingly poisoned herself. She developed cancer and died in 1989.

Jay DeFeo's art has regained the public's attention in the years since her death. She is universally regarded as the primary visual artist of the Beat Generation, and *The Rose* is now on the road, traveling from one museum to another across America.

© C.R. Snyder

Joan Brown with her first husband, Bill Brown, circa 1957.

Joan Brown
Painter and Prodigy
(1938–1990)

"I really felt that I had the respect of all my male friends who were artists. It wasn't an issue maybe because there wasn't any competition for wall space, even any competition for jobs at the time...Joan Brown, who was actually more mature than I—we kind of grew up together—I think Joan would answer the question that same way I do."

—Jay DeFeo, 1989

Artist Joan Brown was nineteen in 1957 when she moved to Jay DeFeo's flat at 2322 Fillmore with her husband Bill. This was the banner Beat year of *On the Road* and the "Howl" obscenity trial. Joan recalls, "It was a very charged period. And I believe most of us who were working at a high peak in terms of energy and feeling. That is, not just the artist but North Beach in general. You felt this with the poets, too. I wouldn't have been anywhere else if I'd had a million dollars and was offered to spend three years in Italy." Joan Brown went on to become an internationally acclaimed artist, recognized chiefly for her primary role in developing the school known as California Figurative art. Her work continues to show in museums around the world.

Joan Brown was widely regarded as an artistic prodigy. A protege of Elmer Bischoff and David Park, Joan had her first show at nineteen and was the youngest artist to be included in the annual show of the Whitney Museum in New York for the year 1960. Joan worked in an expressionist style during the early phase of her career when she began to receive national recognition and acclaim for her strange and compelling self portraits and found object compilations.

Joan's assemblage sculptures helped usher in the San Francisco "funk art" scene

327

co-created by Bruce Conner, Jay DeFeo and Wally Hedrick. Hers were made of the cheapest possible materials, sometimes from actual garbage, but always from non-traditional material. Joan is quoted as stating that "eat, drink, and be merry for to-morrow we die" is the attitude and order of the day. Both Joan's work and her second husband Manuel Neri's assemblages frequently disintegrated soon after they were made and were described as "ephemeral." They both claimed that they weren't meant to last and were an attempt to "seize the moment" and capture it organically, textually and symbolically. Funk art was very Beat in its anti-material stance. Beat poets and funk artists supported and encouraged each other and a show was nearly always also an impromptu reading and, ultimately, a party with red wine flowing freely. One of the creative collectives that evolved from this artistic hybridization was the Rat Bastard Protective Association, founded by Bruce Conner, an homage to the garbage collector tendencies of the new "scavenger" artists. The RBP membership required dues of a mere $3.00 a year and requested members to put the RBP initials on the artworks as seal and insignia. Both Joan and Manuel Neri joined the group along with many other artists and poets— Jay DeFeo, Michael McClure, Wally Hedrick, Art Grant, Alvin Light, Carlos Villa, and Dave Hazelwood. The Association openly hosted guests from all walks and held meetings at out of the way places like the Golden Gate Bridge. One of the more memorable evenings featured a poetic duel between Philip Lamantia and a New York "wannaBeat" poet from New York.

Like her contemporary and housemate, Jay DeFeo, Joan Brown helped draw the

Gui de Angulo

Gui de Angulo's photography caught the emotion and fervor of the fifties and sixties. Originally a painter, as a photographer she remained true to her artistic eye, using exposure techniques and a trained eye to transfer people to film. A native of the San Francisco Bay Area, she participated in many local gallery shows. She and three friends even opened their own space, Freedman's Gallery, where Jay DeFeo's painting career was launched. When the gallery closed, Gui traveled to France and New York, but eventually returned to San Francisco, where she began photographing art exhibits for the famous North Beach bar-cum-gallery Vesuvio's.

Her work was widely known among the hipsters of San Francisco, such as Allen Ginsberg and Peter Orlovsky, who frequently stopped by her apartment to ask her to photograph them. She brought together the art of life and the starkness of film to create a portrait uniquely its own. Two of her photos are included here: portraits of Jay DeFeo and ruth weiss.

eye of the art world away from America's cultural epicenter, New York City. Joan's husband, sculptor Manuel Neri was an influence on her work. They had a child together during this time when Joan came under the public spotlight with features in national magazines like *Mademoiselle*. Joan was under no small amount of pressure to maintain the momentum and type of work for which she was acclaimed, especially from her dealer in New York. More experimentalist than expressionist, Joan surprised the world when she changed her style in 1964, and subsequently, wasn't shown in New York again until the mid-seventies. She continued to show in her native California, however, both as the subject of group- and one-woman exhibitions.

During this post-Beat phase, Joan withdrew and began to change the themes of her work, so much so that a new style seemed to emerge with every exhibition. Her work became more intensely personal with the *Alcatraz Swim* series, inspired by the swims across the San Francisco Bay Joan made and a new, brilliantly colored and cartoonlike group of self portraits on huge canvases with their trademark enamel household paints. Joan's style is most often linked with her mentor and fellow Figurative artist, David Park, and is, thematically, akin to Frida Kahlo for her creepily surreal self portraits where common objects are recontextualized into the bizarre. Joan, like her photographs, is the serene, still center of the piece.

Towards the end of her life, Joan wove Egyptian and Hindu religious icons and imagery into her work and devoted most of her energy into public sculpture. She had a special fascination with obelisks, often found in Egyptian tombs, and put painting aside. In 1990, Joan traveled to India, to the town of Proddaturn to install one of her obelisks. There, tragedy struck when the building collapsed, killing artist Joan Brown at the age of 52.

Worthy Beat Women
Recollection by Ted Joans

"SO YOU WANT TO BE HIP, LITTLE GIRLS?

AND YOU WANT TO LEARN TO SWING?

AND YOU WANT TO BE ABLE TO DIG AND TAKE IN EVERYTHING?

YES, DIG EVERYTHING AS POET ALLEN GINSBERG SAID?

IF YOU WANT TO BE HIP NOW DIG MY SERMON!"

This was the beginning of my popular jazz poem titled, "The Sermon." It was written to be read aloud and it was targeted at the women of America. It was first published in my first chapbook of poems by Shel Derechin of Nuderection Press in the early fifties. I would often read "The Sermon" three times a night on weekends in the many public coffee houses that featured Beat Generation poetry. Greenwich Village was the Beat scene on the Eastern coast of America and thousands of women flocked to that neighborhood. National magazines such as *Holiday, Time,* and *Life* magazine, and even some of the nationally circulated Black magazines sensationalized the Beats generating a total new direction of liberation. My aim was to find strength to change and transform America by getting the wise (hip) words of poetry to the worthy women of this potentially great country. I believed then, and still do, that democracy can never be fully accomplished without the leadership of hip, happy, active women.

Reading in the crowded coffee houses to the wannabe—Beats, the tourists, and those poetic women (who wanted to absorb what it meant to be hipper-than-thou) was almost a religious quest due to the music of the Beat Generation: jazz. It propelled poetry from the page into the ears of the listeners. I being an ex-trumpet player was hip to this unique fact. After all, His High Holy Hipness, Duke Ellington, had wisely musically said: "It Don't Mean A Thing, If It Ain't Got That Swing!" It was my own natural respect for "worthy" women as one individual to another that caused our closeness. If I was not on the scene every night in those days I would not have been able to "discover" women poets. I had known Diane di Prima from the before-Beat-generating days. She, like me, used to hold court in Cafe Rienzi at 107 MacDougal Street (I lived above it in 1952) and when her first book of poems was published, *This Kind of Bird Flies Backwards;* it was I that presented her at the Gaslight Cafe and actually helped place her on top of the piano. Diane and I were not lovers, we were merely poets and bohemian friends.

Beat Generation. I created giggly labels such as: Chicklets (younger than chicks) hipnicks, flipniks, touristniks, jivey leaguer, creepnik, A–Trainer (Black men that took the A–Train from Harlem to Greenwich Village in search of White chicks), Bronx Bagel Babies, and the ultimate, the hipstressnik, who was the most lovable. There were other women poets that did not participate in the Beat scene coffee shop readings, but did read in the Living Theatre and the institutions in Green–which Village. Poets such as Denise Levertov, Barbara Guest. These were some of the poets who did their "thang" back in those good/old days of yore.

This personal Beat memory is of some of the best women poets that were on the Eastern coast of America. I never visited the West Coast scene until decades later when even the Hippie scene was gone on into hysterical history. I met Bob and Eileen Kaufman in New York. I also met many other Wet Coast cast of thousands in New York City. Some of them had come to bite that attractive Apple (Lester Young, tenor-sax man named it) and for many of those West Coast poets, the Apple was too tuff or they found its fruit bitter, therefore not worth nibbling on, thus chose to return to their San Franciscos and Los Angeles. There is one woman whose book of poems was a great inspiration on the late Beat Scene of Greenwich Village (when one could find a copy!), that poet was Lenore Kandel, her book *The Love Book* is a liberating force for all feminists. It should be required reading throughout the world. Too bad her book was never celebrated like Ginsberg's "Howl." She was the first woman poet to use the marvelous word (when used in its original form) f u c k naturally.

I have yet to meet Ms. Kandel to personally thank her for being a self-liberating woman who dared to NOT be. I met Jane Bowles while I was dwelling in Tangier, Morocco.

Hettie Jones I have known for decades and I consider an excellent writer. Her autobiography *How I Became Hettie Jones* is a classic. When I knew Bonnie Bremser, she was not writing, or kept her literary output concealed in the shadow of poet Ray Bremser.

Jan Kerouac I first met a few years ago during a conference in New York, but I had read one of her books and I await a collection of her poems to be published. She is loved by me and perhaps all the "worthy" poets who are hip to the dues that she has paid being the daughter of Kerouac. I did not meet her mother, but did know Jack, her father.

AFTERWORD
by Ann Charters

Berkeley Memories: During 1956-1958 I lived in a cottage in Berkeley, one of the ramshackle, poorly insulated, small wooden buildings scattered throughout the city, usually tucked away in the tree shaded backyard gardens behind larger houses. My tiny cottage was at 2803-$^1/_2$ Forest Avenue in the neighborhood bordered by College Avenue and the Claremont Hotel. That's where I lived while I finished my bachelor's degree at Cal and taught English at San Lorenzo High School, my first teaching job right after graduation.

Unlike Allen Ginsberg's and Gary Snyder's cottages close by, both victims of Berkeley urban development, mine is there still on its pleasant residential side street, a clump of rustling bamboo beside the front door, a tall green hedge by the sidewalk shielding its pocket-handkerchief lawn from the view of the casual passerby. Forty years ago I might have passed Gary on my bicycle taking the long way to campus, or stood in a checkout line with a quart of milk and a couple of bananas watching Allen prowl the late-night supermarket on University Avenue.

Originally my cottage had been built as a gardener's shed alongside the substantial family residence which sheltered it at 2803 Forest Avenue, but by the time I was ready to move in, it had been converted into low-rent student digs. One-third of the space contained a toilet and a shower and a small sink, hot plate, refrigerator, tiny table, and rickety chair.

Two-thirds was my bedroom—a single bed, a three-speed record player perched atop an orange crate, a sagging armchair and a scuffed desk from a Good Will thrift shop. An inadequate bookshelf hugged the wall above my bed, which faced a faded beige burlap curtain on shower rings hiding the metal pole where I hung my clothes. Altogether about as much space as a San Francisco trolley car, except that with all the basic furniture crowded into it, there wasn't much standing room for passengers.

On cold days during the Berkeley winters I ran the hot water in the shower until steam warmed up the bedroom. Then I put on a couple of heavy sweaters and studied under the covers, drinking coffee to keep my hands warm. My favorite meal was a can of ravioli, or—if I could afford the raw ingredients—a pot of stuffed cabbage made after my mother's Polish American Jewish recipe, or my own invention, nutritious liver stew in tomato sauce with chunks of garlic, onions, celery, and carrots hacked with a dull chopping knife with a broken blade I found at the back of the silverware drawer.

I inherited the cottage from my closest friend in Berkeley, an art student named Carolyn. She had been my roommate at Ritter Hall, a private co-op off Dwight Way, until she moved to the cottage which she'd found through a friend of her father's, the art director of the Emporium, a San Francisco department store.

It was Carolyn who arranged my blind date with Peter Orlovsky in March, 1956, my last semester at the co-op. Afterwards I went to the cottage to tell her about the extraordinary reading I attended with Peter in a Berkeley theater, where among a group of young poets I heard his friend Allen Ginsberg give the first public reading of the fully completed "Howl for Carl Solomon."

I was impressed by the poetry I'd heard by Ginsberg, Philip Whalen, Gary Snyder, and Michael McClure that evening, but I was unnerved by the drunken wildness of their friends in the audience and Robert LaVigne's drawings of Orlovsky making love with Ginsberg which were pinned to the walls of the theater. I recognized their artistic power, but I was too naive to understand why Peter and Allen would pose naked for the artist.

Compared with Carolyn, I felt gauche and unsophisticated, and I hoped she'd explain everything to me. Born and raised in San Francisco, she considered herself an intellectual, and I remember that she was decidedly unimpressed by my enthusiasm for a bunch of scruffy, unpublished Berkeley poets.

She would have given me a cool, disbelieving look out of her clear blue eyes before she tossed back the thin strands of her long straight blonde hair, leaned down to tie the supple leather thongs of her well-oiled handmade sandals, reminded me that her favorite poet in San Francisco was Weldon Kees, and invited me to walk along with her to her new boyfriend's apartment near Dwight and Telegraph. He kept a volume of Dylan Thomas' poetry next to the jug of California red wine beside his double bed and made a ritual out of reading aloud to her while they shared a cigarette after making love.

In her series of lovers Carolyn was not attracted to wild-haired "queers" or fast-talking married con men or street-wise junkies or intense students of Buddhism emulating a Japanese lifestyle or handsome but self-absorbed alcoholics just in off the road. She gave the Beat males a wide berth. She might have been self-destructive, but she had her own style.

My friendship with Carolyn taught me there were many worlds within worlds. Her parents lived in a beautiful new house on the slopes of Mount Tamalpais in Mill Valley, where they invited me to come home with Carolyn and join them and their friends in what they called their Sunday afternoon "te' dansants," martinis served in teacups with little canapes at four o'clock while a Dave Brubeck record played softly in the background.

The party would continue until Carolyn took me out of the house to get some fresh air on the winding dirt road leading to the mountain top, her favorite walk. On other afternoons she introduced me to her favorite haunts in San Francisco, the North Beach coffee houses. They modeled themselves on the Parisian cafes where, in the aftermath of World War II, many American GI's had gotten a taste of European existentialism.

Returning to San Francisco, ex-servicemen like Lawrence Ferlinghetti brought an awareness of the French tradition of literature and philosophy back with them to provincial California. On Columbus Avenue in North Beach, Ferlinghetti and his business partner Peter Martin opened the bookshop City Lights, similar to the small Parisian paperback bookshops Ferlinghetti had frequented during his years in Paris studying for his doctorate at the Sorbonne. City Lights was the first paperback bookshop in the United States, with a narrow corner up a rickety flight of wooden stairs devoted to a generous sampling of small press poetry broadsides and magazines.

Since Carolyn loved art more than literature or music, and I had very little money for books, when she took me to North Beach we skipped City Lights in favor of the coffee houses, where we sipped capuccino topped with lots of powdered cocoa and cinnamon and listened to the murmur of serious voices at the other tables discussing Being and Nothingness.

A couple of years later, in the Spring of 1958, the columnist Herb Caen coined the term "beatniks" for the people who hung out in North Beach coffee houses discussing philosophy and poetry, but he inhabited a journalist's world, making quick judgements of people based on how they dressed or acted. Carolyn was a young woman who knew the score. The word she would have used to describe herself was "hip," though she would have been automatically classed as a beatnik if Caen had glanced through the window of the Co-Existence Bagel Shop and not recognized her as the daughter of his friend over at the Emporium.

Perhaps it was the North Beach atmosphere, or our heady sense of privilege at being such carefree women "wandering" (the American writer Gertrude Stein's word) in the City, but I remember that the two of were nearly always serious, even seated at a formica table in a booth downstairs at our favorite Chinese restaurant, anticipating our little white bowls of won ton soup.

Carolyn was quiet most of the time, letting me fantasize that she played the role of Simone de Beauvoir in her unhappy love affairs with graduate students of philosophy, literature, or music at Cal. Each was her Jean Paul Sartre, her real teacher, a member of her own generation, rather than the brilliant older men she struggled to please in her painting and art history courses, of whom she was in awe.

Meanwhile, as an honor scholarship student in the English Department, my favorite reading was in a topic then called Negro theater. Six months later, after Carolyn found out she was pregnant and made the decision to join her latest boyfriend instead of having her third illegal abortion, I moved into what I thought of as "her" cottage with piles of library books on the history of American drama.

I may have inherited her cottage, but I never managed to achieve her cool. The risks of her bohemian lifestyle were so apparent that I never considered hanging out with Ginsberg, Kerouac, and Cassady, older men who were Orlovsky's friends. I moved into the cottage on Forest Avenue despite my parents' strong objections to my leaving the co-op and living alone.

This was adventure enough for me, along with falling in love with Sam Charters, who had graduated Cal and was hitchhiking from Berkeley to New Orleans researching his first book on early jazz. When he left my cottage to go back on the road, I sat at my cramped desk in the cold spring in 1957 with an electric heater at my feet, and wrote up my notes on blackface minstrels and the *Uncle Tom* shows, an independent study project at Cal during my senior year for Professor Travis Bogard in the English Department, who had begun researching his biography of Eugene O'Neill.

My paper resulted in my being awarded a Woodrow Wilson Fellowship for an M.A. Degree at Columbia University. I was excited by the opportunity of graduate study in New York City, even if it meant leaving my friend Carolyn and her baby daughter, and my beloved Berkeley cottage.

Fortunately for me, in 1957 the Russians' apparent advantage with their sputnik space capsule made the United States generous in its support of graduate schools. From all the universities in the country I chose to attend Columbia in the fall of 1958 because I wanted to join Sam Charters in New York City. He turned out to be the right man—we married the next year—and it was certainly the right school.

I went on to study for my doctorate in 1963 when Columbia gave me an additional fellowship. If I'd used the Woodrow Wilson at Harvard, I would have earned what they called a "terminal Master's degree," since Harvard didn't allow women students into their doctoral English program at that time.

Probably if I'd proposed a clearly focused project I could have written a thesis at Berkeley or Columbia on the women writers I admired like Emily Dickinson or the regionalist Sarah Orne Jewitt, who were taught in my American Literature classes. But I was the daughter of first generation Americans. Living on the East Coast, I wanted to explore the idea of the relationship of my country's literary history to its geography.

For my dissertation I concentrated on nineteenth century authors in the

Berkshires, and my thesis advisor Lewis Leary encouraged me to include Catharine Maria Sedgwick and Edith Wharton along with Thoreau, Melville and Hawthorne. In the large classes I was too busy taking notes to protest when my all-male professors' lectured on a mostly male literary pantheon. I knew that in the Columbia library stacks I could browse on my own.

In my independent reading outside the university, the best sources of information about poetry were the popular anthologies edited by Seldon Rodman and Louis Untermeyer which had sold thousands of copies and gone into multiple editions, which Sam culled from the shelves of second-hand bookshops and public libraries. These anthologies taught me there was a women's tradition of creating literature in the United States.

The volumes included work by 1930s and 1940s unconventional American women poets like H.D., Gwendolyn Brooks, and Muriel Rukeyser. Along with others like Gertrude Stein, Tillie Olsen, and Anaïs Nin, these women were committed to literary experimentation and social change and represented a very different tradition from the few women authors on my academic reading lists. Women poets in the 1950s were expected to be polite, like Pulitzer Prize-winning Phyllis McGinley, whose poems were scattered among the cartoons in *The New Yorker.*

Labeled in the 1960s as an "Underground" or alternative press, not even City Lights Books published many women in their Pocket Poets series. In 1956, Ferlinghetti followed *Howl* (number four in the series) with Marie Ponsot's *True Minds*, a book he described approvingly as being "in extreme contrast to the 'bop apocalypse'" of Ginsberg's poem. In 1957, Pocket Poets number six was *Here and Now* by the talented young Denise Levertov, but women poets weren't included in the series again until number twenty-two in 1968, Janine Pommy Vega's *Poems to Fernando.*

Expressing themselves freely in their poetry and prose, the earlier radical women authors developed a tradition for writers in the 1950s like Helen Adam and Jo Miles, both of whom I'd heard about in Berkeley. But the authors who spoke most directly to my sensibilities in the 1960s were Doris Lessing and Elizabeth Bishop, whose poetry I admired most until I encountered Sylvia Plath.

When I read Plath's *Arial* after completing my doctorate in 1965, this supremely gifted, iconoclastic writer became my favorite poet. I cherished her work along with Lessing's *Golden Notebook* and a growing pile of small press Beat paperbacks I found in Greenwich Village at the Eighth Street Bookshop, books like *Dinners and Nightmares* by Diane di Prima, and *Kaddish* by Allen Ginsberg, both of which brilliantly described women's lives closer to home.

In New York City I also read Kerouac's *The Dharma Bums*. There I found a description of cottage life in Berkeley which caught the bohemian flavor of the place—but I read it a few years after I had left its dangers behind me. Kerouac's prose was so seductive that my memories assumed the golden glow of his nostalgia, since I never tested them by living there again.

For my friend Carolyn, the experience wasn't a golden memory. Like Naomi Ginsberg and Sylvia Plath, she was a casualty of her time. A dozen years after graduating from Cal, depressed by the direction her life had taken in an unhappy marriage, my friend committed suicide in Berkeley. Had she lived and managed to continue painting and writing, she might have been one of the women celebrated in this anthology.

Survive! Survive! I wonder if the person currently renting my cottage at 2803-^{1}/$_2$ Forrest Avenue is taking literature courses at the university using anthologies like *Women of the Beat Generation*. For Carolyn's sake, I hope so. Though right now I imagine her in Heaven reading Simone Weil—probably *Waiting for God*.

APPENDIX:

List of Collected Works

Helen Adam

Charms and Dreams from the elfin pedlar's pack, Hodder & Stoughton, 1924.

The Elfin Pedlar and tales told by Pixie Pool, G.P. Putnam's Sons, 1924.

Shadow of the Moon, Hodder & Stoughton, 1929.

The Queen O' Crow Castle, White Rabbit Press, 1958 (with drawings by Jess).

San Francisco's Burning, Oannes Press, 1963. Republished by Hanging Loose Press, 1985.

Ballads, Acadia Press, 1964 (with drawings by Jess).

Counting Out Rhyme, Interim Books, 1972.

Selected Poems and Ballads, Helikon Press, 1974.

Turn Again to Me, Kulchur Foundation, 1977.

Ghosts and Grinning Shadows, Hanging Loose Press, 1979.

Gone Sailing, Toothpaste Press, 1980.

Songs with Music, Aelph Press, 1982.

Stone Cold Gothic, Kulchur Foundation, 1984.

The Bells of Dis, Coffee House Press, 1985.

Jane Bowles

Two Serious Ladies, Knopf, 1943.

In the Summer House, Random House, 1954.

Plain Pleasures, P. Owen, 1966.

The Collected Works of Jane Bowles, Farrar, Straus, 1966.

Quarreling Pair [a puppet play] in *Mademoiselle,* December, 1966.

Contributor to *Harper's Bazaar, Vogue,* and *Mademoiselle.*

Joan Brown

Joan Brown had one-person exhibitions from 1957-1990 in galleries and museums around the country.

Carolyn Cassady

Heart Beat: My Life with Jack and Neal, Creative Arts Book Co., 1976.

Off the Road: My Years with Cassady, Kerouac, and Gins-berg, Morrow, 1990; published in England as *Off the Road: Twenty Years with Cassady, Kerouac, and Ginsberg,* Black Spring Press, 1990.

"Coming Down" in *unspeakable visions of the individual,* vol. 4, *The Beat Book,*1974.

The Pushcart Prize, Number Three: Best of the Small Presses, 1978–79 edition, Pushcart, 1978.

"As I see It" in *Dictionary of Literary Biography,* vol. 16, *The Beats: Literary Bohemians in Postwar America,* Gale, 1983.

Contributor to periodicals including *unspeakable visions of the individual, Beat Scene, Kerouac Connection,* and *Moody Street Irregulars: A Jack Kerouac Newsletter.*

Elise Cowen

"I walk weeping," "Trust yourself—but not too far," "A man speaks a few words to her," "Under the dismal onion," and "No love" in *City Lights Journal,* no. 2, City Lights Books, 1964.

"I wanted a cunt of golden pleasure," "Morning Blessing from Elohim,"

"Heavy-bellied with hero," and "If it weren't for love I'd snooze all day" in *Things,* no. 1, Ron Schreiber and Emmett Jarrett, eds., Fall 1964.

"A cockroach," "The first eye opens by the sun's warmth to stare at it," "Easy to love," and "I took the skin of corpses" in *Fuck You: A magazine of the arts,* Ed Sanders (ed.), February 1965.

"Someone I could kiss" in *The Ladder,* vol. 9, no. 7, Barbara Gittings, ed., April 1965.

"Compassion is a Chinese greeting" in *The Ladder,* June 1965.

"Sloughing death all over each other in slat baskets," "Who will slap," "Death I'm coming," "Faithful paranoid" and "Real as the worn green" in *El corno emplumado* 17, January 1966.

Jay DeFeo

One-Person Exhibitions
1954   The Place, San Francisco, CA
1958   Dilexi Gallery, San Francisco, CA.

1959 *16 Americans,* Museum of Modern Art, New York, N.Y.

1960 Ferus Gallery, Los Angeles, CA.

1967 *The Rose,* Pasadena Museum of Art, Pasadena, CA.

1968 *The Rose,* San Francisco Museum of Modern Art, San Francisco, CA.

The Rose, San Francisco Art Institute, San Francisco, CA.

1969 Pasadena Museum of Art, Pasadena, CA. (traveled).

1970 Oakland Museum, Oakland, CA.

1974 Wenger Gallery, San Francisco, CA.

1975 Isabelle Percy West Gallery, College of Arts and Crafts, Oakland, CA.

1978 University of California Art Museum, Berkeley, CA.

1979 Faith and Charity in Hope (Ed Kienholtz), Hope, ID.

1979 University of Idaho Art Gallery, Moscow, ID.

1980 Gallery Paule Anglim, San Francisco, CA.

Whitman College Art Gallery, Walla Walla, WA

Chico State University, Chico, CA.

1981 Indian Valley College, Novato, CA.

1983 Gallery Paule Anglim, San Francisco, CA.

1984 Boise Gallery of Art, Boise, ID.

1985 Janus Gallery, Los Angeles, CA.

1986 Nave Museum, Victoria, TX

1988 Jan Turner Gallery, Los Angeles, CA.

Gallery Paule Anglim, San Francisco, CA.

1990 *Jay DeFeo: Works on Paper,* University Art Museum, University of California at Berkeley; traveling to the Menil Collection, Houston; Laguna Beach Museum of Art, Laguna Beach, CA.; Fresno Art Museum, Fresno, CA.; and Krannert Art Museum, Champaign, IL; Gallery Paule Anglim, San Francisco, CA.

The New Handbook of Heaven, Auerhahn Press, 1962.

The Man Condemned to Death (trans.), 1963.

Poets' Vaudeville, Feed Folly Press, 1964.

Seven Love Poems from the Middle Latin, Poets Press, 1965.

Haiku, Love Press, 1966.

New Mexico Poem, Poets Press, 1967.

Earthsong, Poets Press, 1968.

Hotel Albert, Poets Press, 1968.

War Poems (ed.), Poets Press, 1968.

L.A. Odyssey, Poets Press, 1969.

Memoirs of a Beatnik, Paris and Olympia Press, 1969.

The Book of Hours, Brownstone Press, 1970.

Kerhonkson Journal, Oyez, 1971.

Revolutionary Letters, City Lights Books, 1971.

The Calculus of Variation, Eidolon Editions, 1972.

The Floating Bear [newsletter] (ed.), Laurence McGilvery, 1973.

Loba, part I, Capra Press, 1973.

Freddie Poems, Eidolon Editions, 1974.

Selected Poems: 1956–1975, North Atlantic Books, 1975.

Loba, part II, Eidolon Editions, 1976.

The Loba As Eve, The Phoenix Book Shop, 1977.

Loba: parts I–VIII, Wingbow Press, 1978.

Memoirs of a Beatnik (revised), Last Gasp Press, 1988.

The Mysteries of Vision, Am Here Books, 1988.

Wyoming Series, Eidolon Editions, 1988.

Pieces of a Song: Selected Poems, City Lights Books, 1990.

Seminary Poems, Floating Island, 1991.

The Mask Is the Path of the Star, Thinker Review International, 1993.

Contributor to more than 300 literary and popular magazines and newspapers; has appeared in at least seventy anthologies; and has been translated into at least thirteen languages.

Diane di Prima

This Kind of Bird Flies Backward, Totem Press, 1958.

Various Fables from Various Places (ed.), G. P. Putnam, 1960.

Dinners and Nightmares, Corinth Press, 1961.

Mary Fabilli

The Old Ones, Oyez, 1966.

Aurora Bligh and Early Poems, Oyez, 1968.

The Animal Kingdom, Oyez, 1975.
Ray Boynton and The Mother Lode, 1976.
Poems 1976–1981, 1981.
Winter Poems, 1983.
Pilgrimage, 1985.
Simple Pleasures, 1987.
Shingles and Other Poems, 1990.

Periodicals
Occident, March/April 1937.
Epitaph, Spring 1938.
Ritual, April 1940.
Experimental Reviews, #2 November 1940; #3 September 1941.
New Directions 8, 1944.
Circle 7 and 8, 1946.
Circle 9, 1946.
Circle 10, 1948.
Occident, Spring 1980.
Talisman 13, 1995.
To, Summer 1995.

Anthologies
I Hear My Sister Singing, 1976.
Contemporary Women Poets, 1977.
Against Infinity, 1979.
Poeti Italo-Americani, 1985.

Artwork
Saints: A Portfolio in Prints, Porpoise Book Shop, 1950.

Madeline Gleason
Poems, Grabhorn Press, 1944.
The Metaphysical Needle, Centaur Press, 1949.
Concerto for Bell and Telephone, Hoyem Press, 1966.
Selected Poems, Dragon's Teeth Press, 1972.
Here Comes Everybody, Panjandrum Press, 1975.
Collected Poems (1944-1979), Madeline Gleason Memorial Fund, 1983.

Joyce Johnson
Come and Join the Dance (under name Joyce Glassman), Atheneum, 1962.
Bad Connections, Putnam, 1978.
Minor Characters, Houghton & Mifflin, 1983.
In the Night Cafe, Dutton, 1989.
What Lisa Knew: The Truth and Lies of the Steinberg Case, Putnam, 1990.

Articles have appeard in *The New Yorker, The New York Times Magazine, Vanity Fair, Harpers, New York, Harpers Bazaar,* and *Mirabella*

Hettie Jones
Poems Now (ed.), Kulchur Press, 1968.
The Trees Stand Shining, Poetry of the North American Indians, The Dial Press, 1971
(reissue 1993). Dial Books for Young Readers, a division of Viking-Penguin USA.
Coyote Tales, Holt, Rinehart & Winston, 1972.
Longhouse Winter, Holt, Rinehart & Winston, 1972.
Big Star Fallin' Mama, Five Women In Black Music, Viking Press, 1974. Revised and updated, February 1995.
Living With Wolves, Macmillan, 1975.
Forever Young, Forever Free, Berkley Publishing, 1976.
How To Eat Your ABCs: A Book About Vitamins, Four Winds Press (Scholastic), 1976.
Mustang Country, Pocket Books, 1976.
You Light Up My Life, Pocket Books, 1977.
I Hate to Talk About Your Mother, Delacorte Press, 1979.
In Search of the Castaways, Pocket Books, 1979.
Promises in the Dark, Bantam Books, 1979.
Having Been Her, Number Press, 1981.

"A Woman Remembers Her Past," *Noose* Memorial Issue, 1982.
"The Big Fish," *Infinite Number,* Number Press, 1983.
"The Ironing Board" in *Giants Play Well in the Drizzle,* 1983.
"The Pause That Refreshes," *IKON,* Winter/Spring, 1983-84.

Missing Sweet Rose, Delacorte Press, 1984.

"From Four Hetties" in *Giants Play Well in the Drizzle,* 1986.

"This Time It Was Different At the Airport," IKON *Art Against Apartheid Anthology,* "The Summer House Secret," *Secrets and Surprises,* Macmillan Publishing Company, 1986.

Supplement, June 1988.

How I Became Hettie Jones, a memoir. E. P. Dutton, 1990 (hardcover); Penguin USA,1991. Reissue August 1996.

"Bernstein on Jazz" in *Bernstein Remembered,* Carroll & Graf, 1991.

The Portable Beat Reader, Viking Penguin, January 1992. Also *The Penguin Book of the Beats* (UK).

"Mother Moon" and "Sharing The Image" in *More In Than Out,* also edited by Hettie Jones, Bedford Hills Correctional Facility, 1992.

"Home Free," *Your House Is Mine,* a book and street project by Bullet Space Urban

Artists Collaborative. Last showing, New Museum of Contemporary Art, 1993.

"Lost and/or Gained," *Artist and Homeless Collaborative,* Visual Arts Gallery, Henry

Street Settlement, February 26–April 4, 1993.

"Enough of This" and "How She Recognized Her Last Fling When She Found It," *Frontiers, A Journal of Women Studies,* vol. 13, no. 2, Winter 1993.

"Manhattan Special," "Racing with the Moon," "Winsome, Lose Some," and others, *Owen Wister Review,* University of Wyoming, Fall 1993.

"Sisters, Right?" in *Time Capsule: A Concise Encyclopedia by Women Artists,*

"The Third Poem," "My friend in love," "Lottie and Oscar," "Welcome to Our Crowd," "Manhattan Special" in *Hanging Loose,* Spring 1996.

Contributor to many literary and popular magazines and newspapers.

Forthcoming:

"Lunch Poem" and "One Hundred Love Poems for Lisa" in *El Signo del Gorrion,* 1996.

"Saturday the stuffed bears," "Paleface," "The woman in the blue car" in *Ladies*

Start Your Engines, Faber and Faber, 1996.

"Song at Sixty" [bookmark], Alternative Press, 1996.

Spooky Tales From Gullah Gullah Island, Simon & Schuster, 1996.

Lenore Kandel

An Exquisite Navel, Three Penny Press, 1959.

A Passing Dragon, Three Penny Press, 1959.

A Passing Dragon Seen Again, Three Penny Press, 1959.

The Love Book, Stolen Paper Editions, 1966.

Word Alchemy, Grove, 1967.

Anthologies

Beards and Brown Bags, Grover Haynes (ed.), Three Penny Press, 1959.

Word Alchemy, Grove, 1967.

Best Poems of 1961: Borestone Mountian Poetry Awards 1962, Pacific Books, 1962.

San Francisco Art Festival: A Poetry Folio, East Wind Printers, 1964.

Edie Parker Kerouac

You'll Be Okay, unpublished autobiography.

Jan Kerouac

Baby Driver: A Story About Myself, St. Martin's, 1981.

Trainsong, Henry Holt, 1988.

Joan Haverty Kerouac

Nobody's Wife, unpublished autobiography.

Mary Norbert Körte

The Beginning is the Life, 1967.

Hymn to the Gentle Sun, Oyez, 1968.

Beginning of Lines, Oyez, 1968.

Two Poems, 1969.

The Midnight Bridge, Oyez, 1970.

A Brievary in Time of War, Cranium Press, 1972.

Mammals of Delight, Oyez, 1978.

Lines Bending, 1978.

Throwing Firecrackers out the Window While the Ex-Husband Drives By, Rainy Day Women Press, 1991.

Numerous broadsides.

Brenda Frazer

Troia: Mexican Memoirs, Croton Press, 1969. Republished as *For Love of Ray,*

London Magazine Editions, 1971.

Anthologies:
Cherry Valley Anthology, 1973.

Also published in:
Fuck You, a Magazine of the Arts, 1963.

Blue Beat, 1963.

Intrepid, 1963.

Joanne Kyger

The Tapestry and the Web, Four Seasons Foundation, 1965.

The Fool in April: A Poem, Coyote Books, 1966.

Joanne, Angel Hair Books, 1970.

Places to Go, Black Sparrow Press, 1970.

Desecheo Notebook, Arif Press, 1971.

Trip Out and Fall Back, Arif Press, 1974.

All This Every Day, Big Sky, 1975.

Lettre de Paris, with Larry Fagin, Poltroon Press, 1977.

The Wonderful Focus of You, Z Press, 1980.

Japan and India Journals 1960–1964, photographs by Gary Snyder and Allen Ginsberg, Tombouctou Books, 1981.

Mexico Blonde, Evergreen Press, 1981.

Up My Coast (adapted from the stories of C. Hart

Merriam; illustrated by Inez Storer), Floating Island Books, 1981.

Going On: Selected Poems 1958–1980, Dutton, 1983.

The Dharma Committee, Smithereens Press, 1986.

Man-Women, with Michael Rothenberg, illustrated by Nancy Davis, Big Bridge Press, 1988.

Phenomenological, Institute of Further Studies, 1989.

Just Space: Poems 1979–1990, illustrated by Arthur Okamura, Black Sparrow Press, 1991.

Contributor:
The American Literary Anthology, George Plimpton and Peter Ardery (eds.), Random House, 1969.

The World Anthology, Anne Waldman (ed.), Bobbs-Merrill, 1969.

Rising Tides, Laura Chester and Sharon Barba (eds.), Pocket Books, 1973.

Big Sky Mind, Carole Tonkinson (ed.), Riverhead Books, 1995.

The Beat Book: Poems & Fiction from the Beat Generation, Anne Waldman (ed.), Shambhala, 1996.

Contributor of poems to periodicals, including *Coyote's Journal, Paris Review, Poetry, Rockey Ledge, Turkey Buzzard Review,* and *World.* A collection of Kyger's work is held at the Archive for New Poetry, University of California, San Diego.

Eileen Kaufman

Poems for Women, Carol Berg (ed.), 1967.

Who Wouldn't Walk with Tigers? [first chapter published in 1985], Alix, 1973.

"Eileen, Pat and the Light Light People" in *Past Lives, Future Loves* by Dick Sutphen, Valley of the Sun Press, 1977.

Publisher, *Beatitude International,* 2 vols.: April 1992 and June 1992.

Columnist on music criticism for *Los Angeles Free Press* [weekly underground newspaper—"Sounds" column and other], 1966 through 1968. Articles include those on Monterey Pop Festival (1967) and Monterey Jazz Festivals (1967–1968).

Also wrote on musical events for *World Countdown, Los Angeles Oracle,* John

Bryan's *Open City, World Pacific Records* (1966), and *Billboard.*

Denise Levertov

The Double Image, Cresset Press, 1946.

The New British Poets, Kenneth Rexroth (ed.), New Directions, 1948.

The Freeing of the Dust, New Directions, 1975.

Life in the Forest, New Directions, 1978.

Collected Earlier Poems 1940–1960, New Directions, 1960.

Light up the Cave, New Directions, 1981.

Candles in Babylon, New Directions, 1982.

Poems 1960–1967. "The Jacob's Ladder" (1961), "O Taste and See" (1964), and "The Sorrow Dance" (1967) in their entirety, New Directions, 1983.

Oblique Prayers [poetry with 14 translations from Jean Joubert], New Directions, 1984.

Breathing the Water, New Directions, 1987.

Poems 1968–1972. "Footprints" (1972), "Relearning the Alphabet" (1970), and "To Stay Alive" (1971) in their entirety, New Directions, 1987.

A Door in the Hive, New Directions, 1989.

New & Selected Essays, New Directions, 1992.

Evening Train, New Directions, 1993.

Tesserae, New Directions, 1995.

Sands of the Well, [forthcoming] 1996.

Joanna McClure

Wolf Eyes, Bearthm Press, 1974.

Extended Love Poems, Arif Press, 1978.

Hard Edge, CoffeeHouse Press, 1987.

Josephine Miles

Lines at Intersection, Macmillan, 1939.

Poems on Several Occasions, New Directions, 1941.

Local Measures, Reynal & Hitchcock, 1946.

After This Sea, Book Club of California, 1947.

Eras & Modes in English Poetry, University of California Press, 1957; revised and enlarged, 1964.

Poems, 1930–1960, Indiana University Poetry Series, no. 18, Indiana University Press, 1960.

Renaissance, Eighteenth-Century, and Modern Language in English Poetry: A Tabular *View,* University of California Press, 1960.

Kinds of Affection, Wesleyan University Press, 1962.

Ralph Waldo Emerson, University of Minnesota Press, 1964.

Civil Poems, Oyez Press, 1966.

Style and Proportion: The Language of Prose and Poetry, Little, Brown, 1967.

Saving the Bay, Open Space, 1967.

Fields of Learning, Oyez Press, 1968.

American Poems, Cloud Marauder Press, 1970.

Poetry and Change: Donne, Milton, Wordsworth, and the Equilibrium of the Present, University of California Press, 1974.

To All Appearances: Poems New and Selected, University of Illinois Press, 1974.

Coming to Terms: Poems, University of Illinois Press, 1979.

Working Out Ideas: Predication and Other Uses of Language, University of California, Berkeley Bay Area Writing Project, 1979.

Collected Poems, 1930-83, Urbana, Ill.: University of Illinois Press, 1983.

Contributed articles to many periodicals.

Janine Pommy Vega

Poems to Fernando, City Lights Poet Pocket Series no. 22, 1968.

Journal of a Hermit, Cherry Valley Editions, 1975, 1979.

New Year's Crossing, Poets Who Sleep, 1975.

Star Treatise [broadside], Cranium Press, 1975.

Morning Passage, Telephone Books, 1976.

Song for Cesar [broadside], Longhouse, 1977.

Here at the Door, Zone Press, 1978.

The Bard Owl, Kulchur Press, 1980.

Apex of the Earth's Way, White Pine Press, 1984.

Drunk on a Glacier, Talking To Flies, Tooth of Time Books, 1988.

Letter from the Woods [broadside], Poetry Project, 1988.

Pokhara [broadside], Mad River Press, 1989.

Island of the Sun, Longhouse, 1991.

Threading the Maze, Cloud Mountain Press, 1992.

Anthologies

The Aspect Anthology, A Ten Year Retrospective, Aspect.

On Turtle's Back, New York State Anthology, White Pine Press.

New America, A Review, University of New Mexico.

Hudson River Anthology, Vassar College.

Sitting Frog, Naropa Institute.

Up Late: American Poetry Since 1970, 4 Walls 8 Windows.

Out of This World, Crown.

Traveling with the Spirit: A Woman's Journey, work in progress.

Anne Waldman

The World Anthology: Poems from The St. Mark's Poetry Project, Bobby Merrill, 1969.

Fast Speaking Woman, City Lights, 1975.

Baby Breakdown, Bobby Merrill, 1970.

Giant Night, Corinth Books, 1970.

Another World: A Second Anthology of Works from the St. Mark's Poetry Project, Bobby Merrill, 1971.

No Hassles, Kulchur Foundation, 1971.

Life Notes, Bobby Merrill, 1973.

Sun the Blond Out, Arif Press, 1975.

Hotel Room, Songbird Editions, 1977.

Talking Poetics from Naropa Institute: Annals of The Jack Kerouac School of Disembodies Poetics, Shambhala, 1978.

Four Travels, Sayonara, 1979.

Countries, Toothpaste Press, 1980.

Sphinxeries, Smithereens Press, 1981.

First Baby Poems, Hyacinth Girls Editions, 1983.

Cabin, Z Press, 1984.

Makeup on Empty Space, Toothpaste Press, 1984.

Invention, Kulcher Foundation, 1985.

Skin Meat Bones, Coffee House Press, 1985.

The Romance Thing: Travel Sketches, Bamberger Books, 1987.

Blue Mosque, United Artists Books, 1988.

Helping the Dreamer: New and Selected Poems, Coffee House Press, 1989.

Not a Male Pseudonym, Tender Buttons, 1990.

Nice to See You: Homage to Ted Berrigan, Coffee House Press, 1991.

Out of This World: An Anthology of the St. Mark's Poetry Project, 1966–1991, Crown, 1991.

Iovis, Coffee House Press, 1993.

Troubairitz, Fifth Planet Press, 1993.

Disembodied Poetics: Annals of the Jack Kerouac School, with Andrew Schelling, University of New Mexico Press, 1994.

Kill or Cure, Penguin Books, 1994.

The Beat Book: Poems & Fiction from the Beat Generation, Shambhala, 1996.

ruth weiss

Steps, Ellis Press, 1958.

Gallery of Women, Adler Press, 1959.

South Pacific, Adler Press, 1959.

Blue in Green, Adler Press, 1960.

Light and Other Poems, Peace and Pieces Foundation, 1976.

Desert Journal, Good Gay Poets, 1977.

Single Out, D'Aurora Press, 1978.

13 Haiku, Attic Press, 1986.

Anthologies:

Beatitude #2-8, 11, 1959.

Semina #5, 1959.

Beatitude Anthology, 1960.

Outburst #2, 1962.

Matrix #1, 1970.

Matrix #2, 1971.

Mark in Time, 1971.

Peace & Pieces: An Anthology of Contemporary American Poetry, 1973.

Panjandrum Poetry #2 & #3, 1973.

185, 1973.

This Is Women's Work, 1974.

Contemporary Fiction: Today's Outstanding Writers, 1976.

Contemporary Women Poets Anthology, 1977.

Anthology: Women's Poetry Festival, 1977.

19+1, 1978.

Second Coming Anthology, 1984.

Beatitude 33, 1986.

Beatitude 34, 1987.

Minnie's Can-Do-Club Memories of Fillmore St., 1991.

Poetry at the 33, 1994.

Poetry at the 33, 1995.

Poetry at the 33, 1996.

Beatitude 35, 1996.

Contemporary Authors Autobiography Series, Gale Research, 1996.

Video, Audio, and Film

The Brink, originally 16mm, 40 min., B&W, 1961; videocassette, 1986.

Poetry & Allthatjazz, vol. 1, audio & videocassette, live performance with acoustic bass accompaniment, 1990.

Poetry & Allthatjazz, vol. 2, audio cassette, live performance with jazz trio, 1993.

Interview: Holocaust Oral History Project, videocassette, 5 hours, 1993.

Films by Steven Arnold with ruth weiss in Major Roles

Liberation of Mannique Mechanique, 16mm, B&W, 1967.

The Various Incarnations of a Tibetan Seamstress, 16mm, B&W, 1967.

Messages Messages, 16mm, B&W, 1968.

Luminous Procuress, 35mm, color, 1971.

Acknowledgments

The following people have been essential to the creation of this book. I will always be grateful for their help and support.

Jay Kahn, a living, breathing encyclopedia of all things Beat, who kept this book on track. You did Neal Cassady proud.

Andrea Dabbs, a fine researcher whose enthusiasm and hard work helped take the project from idea to book. You have a bright future in books.

Tosha Schore, upon whom I could always rely for her sharp intelligence, keen sense of responsibility, and for caring as much as I do for these special Beat women, especially Elise Cowen.

Chandrika Madhavan and Kevin Trotter helped immensely in compiling the anthology with their endless trips to the rare archives of U.C. Berkeley's Bancroft Library and their dedication to the selection of poetry and prose.

I also owe many thanks to all my colleagues at Conari Press who helped every step of the way and listened to me talking about the Beat Generation nonstop for eight months! I wish to thank Emily Miles for her unfailing support from the inception, Ame Beanland for her singular aesthetic and vision, Jennifer Brontsema for making a beautiful book, Laura Marceau for cheerful balance and enthusiasm, Maya Van Putten for assiduous skill and uncompromising standards, Will Glennon for his good listening and excellent advice, and a very special thanks to editor par excellence, Mary Jane Ryan, for turning this into an actual book instead of a six-hundred-page encyclopedia of Beat women.

I am grateful to these women of the Beat Generation for sharing their time, their lives, and their writings with me: Anne Waldman, a guiding light throughout; Diane di Prima, who set the standard; Hettie Jones, who helped out again and again; Janine Pommy Vega for her fascinating stories; Lenore Kandel for her strength; Jan Kerouac for her generosity; Brenda Frazer for her honesty; ruth weiss for always being there; Joyce Johnson for illuminating memories; Joanna Kyger for second chances; Joanna McClure for her understanding; Eileen Kaufman for her indomitable spirit; Mary Norbert Körte for her willingness; and Carolyn Cassady for showing us all what grace really means.

A

Adam, Helen, xi, xii, 2, 3, 5, 8–17, 31, 126, 340
Adams, Joan Vollmer. *See* Burroughs, Joan Vollmer Adams
Adams, Paul, 50
Admiral, Virginia, 118
Akamatova, 125
Albiach, Anne Marie, 125
Amram, David, 288
Antoninus, Brother. *See* Everson, William
Ark II/Moby I, 217
Arnold, Steven, 246
Auden, W. H., 20, 217

B

Baraka, Amiri, 184, 186. *See* Jones, LeRoi
Beatitude, 105, 242
Beattie, Paul, 322
Berkeley Poetry Conference, 258, 262
Berkeley Poetry Festival, 289
Berman, Shirley, 217
Berman, Wallace, 126, 217, 242, 324
Berrigan, Ted, 289
Bishop, Elizabeth, 340
Black Mountain College, 4–5, 199, 208, 216, 279, 288
Black Mountain Review, 208
Black Power movement, 186
black Rimbaud, 103. *See also* Kaufman, Bob
Black Sparrow Press, 198
Blake, Paul, 246, 247
Blake, Paul (Ti-Paul), 97–100
Blake, William, 2, 11, 41, 56, 229
Blaser, Robin, 12, 41

Blumenthal Award for Poetry, 42
Bowers, John, 91
Bowles, Jane, 7, 18–27, 183, 333
Bowles, Paul, 7, 18, 19–22
Boyce, Jack, 198
Brahms, 205
Bremser, Bonnie. *See* Frazer, Brenda
Bremser, Rachel, 269–270, 272, 276, 278
Bremser, Ray, 269–270, 272–278, 333
Britten, Benjamin, 20
Brooks, Gwendolyn, 340
Broughton, James, 12, 28, 29, 30
Brown, Joan, 322, 326–329
Browning, Robert, 207
Buddhism, 2, 125, 127, 128, 198, 199, 244, 279, 288, 289, 337
Burroughs, Joan Vollmer Adams, xi, 48–56, 73, 76, 77, 168
Burroughs, William, 4, 7, 18, 20, 21, 25, 49, 51–54, 55, 61, 77–78, 79, 87, 168, 185, 227, 287, 288, 311

C

Caen, Herb, 241, 338
Cage, John, 4
Cagney, James, 279
Cameron, 244
Camus, Albert, 229
Cannastra, Bill, 87, 89, 92, 310
Cannes Film Festival, 246
Capote, Truman, 18, 20
Carlson, Wil, 242
Carr, Cessa, 179-180
Carr, Lucien, 51, 77–78, 179-180
Cassady, Carolyn, xi, 2, 52, 55, 57–75, 280, 281, 311, 315

Cassady, Cathy, 61, 66
Cassady, Jami, 62, 66
Cassady, John Allen, 62, 75
Cassady, Neal, 31, 47, 52, 57, 59–75
  79–85, 92, 107, 242, 310, 315,
  316, 323, 339
Catholicism, 2, 29, 77, 78, 88, 99,
  119, 120, 149, 171, 257–267
Catullus, 229
Cayce, Edgar, 63
Cedar Tavern, 5, 176
Charles, Ray, 276
Charters, Ann, 335–341
Charters, Sam, 339
Chase, Hal, 51, 53
Cherifa, 19, 21
City Lights, 62, 105, 217, 224, 281, 338,
  340
Co-Existence Bagel Shop, 112, 114, 338
Cohen, Hettie. *See* Jones, Hettie
Collins, Jess, 11, 12
Conner, Bruce, 322, 323, 328
Copeland, Aaron, 19
Corinth Press, 125
Corman, Cid, 208
Corso, Gregory, 103, 125, 141, 185,
  225, 311
Cowen, Elise, xi, xii, 2, 4, 141–165,
  167, 168, 178, 223, 228, 230
Cowley, Malcolm, 85
Coyote, Peter, 126
Creeley, Robert, 5, 208, 258
Cru, Henry, 77, 80
Cullenbine, Roy, 84
cummings, e. e., 113
Cunningham, Merce, 4

D

Daumal, Rene, 230
Davis, George, 20
Davis, Miles, 174
de Angulo, Gui, 328
DeFeo, Jay, 126, 216, 217, 320–325, 328
DeFeo, Joan. *See* Defeo, Jay
DeKooning, Willem, 176
Derechin, Shel, 331
di Prima, Diane, xi, 2, 5, 115, 123–140,
  185, 219, 258, 269, 279, 280, 332,
  341
Dickens, Charles, 229
Dickinson, Emily, 4, 30, 117, 229, 339
Diebenkorn, Richard, 216
Diggers, the, 126, 258, 279, 280
Donnelly, Lee, 84–85
Donovan, 244
Doolittle, Hilda, ix, 4, 125, 340
Doors, the, 105
Dorn, Ed, 289
Dostoyevsky, 230
Doyle, Kirby, 126
drugs, 21, 51–52, 55, 57, 61, 70,
  112, 114, 156, 223, 225, 246,
  269, 270, 277, 311
  Benzedrine/speed, 50, 51, 52, 55, 65
  heroin, 51, 155, 186, 225, 269
  LSD, 65, 310
  marijuana/hashish, 51, 114, 225, 277
  peyote, 107, 112, 155
Duncan, Isadora, 287
Duncan, Robert, 5, 10, 11, 12, 28, 29,
  30, 117, 118, 119, 120, 126, 127,
  198, 208, 216, 258, 279, 288

E

East-West House, 197, 279
Eberhardt, Richard, 41
Eliot, T. S., 2, 113, 141, 205, 210
Ellington, Duke, 332
Everson, William, 30, 119, 120, 257

F

Fabilli, Mary, xi, 2, 30, 41, 116–122
Ferlinghetti, Lawrence, 62, 124, 217,
    224, 280, 289, 311, 337, 340
Festival of Contemporary Poetry, 29
Fields, W. C., 72, 73
Fisher, Grant, 127
Floating Bear, 125, 126
Frazer, Brenda, xi, 268–278, 233, 288, 333
Freud, Sigmund, 148
Fritsch, William, 281
Furthur, 65

G

Gardiner, Charles Wrey, 205
Genet, Jean, 126
Getz, Stan, 174
Ginsberg, Allen, 2, 12, 20, 29, 31, 41,
    49, 50, 51, 53, 54, 55, 57, 60,
    61, 62, 71–75, 77, 95, 103, 107,
    124, 125, 127, 142, 144, 148, 149–
    151, 154, 155, 167, 168, 169, 170,
    171, 185, 199, 208, 216, 217,
    223, 225, 227, 228, 229, 230,
    242, 258, 270, 287, 288, 289,
    310, 311, 314, 323, 328, 335, 336,
    339, 341

Ginsberg, Naomi, 341
Gleason, Madeline, xii, 3, 5, 12, 28–38,
    246
Goodman, Mitchell, 207, 210
Gould, Jean, 207
Grateful Dead, the, 105
Green, Mark, 107, 108
Greer, Alex, 142
Greer, Mary, xii, 31
Grogan, Emmet, 126
Guest, Barbara, 125, 332
Guillevic, Eugene, 210
Guravich, Donald, 199

H

Hansen, Diana, 62
Hart, Howard, 245
Hawley, Robert, 258
Hawley, Robert and Dorothea, 119
HD. *See* Doolittle, Hilda
Heard, John, 315
Hedrick, Wally, 322, 323, 328
Henderson, David, 126
Henderson, LuAnne, 52, 59, 60, 61
Hendrix, Jimi, 105
Herko, Fred, 126
Herms, George, 244
Hesse, Herman, 230
Hinkle, Al, 52
Hinkle, Helen, 52
Hirschman, Jack, 247
Holiday, Billie, 174, 186
Holmes, John Clellon, 2, 80, 225
Hopkins, Gerard Manley, 261
Hopps, Walter, 321, 325

Huncke, Herbert, 2, 49, 50, 52, 53–54, 55, 56, 126, 142, 223, 225, 226, 227, 228
Hyman, Stanley Edgar, 288

I

Imagist poets, 4, 125
Isbell, Roy, 246

J

Jack Kerouac School of Disembodied Poetics, 169, 199, 287, 289
Jackson, Natalie, 311
jazz, 81, 105, 106, 113, 241, 242, 246, 247, 288, 331–332, 339
Jess. *See* Collins, Jess
Jewitt, Sarah Orne, 339
Joans, Ted, 331–333
John, Elsie, 225
Johnson, James, 176
Johnson, Joyce, xi, 4, 5, 76, 141, 142, 154, 157, 166–181, 173, 176, 194
Jones, Hettie, xi, 4, 5, 18, 125, 167, 168, 179, 182–195, 219, 269, 333
Jones, LeRoi, 125, 126, 167, 179, 184–186, 219
Joplin, Janis, 105
Joycey. *See* Johnson, Joyce

K

Kael, Pauline, 42
Kahlo, Frida, 260, 329
Kammerer, Dave, 77–78
Kandel, Aben, 279

Kandel, Lenore, 126, 127, 258, 279–285, 289, 332
Karmapa, Gyalwa, 199
Kaufman, Bob, 103–114, 228, 332
Kaufman, Eileen, xi, 103–114, 332
Kees, Weldon, 337
Kerouac, Caroline, 95–98
Kerouac, Edie Parker, 49, 50, 54, 55, 76–85
Kerouac, Gabriele "Mémère," 88, 93–102, 180
Kerouac, Jack, xii, 2, 5, 6, 12, 20, 21, 31, 49, 50, 54, 57, 60–61, 62–63, 65–68, 71, 72, 77–85, 87–89, 91, 92, 93, 102, 103, 107, 125, 167, 168–175, 179, 180–181, 184, 185, 199, 224, 225, 242, 280, 281, 309, 315, 323, 333, 339, 341
Kerouac, Jan, xii, 2, 78, 89, 90–93, 308–318, 333
Kerouac, Joan Haverty, 86–102, 310, 311, 314
Kesey, Ken, 57, 64
King Jr., Martin Luther, 258
Kingsland, John, 51
Kinsey Sex Report, 225, 227
Klapper, Ilse, 25
Kline, Franz, 176
Koestler, Arthur, 229
Körte, Mary Norbert, xi, 3, 209, 257–267
Krasny, Michael, 1
Kyger, Joanne, xi, 196–204, 280, 288

L

Lamantia, Philip, 217, 242, 328
Lashinsky, Herb, 91
LaVigne, Robert, 336
Leary, Timothy, 126
Lessing, Doris, 340
Levertov, Denise, xi, 3, 185, 205–213, 259, 332, 340
Levin, Arnie, 227
Long, Philomene, 244
Lorca, 113
Lorde, Audre, 126

M

MacDowell, John Herbert, 126
Maidens, The, 12
Malamud, Bernard, 288
Markowsky, Barney, 84
Marlowe, Alan, 126
Márquez, Gabriel García, 261
Martin, Peter, 337
Marx, 55
Matson, Clive, 126
McCarthy, Eugene, 260
McClure, Joanna, 214–222, 323
McClure, Michael, 29, 124, 126, 127, 216–219, 288, 322, 323, 328, 336
McCullers, Carson, 19, 20
McGinley, Phyllis, 340
McKeever, Anne, 242, 245
McNaughton, Duncan, 127
McNeill, William, 11
Melody, Little Jack, 50, 142
Meltzer, David, 127, 258
Merry Pranksters, 64
Merton, Thomas, 259

Mexico, 64, 65, 66, 68, 71, 74, 105, 242, 269–270, 272–278, 273, 310
Mexico City, 49, 52, 56, 174, 245, 273
Micheline, Jack, 228, 229
Miles, Josephine, xi, 39–45, 118, 340
Minger, Jack, 242
Monterey Pop and Jazz Festival, 105
Morgan, Ted, 54
Moriarity, Dean, 65
Morocco, 20, 230
Tangier, 18, 19, 20–21, 333
Moses, Ed, 323
Murphy, Ann, 47, 64
Mutti, Tambi, 205

N

Naropa Institute, 12, 141, 199, 287, 289
National Endowment award, 259
Nelson, Sonny, 242
Nemerov, Howard, 288
Neri, Manuel, 328, 329
New Directions, 105, 208
New York Poets Theatre, 126
New York School of Poets, 288
Nicosia, Gerald, 312–314
Nin, Anaïs, 340
Nolte, Nick, 65, 315–316

O

O'Connor, Sinead, 260
O'Hara, Frank, 124, 176, 185, 219, 288
Olsen, Tillie, 340
Olson, Charles, 4, 124, 208, 258, 289
O'Neill, Eugene, 339
Orlovsky, Lafcadio, 223, 230

Orlovsky, Peter, 21, 125, 142, 148, 149–151, 153, 155, 168, 223, 225–227, 228–230, 311, 328, 336, 339
Ostriker, Alicia, 198
Oyez, 258

P

Park, David, 329
Parker, Charlie, 174
Patchen, Kenneth, 124, 217
Patler, Louis, 127
People's Park, 259
Pittsburgh John, 146, 147
Pixy Pool, 10. *See* Adam, Helen
Plath, Sylvia, 340, 341
Pound, Ezra, 4, 123, 141, 147
Powell, Sheppard, 127
Prevallet, Kristin, 13
Proust, 55, 60

R

Rat Bastard Protective Association, 328
Rauschenberg, Robert, 4
Read, Herbert, 205
Rexroth, Kenneth, 30, 41, 205, 208, 210, 217, 281
Rhys, Jean, 177
Rilke, 205
Rimbaud, 148
Rinpoche, Chatral Sangye Dorje, 288
Rinpoche, Chogyam Trungpa, 128, 199
Rios, Frankie, 244
Romanticism, 205
Romero, Lee, 244
Romero, Victor, 140
Rose, The, 320, 324, 325

Roshi, Shunryu Suzuki, 197, 244, 280
Royere, William, 244
Rukeyser, Muriel, 340
Russell, Vickie, 50, 51, 142

S

Sampas, Stella, 78, 312
San Francisco Institute of Magical and Healing Art, 128
San Francisco Poetry Festival, 3, 30
San Francisco Poetry Guild, 29
San Francisco Renaissance, 5, 9, 10, 13, 31, 118, 208, 279, 288
Saroyan Jr., William, 260
Sartre, Jean Paul, 338
Sasaki, Ruth Fuller, 198
Schoer, Mark, 41
Sedgwick, Maria, 340
Shakespeare, 51, 60, 148, 171
Shelley Memorial Award for Poetry, 40
Sikelianos, Anghelos, ix
Simon, Dave, 227
Sinclair, Duncan, 140
Six Gallery, 319, 323
Skir, Leo, 142, 143–158
Smart, Christopher, Catullus, 229
Smith, Barbara Hernstein, 288
Snyder, Gary, 29, 103, 197, 198, 217, 258, 279, 280, 288, 335, 336
Solomon, Carl, 50, 142
Soyer, Moses, 140
Spacek, Sissy, 65, 315
Spicer Circle, 11, 41
Spicer, Jack, 11, 41, 198, 209, 258, 323
Spock, Benjamin, 210
Starr, Ringo, 244

Stein, Gertrude, ix, 4, 20, 229, 261, 338, 340
Still, Clyfford, 245
Strauss, René, 138
Suzuki, Shunryu Roshi, 280

T

Tarlow, Aya, 244, 245
Thomas, Dylan, 337
Toklas, Alice B., 20
Triem, Eve, 12
Tysons, the, 79–85

U

Ulewicz, Laura, 245

V

Vega, Janine Pommy, xi, 223–240, 268, 270, 340
Venice Biennale Film Festival, 247
Vietnam War, 209, 322
Vigné, Dion, 245

W

Wakefield, Dick, 84
Waldman, Anne, ix–xii, 124, 199, 286–307
Wangyal, Geshe, 288
Waring, James, 125
Watts, Alan, 199
Wavy Gravy, 127
Weil, Simone, 341
Weiners, John, 229
weiss, ruth, 241–256, 328
Weitsman, Mel, 245

Welch, Lew, 279, 280, 288
Whalen, Philip, 103, 185, 217, 288, 336
Wharton, Edith, 340
White, Ed, 79
Whitey, 55
Whitman, Walt, 4
Williams, William Carlos, 217
Williams, Tennessee, 18, 19, 20
Williams, William Carlos, 4
Wright, Richard and Ellen, 20

Y

Yeats, 41
Young, Celine, 51, 78
Young, Lester, 174, 332
Yugen, 185

Women of the Beat Generation
is also available on audio

Read by Debra Winger with contributions by Carolyn Cassady, Anne Charters, Diane di Prima, Joyce Johnson, Hettie Jones, Anne Waldman, ruth weiss, and many more! Available from Audio Literature (800) 383-0174. ISBN: 1-57453-069-0, abridged, four cassettes, six hours, $24.95.

Conari Press, established in 1987, publishes books on topics ranging from spirituality and women's history to sexuality and personal growth. Our main goal is to publish quality books that will make a difference in people's lives—both how we feel about ourselves and how we relate to one another.

Our readers are our most important resource, and we value your input, suggestions, and ideas. For a complete catalog or to get on our mailing list, please contact us at:

Conari Press

2550 Ninth Street, Suite 101
Berkeley, California 94710
800-685-9595 • FAX 510-649-7190 • E-MAIL Conaripub@aol.com

Women of the Beat
generation.

DATE			